KINGS & QUEENS
OF ENGLAND
A DARK HISTORY

KINGS & QUEENS
OF ENGLAND
A DARK HISTORY

Brenda Ralph Lewis

amber
BOOKS

This updated Amber edition first published in 2019

First Amber edition published in 2015

Copyright © 2019 Amber Books Ltd

First published in 2003 as *Dark History of the Kings & Queens of England*

Published by Amber Books Ltd
United House
North Road
London N7 9DP
United Kingdom
www.amberbooks.co.uk
Instagram: amberbooksltd
Facebook: www.facebook.com/amberbooks
Twitter: @amberbooks

ISBN: 978-1-78274-858-8

Project Editor: James Bennett
Picture Research: Natasha Jones
Design: Jerry Williams

Printed in China

CONTENTS

MAP OF GREAT BRITAIN
AND ASSOCIATED PLACES IN EUROPE

ATLANTIC OCEAN

Fort William
Balmoral Castle
Glencoe
SCOTLAND
Inveraray
Dunbar
Edinburgh

NORTH SEA

NORTHERN IRELAND

R. Boyne

REPUBLIC OF IRELAND

Middleham
Lancaster
York
Pontefract
Wakefield
Llantrisant
ENGLAND
Anglesey
Conwy
Chester
Lincoln
Caernarfon
Derby
Nottingham
Sandringham House
Leicester
WALES
Naseby
Brampton
Warwick
Althrop House
Worcester
Framlingham
Evesham
Edgehill
Milford Haven
Hereford
Tewkesbury
Gloucester
Oxford
St. Albans
Hoddeston
Stoke
Barnet
Berkeley
Richmond
London
Bristol
Windsor
Hampton Court
Taunton
Winchester
Dover
Devonshire
New Forest
Brighton
Calais
Cornwall
Torbay
Portsmouth
Isle of Wight

IRISH SEA

ENGLISH CHANNEL

Rouen

Falaise
Paris

Normandy

Brittany
Le Mans

Chinon

Poitou

Angoulême

Aquitaine

KEY TO THE SYMBOLS
USED THROUGHOUT THIS BOOK

The family trees at the start of each chapter show the relationships between persons mentioned in the text and are not intended to be comprehensive. The dates given for each monarch denote the period of their reign. The following symbols are used:

The Normans

The Plantagenets

The Tudors

The Stuarts

The Hanoverians

The House of Saxe-Coburg-Gotha

The Windsors

Illegitimate

Heir who did not succeed

Crown won in battle

Usurper

Abdicated

Murdered

Died in battle

Executed

INTRODUCTION

✦

The British royal family is considered by many to be the most prestigious in the world.

Yet its sensational and often lurid past contains deeds so dark and dastardly that they were covered up and remained secret for centuries.

Over the last thousand years or so, many of the kings and queens of England have played their part in betrayals, regicides, plots, treason, atrocities, and revolts. The English throne has been usurped four times. There have been five pretenders to the crown, two of them impostors. Four kings have been forcibly deposed. All were subsequently murdered. One of them was publicly executed.

Kings and queens of England have been responsible for thousands of executions and deaths. Tudor king Henry VIII set out to exterminate every surviving member of the Plantagenets, the dynasty that preceded his own. And Henry's daughter, Queen Mary I, burned 300 Protestants at the stake.

English royalty was a regular target for conspiracies and assassination attempts. Queen Elizabeth I was at constant risk from plotters who wanted to kill her and replace her with her cousin, Mary, Queen of Scots. The Gunpowder Plot of 1605 was a Catholic conspiracy to blow up King James I, his government and the Houses of Parliament.

Two kings of England went mad. One was kidnapped, and another was mercilessly bullied by his own nobles. King Henry VIII, who married six times, hounded his first wife, Catherine of Aragon, to her death in 1536. Later, he executed his second and fifth wives.

While King George IV was Prince of Wales and heir to the throne, he incurred so many debts that he had

Henry VIII, shown here with Pope Leo X, was a sincere Roman Catholic, but that did not stop him from breaking his ties with Rome when the pope would not grant him a divorce.

to be bailed out – twice – by Parliament. His father, King George III, derived little pleasure from his family of 15 children, many of whom were enveloped in scandal. Two of his offspring were suspected of incest, and his sons provided him with an army of illegitimate grandchildren.

Queen Victoria and her husband, Prince Albert, tried to raise the moral standards of royalty, but they were frustrated by their eldest son, the future King Edward VII, who enjoyed nothing more than drinking, gambling and womanizing to excess.

In 1936 King Edward VIII nearly wrecked the monarchy when he abdicated to marry the unsuitable, twice-divorced Wallis Simpson. More recently, the royal family has been rocked to its foundations by the Charles and Diana scandals.

This book pulls no punches in telling the whole shameful story of royal deeds that were never intended to be revealed.

A detail from the invitation to the fireworks display held to celebrate the coronation of King Edward VII in 1902.

CONSPIRATORS AND CONQUERORS
A DIRTY BUSINESS

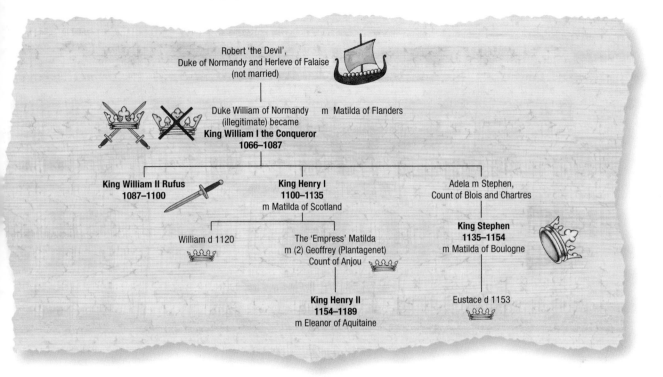

Robert 'the Devil',
Duke of Normandy and Herleve of Falaise
(not married)

Duke William of Normandy   m Matilda of Flanders
(illegitimate) became
**King William I the Conqueror
1066–1087**

**King William II Rufus
1087–1100**

**King Henry I
1100–1135**
m Matilda of Scotland

Adela m Stephen,
Count of Blois and Chartres

William d 1120

The 'Empress' Matilda
m (2) Geoffrey (Plantagenet)
Count of Anjou

**King Stephen
1135–1154**
m Matilda of Boulogne

**King Henry II
1154–1189**
m Eleanor of Aquitaine

Eustace d 1153

Exactly what happened in the New Forest in southern England on 2 August 1100, remains a mystery, despite the fact that it was broad daylight and there were several eyewitnesses.

◆

On that morning King William II, nicknamed Rufus for his red hair, red face, and violent temper, ate an early breakfast and set off for the forest, equipped with bows and arrows for a day's hunting. His close friend Walter Tirel went with him.

Once inside the forest, the royal hunting party spread out in search of prey. Tirel remained with the king and soon the beaters accompanying the hunt drove a herd of stags toward the pair. King William shot at them but missed. According to a witness named Knighton, the king shouted to Tirel: 'Draw, draw your bow for the devil's sake or it will be the worse for you!' It has long been accepted that Tirel did as he was told, but his arrow ricocheted off a tree, missing the stag and striking the king in the chest.

The English chronicler and historian William of Malmesbury, writing a few years later, described what happened next.

A late 15th-century portrayal of the death of William II. The King is shown lying on the ground with the fatal arrow in his chest at the top left of the picture.

An account of King William II's death from 'A Chronicle of England', published between 1300 and 1325. William sits on a bench, an arrow in his chest, but still, curiously enough, very much alive.

'On receiving the wound, the king uttered not a word; but breaking off the shaft of the weapon where it projected from his body, fell upon the wound, by which he accelerated his death.'

Horrified, Tirel rushed to the king, but he was dead.

Now Tirel's only concern was to escape. He leapt onto his horse and spurred it on through the dense forest, galloping furiously without stopping until he reached the English Channel and crossed to France. From there, Tirel vehemently denied killing the king and continued to deny it for the rest of his life.

A royal death foretold

When news of the king's death spread, many people in Europe claimed they had experienced premonitions of the event. In Belgium, Abbot Hugh of Cluny revealed he had received a warning on the night of August 1 that the king of England would die the next day. A monk told that on 2 August, while his eyes were closed during prayer, he had had a vision of a man holding a piece of paper bearing the message 'King William is dead'. When the monk opened his eyes, the vision disappeared.

The circumstances of the king's death remained shrouded in secrecy. Tirel, the prime suspect, was never punished in any way, and most people were inclined to believe his denials. Yet no further investigations into the death took place, nor was any evidence ever submitted. So the death of King William II went down in history as a tragic accident.

A murder in the family

The story quickly spread that the king's death was really a murder that had been disguised as an accident. The disrespectful way in which the king's body was handled after the fatal hunt seems to point to a murder plot. A lowly charcoal burner named Purkiss was ordered to remove the corpse. Purkiss placed the king on a wooden cart and covered him with an old work cloth. Then he trundled the cart to Winchester Cathedral where William was hastily buried by the monks. This was certainly no funeral fit for a king.

Motives for murder

While Tirel was generally presumed innocent, there were several suspects who might indeed have wanted

King William dead. The king had never married, and the heirs to the throne were his two brothers: Duke Robert of Normandy, known as Curthose for his short

When news of the king's death spread, many people in Europe claimed they had experienced premonitions of the event.

legs, and Prince Henry, known as Beauclerc because he could read and write. Of the two, Henry was the more likely culprit. He had been one of the hunting party and had probably witnessed the king's death.

As he had been present at the grisly scene, Henry had had the opportunity to act quickly and grab what

he most wanted – the throne of England – before Robert, or anyone else, could stop him. He wasted no time mourning his dead brother. Instead, he went straight to Winchester, where he seized the royal treasure, then raced the 60 miles to London and had himself crowned king. It was all over within three days. By 5 August, Henry was England's new sovereign.

Resentful and greedy, Henry had plenty of reasons for having wanted the king dead. When his father, King William I the Conqueror, had died in 1087, Henry had been overlooked and received neither titles nor land. Robert Curthose, on the other hand, was awarded the family duchy of Normandy, in France, and William was placed on the throne of England. All Henry

Archers, seen here in a reenactment, were the 'artillery' of medieval armies. They could fire a barrage which filled the air with a mass of deadly barbs that could fell knights in chainmail – and kill their horses, too.

FACT *or* **FICTION**

A CULT KILLING?

MANY CHURCHMEN BELIEVED that William, who was upheld as a Christian king, was really a pagan – a practitioner of sorcery and witchcraft. In medieval times people were terrified of witchcraft, so much so that the *Anglo-Saxon Chronicle* dared not even hint at such inflammatory gossip. This was all due to William's grandfather, Robert, Duke of Normandy. The duke's father, it was believed, was the devil. That is why the duke was nicknamed Robert the Devil, making King William II the great-grandson of the devil.

EVIDENCE OF BLASPHEMY

He certainly acted in a devilish manner. He was a blasphemer and often swore 'by the devil'. Nor had he any respect for the Church. When he attended services, he spent his time doodling or gossiping with his courtiers. William was also homosexual. This was considered a scandalous sin in the eleventh century. One chronicler described William's 'camp' court in scathing terms:

'…then there was flowing hair and extravagant dress, and was invented the fashion of shoes with curved points; then the model for young men was to rival women in delicacy of person, to mind their gait, to walk with loose gesture and half naked….'

In 1094, Anselm, the Archbishop of Canterbury, publicly accused King William of sodomy and other 'unnatural sins of the flesh.' Most people tended to side with Anselm, who was later made a saint. With this in mind, it was easy to believe that the 'devil' king was indeed a secret pagan.

Centuries later, this belief formed part of a theory that William II was killed by a pagan cult that practiced royal sacrifice. In her book *The Witch Cult in Western Europe*, published in 1921, Margaret Alice Murray wrote that this cult was widespread throughout pre-Christian Europe. According to the author, the Norman family itself belonged to a cult that demanded the ritual killing of the monarch for the good of the community.

This seems in line with King William's strange behavior on the night before his death. He behaved as if he knew that he was going to be the target of a cult killing. On the evening of 1 August 1100, the king ate and drank more than usual and slept badly.

AN UNWELCOME GIFT

Next morning, William was given a surprise gift of six newly made arrows. He gave two of them to Walter Tirel, saying cryptically: 'Walter, take good care to carry out the orders I gave you.' Some have suggested that Tirel, too, belonged to the pagan cult. A monk named Serlo warned the king not to go hunting that day, but William ignored his advice. Minutes after he reached the forest, he was dead.

Sensational gossip about William's death continued for many years. In 1107, the tower of Winchester Cathedral collapsed. The fact that William was buried there was blamed for the disaster. God, it was said, had cursed the king for his many sins.

The 12th century was a very superstitious time, in which the remains of holy men were believed to have supernatural powers. This 15th-century chronicle shows Norman knights at prayer before the relics of Saint Valery.

ROUGH JUSTICE

HENRY'S CRUELTY WAS LEGENDARY throughout the country. For instance, in 1118, he demonstrated his idea of justice when he refused to execute one Herbert, a treasurer in the royal household. Herbert had been plotting against Henry, but the king was fond of Herbert so, instead of executing him, he had him blinded and castrated. With a king capable of such rough justice, even powerful men such as the land-owning barons thought it best to defer to his wishes.

A representation of King Henry I. Though more refined and educated than other Normans, he was just as brutal.

received was £5,000 in silver. Although this was a huge amount of money in the 11th century, it was not nearly enough for a cunning, hard-nosed prince who felt he had been wronged.

Robert Curthose was also suspected of wanting the king dead, but it is unlikely that he was involved in the affair. Robert dearly wished to rule England and had been deeply disappointed when his father chose William to succeed him on the English throne. After all, Robert was the elder brother. Twice Robert

> **Other than the Norman royal family there were many ordinary people who would have been glad to see William II dead. They had good reason. The Norman conquest of England after 1066 had been a savage business.**

had tried to seize the kingdom – at the start of King William II's reign in 1087, and again in 1088 – and twice he had failed.

But William the Conqueror had had good reason for passing Robert over. William had won his crown at the battle of Hastings in 1066, and from then on ruled England by force. He considered Robert weak and easily led. It would have been easy for his stronger-willed barons to get the better of him – and that was the last thing William the Conqueror had in mind. The Conqueror wanted a brute like himself to succeed him. That brute was not Robert. It was William.

Ultimately the wily Henry I found it easy to outwit Robert. At the time of William II's death in the New Forest, Robert had been halfway across the world in the Holy Land, fighting in the crusades. He returned to find his younger brother well and truly in the saddle. Besides claiming the throne, Henry had married Matilda, daughter of King Malcolm III of Scotland, who would soon be pregnant with their first child, the heir to Henry's throne.

There was no place for Robert at court, and eventually Henry imprisoned him for life until his death in 1134 at the age of 81. Robert never tried to escape, and spent his time learning Welsh and writing poetry.

Justice for the people

Other than the Norman royal family there were many ordinary people who would have been glad to see William II dead. They had good reason. The Norman conquest of England after 1066 had been a savage business. Anyone who resisted Norman rule was

Hand-to-hand fighting, as seen in this reenactment, was a bloody and barbarous business. Although Norman soldiers wore the chainmail, helmets and kite-shaped shields shown here, they were not immune to the blows of swords and axes.

cruelly punished. In the rebellious north of England, for instance, Normans burned crops and destroyed hundreds of villages. They slaughtered cattle and sheep, and killed inhabitants by the thousands. Only when the whole area was laid waste were the Normans satisfied.

Normans were just as brutal about the rights they claimed to English forests. Throughout history, peasants had relied on the forests to gather wood for their fires and kill animals for food. Now, anyone who entered the forests faced appalling punishments. Poachers who shot deer had both hands cut off; even if they merely disturbed the deer they were blinded. And intruders who played music to draw the deer out into the open suffered the same fate. This, though, did not stop the peasants, who continued to enter the forest illegally. So it is possible that the arrow that killed King William II in 1100 was fired by a trespasser hidden among the trees.

Perversion, blasphemy and pagan sacrifice

The list of King William's enemies did not end there. The English Church hated him, too. Churchmen wrote

This 19th-century engraving of King William II Rufus bears a close resemblance to depictions of King Stephen. In fact, no one really knows what either of these kings looked like.

the chronicles and histories of the time, and took every opportunity to give William a bad 'press'. This was the entry for the year 1100 in the most famous of all the medieval histories – the *Anglo-Saxon Chronicle*:

'He was very harsh and fierce with his men, his land and all his neighbours and very much feared. He was ever agreeable to evil men's advice, and through his own greed, he was ever vexing this nation with force and with unjust taxes. Therefore, in his days all justice declined ... he was to nearly all his people hateful, and abominable to God.'

Divine retribution

William was not the only royal in his family to suffer. People believed that King Henry I and the entire Norman dynasty were also cursed by God. This seemed to be confirmed when Henry suffered the worst disaster that could befall a medieval monarch.

In medieval times, a king was required to be a warrior. This was why he needed male heirs to succeed him. Henry had sired around 25 children by eight or more mistresses. But they were illegitimate and there-

fore could not inherit the English throne. So it was a terrible blow for Henry when his only legitimate son, Prince William, drowned in the English Channel on 25 November 1120. Henry's courtiers did not dare tell him for two days. When they did, he fainted from shock.

That left Henry's daughter Matilda as his only legitimate heir. This was a great problem for the king. The 12th century was dominated by men and war, and women were regarded as unsuitable to reign as queens. Henry's first wife, Matilda, was dead, so he remarried, hoping to have more sons. But Henry, now 53, was unable to father more children. So the king resolved that his only heir Matilda would, after all, reign.

Although she was only 19, Matilda was very much like her father. She was intelligent, forceful, well-educated and self-confident. She was also highly disagreeable. Henry felt sure that Matilda could continue his policy of strong-arm rule. But the decision was not his alone. Matilda had to be accepted by the country's powerful barons. The barons of England and Normandy were semi-independent, with their own private armies, fortified castles, and extensive landholdings. These were powerful men who were not afraid to voice their opinions to the king.

Henry realized that the barons were much too pig-headed to welcome the idea of a woman reigning over them, but he was desperate. So he commanded the nobles to swear an oath before God accepting Matilda as his rightful successor. Henry made them swear four times – in 1127, 1128, 1131, and 1133. Although the barons resented being forced to take the oath, they were only too well aware that Henry was not a man to be refused.

Matilda is betrayed

The barons, however, were just biding their time. As soon as Henry died in 1135, they went back on their oaths, but not because Matilda was a woman. The bar-

King Henry I lost Prince William, his only surviving son and heir, when the *White Ship* sank in the English Channel in 1120. The tragic story was told in this manuscript produced two centuries later, in 1321.

qui successit Henricus frater
eius et regnauit annis xxxvi
hic erat pastor ferax et custos
nemorum fuit et sapiens et stre
nuus Dux normannie que
auersimus Ambrosius Leonem iusticie
in historia Regum noiauit secit eni
iudicium et iusticiam in terra Dixit q̄
vxorem generosam et optimam de
nobili genere anglorum et Britonum p
quam multum sibi confederauit reg
num scilicet filiam principis sui Alba
nie vita et moribz ornatam sororem
scilicet Alexandri principis sui scotie
et Dauitis scotie qui postea fuit princeps
Albanie. Qui uero Rex Henricus pfa
tus dedit honorem de huntingdon
cum matilda cognate sua que erat
vxor prius primi Simonis de Seenlis
comitis de huntingdon et norhamp
ton cum custodia pueror suor et die
concordes ad inuicem deinde effecti
fuerunt quia prefatus Alexander ven
sicauit filia iure hereditario coronam
et monarchiam tocius Regni predi
sicut uerus Heres et iustus de iure boni
Regis Edwardi ultimi. Alexr q̄ dm
sup omnia diauit q̄ scdm ecciam in
multis p loca secit q̄ bonu in genitu
tocius malum q̄ descruit vocabitur
matildis Regina optima Obiit uo
predictus henricus in normannia
apud S. Johns. sepultus enim fuit
in anglia apud Redinges in Alba
thia quam construxerat. matilda
vero Regina predicta sepulta fuit
in anglia apud westmonasterium
cuius anime aspicietur deus.

Henricus primus genuit

Willm
qui periit
in mari

Ricm
qui piit
in mari

Matil
dam im
patrice

Ricdm
q obiit

Henria
Regis se
cundi

ons knew that she was more than a match for them and that they would never be able to get the better of her. They had their eyes on a far more malleable candidate.

Stephen de Blois, Matilda's first cousin, was a

The effects of the conflict in England were devastating. Towns and villages were pillaged by both sides. Refugees wandered the countryside and trade slumped

---

gentleman. He was kind-hearted, good-natured, and tolerant. In other words, he was a promising soft touch. This did not mean, though, that Stephen lacked cunning. As soon as he heard that his uncle, Henry I, was dead, he left France for England. Within three weeks, he had raised enough support for his claim to the throne among barons, government officials, and the Church.

He also seized the royal treasure. On December 22, 1135, Stephen had himself crowned king at Westminster Abbey.

The result was civil war, because Stephen was a usurper with no legal right to the throne. Also, Matilda had her supporters among the barons who believed in her legal succession. They soon lined up against Stephen but they had to wait for Matilda. She finally brought her army across the Channel to England from Normandy in 1139.

The civil war was a miserable affair. Neither Stephen nor Matilda was strong enough to win a final victory. So, the war ended as a succession of long sieges of castles and other strongholds. The effects on England were devastating. Towns and villages were pillaged by both sides. Refugees wandered the countryside, seeking shelter in monasteries and

In December 1142, Empress Matilda and four of her knights escaped from confinement in Oxford Castle wearing white robes to disguise themselves against the thick snow. King Stephen's guards were too busy carousing to notice them.

nunneries. Trade slumped and the barons took advantage of the anarchy caused by the civil war to raid, rob, and rape. A contemporary chronicler, Henry of Huntingdon, described the scenes of suffering:

'There was universal turmoil and desolation. Some, for whom their country had lost its charms, chose rather to make their abode in foreign lands; others drew to the churches for protection, and constructing mean hovels in their precincts, passed their days in fear and trouble.

'Food being scarce, for there was a dreadful famine throughout England, some of the people disgustingly devoured the flesh of dogs and horses; others appeased their insatiable hunger with the garbage of uncooked herbs and roots.... There were seen famous cities deserted and depopulated by the death of the inhabitants of every age and sex, and fields white for the harvest... but none to gather it, all having been struck down by the famine. Thus the whole aspect of England presented a scene of calamity and sorrow, misery and oppression....

'These unhappy spectacles, these lamentable tragedies...were common throughout England.... The kingdom, which was once the abode of joy, tranquillity, and peace, was everywhere changed into a seat of war and slaughter, and devastation and woe.'

Henry Plantagenet: a new hope for England

The obnoxious Matilda cared nothing for the sorry plight of the population. In June 1141, while she was in London preparing for her coronation, she demanded huge sums of money from the citizens. But the civil war had ruined them and they could not pay.

When officials and bishops tried to explain the situation, Matilda cursed and swore at them. Very soon, London had had enough. A raging mob burst in on Matilda's pre-coronation banquet at Westminster. They drove her out of the city. She never returned.

The civil war dragged on, but Matilda's chances of success were fading. In 1148, she finally gave up and returned to Normandy. King Stephen, it seemed, had won. But within five years, fate gave a bitter twist to his success. His eldest son and heir Eustace died suddenly in 1153. His wife, Queen Matilda, had died the year before. Losing his wife and son was too much

This strong, determined-looking king, dressed in armour, is King Stephen. The portrait is somewhat flattering: the soft, gentlemanly and sensitive Stephen wasn't nearly as resolute as the picture makes him appear.

for Stephen. Although he had other sons, he was too heartbroken to groom them for the throne. Instead, in 1153, he made a deal with Matilda and her 20-year-old son, Henry Plantagenet. Henry was named as Stephen's successor on the condition that he allow Stephen to remain king in England while he lived.

But Henry did not have to wait long. Less than a year later, on October 25, 1154, Stephen, the last of the Norman kings, died. Now, Henry Plantagenet became the first monarch of the new Plantagenet dynasty.

Henry was a lot like his mother – hot-tempered, masterful, and stubborn. He was also like a time bomb waiting to go off. What followed was the most vicious royal family quarrel England had ever seen. And it was a fight to the death.

UNHOLY ALLIANCES

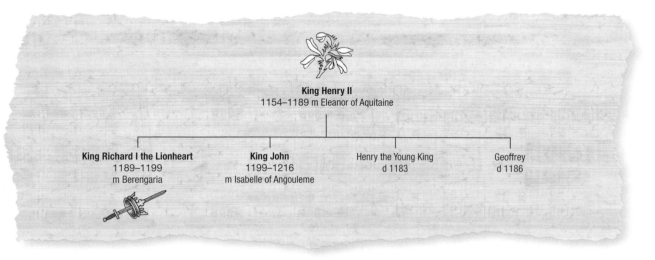

King Henry II
1154–1189 m Eleanor of Aquitaine

King Richard I the Lionheart	**King John**	Henry the Young King	Geoffrey
1189–1199	1199–1216	d 1183	d 1186
m Berengaria	m Isabelle of Angouleme		

When Henry II became King of England in 1154, he was just 21 years old. But he was neither an ordinary man, nor an ordinary king. Despite his youth, he had a natural air of command. He was greatly admired and also greatly feared.

Yet 35 years later, Henry was a worn out, sick old man. He died deserted by his family and his barons, and humiliated by his great rival, the king of France. The monk chronicler Gerald of Wales wrote that Henry was 'without ring, sceptre, crown and nearly everything which is fitting for royal funeral rites.'

How could such a brilliant monarch, one of England's greatest, come to such a miserable end? It all came down to a single, fatal flaw: Henry's ferocious temperament. First of all, his fiery nature involved him in the most sensational murder of his time. Later, it made his family and his nobles conspire together to destroy him.

Canterbury Cathedral, the scene of the murder of Archbishop Thomas Becket on 29 December 1170. Henry II was thought to have ordered his knights to kill Becket.

A passionate pairing

Henry II was not only King of England. He also ruled Normandy, Anjou, Maine, Touraine and Poitou in France. When he married Eleanor, a former queen consort of France, in 1152, he acquired his new wife's own territory, Aquitaine, the largest duchy in France. Together, these lands made up the Angevin Empire. It stretched from England's northern border with Scotland down to the Pyrenees mountains in southwest France. No monarch of England ever came to the throne with a more splendid inheritance.

The marriage of Henry II and Eleanor of Aquitaine was a marriage of two dynamic personalities. Sooner or later, a violent clash between them was inevitable. Eleanor was not a traditional royal wife. She was heiress to Aquitaine in her own right, and the former wife of King Louis VII of France. She had

REGAL PROFILES

ELEANOR OF AQUITAINE: A SCANDALOUS QUEEN

ELEANOR'S FIERCE INDEPENDENCE and wayward nature led, naturally, to accusations of immorality. One of her courtiers, named Andrew, seems to have cashed in on Eleanor's reputation in a piece of salacious fiction that he wrote in 1186. Andrew's *De Amore or The Art of Courtly Love*, was set against the background of Eleanor's court at Poitiers between 1167 and 1173. Here, according to Andrew, Eleanor and Marie de Champagne, one of her two daughters by King Louis VII, were the focus of a cult that practiced adultery.

Eleanor's real love life was hardly less sensational. Gossip linked her with her father-in-law, Geoffrey d'Anjou, and with her own uncle, Raymond de Poitiers, the crusader Prince of Antioch. Eleanor's affair with Raymond was supposed to have taken place when she accompanied King Louis on the second crusade to the Holy Land, where Christians and Muslims waged war over Christ's birthplace between 1147 and 1149. The smears, however, went even further than this.

'She carried herself not very holily,' wrote Sir Richard Baker in *A Chronicle of the Kings of England*, published in 1643, 'but led a licentious life; and, which is the worst kind of licentiousness, in carnal familiarity with a (Muslim) Turk.'

Beautiful, charismatic and clever, Eleanor of Aquitaine was too sexy to meet with the approval of the prudish clerics of her day.

tasted power long before she married Henry, who was ten years her junior.

None of these credentials equipped Eleanor to conform to the 'ideal' consort of her time – the type of wife who stayed in the background while her husband took the limelight, or was expected to put up with her husband taking mistresses. Sometimes, in such circumstances, the wife and mistress actually became friends. Eleanor was most decidedly not that sort of woman.

A page from a medieval history of England showing (clockwise from top left) King Henry II, Richard I the Lionheart, King Henry III and King John. Each is holding a representation of a church with which he is associated.

She was strong-minded, self-confident and very independent. She objected fiercely to King Henry's numerous affairs and to his two known illegitimate children. When Rosamund Clifford, considered by some to be the great love of Henry's life, died suddenly in 1176, it was hinted that Eleanor had had her poisoned. Whatever the truth of the matter, Eleanor seems to have paid back her husband in kind by taking lovers of her own.

Hot-headed and unkempt

Henry II was not a regular medieval king, either. In the twelfth century, kings needed to be visibly impressive. Henry was hardly that. He had no interest in the

King Henry II and Thomas Becket, once friends, argued fiercely about the rights of the Pope over the Church in England. In this medieval manuscript, their hand movements represent their diametrically opposed opinions.

outward show and fashionable finery that surrounded other kings. Known as 'Curtmantle' or 'short coat', he was squat, square and freckle-faced. He often appeared unkempt and even grubby, and thought nothing of appearing at court straight from riding his horse, his clothes and boots covered in mud.

In a religious age, Henry cared nothing for religion. He frequently missed church services, and when he did attend, he spent his time sketching and chatting with his courtiers. All the same, beneath this rough and casual exterior, Henry II had a personality that hit people between the eyes. He was stubborn, autocratic and a powerhouse of energy, just like his mother.

But also like his mother, his temper was terrifying to witness. When in a rage, Henry went completely over the top: his pale eyes became fiery and bloodshot and he would literally tear his clothes apart, fall to the floor and chew the carpet. Luckily for him, in medieval times, 'carpets' were made of loose straw.

Anyone who crossed King Henry II was taking a huge risk. The one man who did so, not once but many times, set the scene for an epic tragedy. Henry appointed Thomas Becket as Chancellor of England at the start of his reign in 1154. Although Becket was 15 years older than Henry, the two men were close friends. They went hunting, gaming and hawking

> **When Becket appeared in court, dramatically carrying a large cross, he claimed that, as a churchman, the secular judges had no right to try him.... Even for Becket, this was going too far.**

together. Henry gave Becket so many estates and royal grants that Becket became a very wealthy man.

Excess and extravagance
Unlike the king, Becket had a taste for the high life. When Henry sent him on an embassy to Paris in 1158, Becket took with him 250 servants, 8 wagons full of provisions and expensive plates, and a wardrobe of 24 different outfits. In England, Becket kept a personal household of some 700 knights and employed 52 clerks to manage his estates. Devoted to the finest foods, he once ate a dish of eels that cost 100 shillings – at the time a phenomenal price for a meal.

Friends become foes
Henry came to trust Becket absolutely. In 1162, Becket became the most important churchman in England when he was appointed Archbishop of Canterbury. But this was more than just the latest in a long line of royal gifts. Ever since the time of William the Conqueror, the kings of England had tried to diminish the power of the Pope over their realm. Making Becket Archbishop of Canterbury was Henry's

way of putting in place a man who would fend off the Pope's demands. But if this was what Henry believed Becket would do for him, he was completely wrong.

Instead, a complete change came over Becket. He at once resigned as chancellor. He abandoned the good life and all its pleasures, giving away his expensive wardrobe, his fine plates and exquisite furniture. Instead, he devoted himself to study, prayer and acts of charity.

The fact that Henry's luxury-loving friend had become an ascetic was startling enough. But Becket's conversion went deeper than outward show. Instead of backing up Henry in dealings with the Pope, he obstructed the king at every turn.

Accusations and insults
The crunch came when the king demanded that clerks found guilty of crimes in the independent church courts should be handed over to the ordinary, secular courts for punishment. Becket turned this down flat. His relations with Henry, already strained, turned from friendship to black hatred. Henry hit out at Becket by fabricating various criminal charges against him. These included embezzling public funds while serving as chancellor.

When Becket appeared in court, dramatically carrying a large cross, he claimed that, as a churchman, the secular judges had no right to try him. He also appealed directly to the Pope for assistance. Even for Becket, this was going too far. In 1164, realizing his life was in danger he fled to Sens in France.

Becket's exile lasted six years. During that time, the king of France and the Pope managed to patch things up between the former friends-turned implacable enemies. This allowed Becket to return to England on 1 December

An engraving of a 12th century crown, which was meant to fit across the wearer's brow. It might have been worn in battle over the king's head armour in order to identify him to his soldiers – and his enemies!

DEEDS *of* **POWER**

MURDER IN THE CATHEDRAL

At around 5:00 p.m. on 29 December 1170, Henry's four knights marched into Canterbury Cathedral where they found Becket at prayer before the altar. In front of a large, frightened crowd of worshippers, they demanded that he cancel the excommunications. Becket ordered them to leave, in no uncertain terms.

Nearby, a young monk, Edward Grim, was watching the scene from behind the altar. Later, he wrote the following account of everything he saw and heard on that tragic evening.

'"You shall die!" the knights threatened Becket, only to receive the answer: "I am ready to die for my Lord that in my blood the Church may obtain liberty and peace."'

'Then,' wrote Edward Grim, 'they laid sacrilegious hands on him, pulling and dragging him that they may kill him outside the church, or carry him away a prisoner.... But when he could not be forced away...one of them pressed on him and clung to him

Archbishop Thomas Becket was unarmed and at prayer when King Henry's four knights burst into Canterbury Cathedral and attacked him as he prayed at the altar.

more closely. Him he pushed off... crying, "Touch me not, Reginald; you owe me fealty and subjection! You and your accomplices act like madmen!"

'The knight, fired with a terrible rage...waved his sword over (Becket's) head. "No faith," he cried, "nor subjection do I owe you against my fealty to my lord the king."

'Then (Becket), seeing the hour at hand which should put an end to this miserable life...inclined his neck as one who prays and, joining his hands, he lifted them up and commended his cause and that of the Church to God.... Scarce had he said the words than the wicked knight, fearing lest he should be rescued by the people and escape alive, leapt upon him suddenly and with his sword struck him on the head, cutting off the top of the crown.... (Becket) received a second blow on the head, but stood firm. At the third blow, he fell on his knees and elbows...saying in a low voice: "For the name of Jesus and the protection of the Church, I am ready to embrace death."

'Then the third knight inflicted a terrible wound as he lay (on the ground) by which the sword was broken against the stones and the crown, which was large, was separated from the head.... (Another) knight...put his foot on the neck of the priest and, horrible to say, scattered his brain and blood over the stones, calling out to the others: "Let us away, knights. He will rise no more".'

The 'meddlesome priest', his skull hacked to pieces, his brains splattered on the cathedral floor, was dead. But Henry was still not rid of him. Becket dead became just as irksome for the king as Becket alive.

The scene of the crime can still be seen today, at the altar in Canterbury Cathedral, Kent. Becket's death was known as The Martyrdom, since he was regarded as a martyr who died for the Church.

The murder caused anger and outrage throughout Christian Europe. In 1173, Becket was made a saint and a martyr. Canterbury became a place of pilgrimage and the cathedral a shrine to the murdered archbishop.

Bloodthirsty, headstrong and then remorseful in equal measure, Henry II was a far more hot-tempered and hasty character than this 19th century portrait suggests.

came to crowning English monarchs. As archbishop – even a disgraced archbishop – Becket's rights had been usurped. He was not prepared to let the insult pass. Instead, he excommunicated the Archbishop of York and the six bishops involved in the Young King's coronation.

Henry was in Normandy that Christmas, and when the news reached him he flew into one of his terrifying rages, shouting:

'What miserable drones and traitors have I nourished and promoted in my household who let their lord be treated with such shameful contempt by a low-born clerk? Will no one rid me of this meddlesome priest?'

Four of Henry's knights, Hugh de Moreville, William de Tracey, Reginald FitzUrse and Richard le Breton, took Henry at his word. They crossed to England, arrived at Canterbury whereupon they stormed into the cathedral, fully armed, and slaughtered Thomas Becket.

Far from being rewarded for their deed, the four knights were disgraced. They were forced to do penance by fasting. Then they were banished to the Holy Land. But the greatest display of remorse had to come from the king. Soon after the murder, Henry went to Ireland and laid low for a year or more. But the Angevin Empire could not, of course, be properly ruled by a fugitive, so eventually King Henry had to return to England and face the music.

Canterbury Cathedral became a place of pilgrimage after the murder of Thomas Becket. Becket's shrine was visited by thousands of pilgrims, until it was destroyed by King Henry VIII in the 16th century as an unwelcome reminder of how a subject had defied a king.

1170. But deep down his quarrel with the king was not resolved. Once home, Becket proved even more recklessly defiant than before.

Defiance leads to death

On 14 June 1170, Henry's eldest surviving son, eight-year-old Prince Henry, had been crowned by the Archbishop of York and became known as the Young King. The crowning of an heir in his father's lifetime was a failsafe device: it was meant to deter powerful rivals and would-be usurpers. What King Henry had forgotten, or more likely ignored, was the fact that archbishops of Canterbury had a monopoly when it

King Henry II was made to suffer for the murder of Thomas Becket. Here he is pictured doing penance at Becket's tomb in Canterbury, a public demonstration of remorse demanded of him by the Pope.

A king is humbled

His punishments were grave, but they were not too damaging, except perhaps to the royal ego. Henry was not excommunicated, though he was banned from entering a church. This would hardly have troubled Henry, who was not particularly religious anyway. In addition, his lands in France were laid under interdict: this meant the protection of the Church no longer applied there. So any rival could invade them. And if that happened, Henry could not seek aid from the Pope. But there was more to come.

On 12 July 1174, King Henry walked barefoot through the streets of Canterbury dressed in sackcloth, the traditional garb of humility. He prayed at the cathedral and was afterwards scourged by 80 monks, who beat him with branches. Sore, bleeding and half-naked, the king spent the following night in the freezing crypt where Thomas Becket was buried. Only after this was Henry given a pardon for the sin he had committed.

Unfortunately, King Henry did not learn very much from the Becket affair. He certainly made no attempt to tame his temper or to think before speaking. Far from it. Three years after Becket's murder, his fiery nature led him into another, much more damaging, quarrel. This time, it led to disaster.

Apple of the king's eye

In 1169, at Montmirail, some 40 miles (64km) east of Paris, King Henry shared out his vast empire between three of his four surviving sons. Prince Henry, heir to the throne and now aged 14, would have England and Normandy. Richard, 12, the future King Richard the Lionheart, received his mother's Duchy of Aquitaine. The fourth surviving son, Geoffrey, aged 11, was to have Brittany in France. The youngest, John, received no lands, for he was only two years old when the

---

Henry was not going to get away with handing out empty promises. In 1173, his sons' resentment boiled over into open rebellion.

---

arrangements were made. But this was not due to any lack of fatherly affection.

John, who was given the nickname of 'Lackland', was Henry's best-loved child. The king made several efforts to provide for him. These efforts included marriage to a wealthy French heiress, but it never came about. In 1177, when John was aged 10, Henry made him Lord of Ireland. Eight years later, John visited Ireland. But he spent his time frittering away his father's money on luxury living, and annoyed the Irish by poking fun at them.

Family feud

As for Henry's other sons, they fully anticipated ruling the lands they had been given. They also expected to receive the revenues their lands produced. But King Henry had never intended his sons to have any real power in his lifetime. They were simply figureheads. All power and revenues remained in their father's hands.

But Henry was not going to be able to get away with handing out empty promises. In 1173, his sons' resentment boiled over into open rebellion. Queen Eleanor, who had grudges of her own against the king, was their chief ally. Henry's sons also found

many malcontents to join them, including barons in both England and Normandy who chafed under King Henry's control. But by far their most important supporter was King Louis VII of France, their mother's former husband.

Louis coveted Henry's Angevin lands and was only too pleased to help his rival's sons destabilize their father's power. Not this time, however. In 1173, King Henry had sufficient military punch to put down the family rebellion and it came to nothing.

Even before the actual rebellion, Queen Eleanor had realized what a dangerous game she was playing. She tried to slip away across the English Channel to Chinon, in Anjou, disguised as a man. But she was recognized and brought back to England. Henry placed her under house arrest at Winchester, where she remained for the next 16 years.

The seal of King Henry II, showing him seated on his throne, sword in one hand and in the other the orb that was an indication of his royal authority. Royal seals on documents and charters showed they had royal sanction and were therefore legal.

Philip, the robber king

Once the rebellion was over, King Henry was arguably more generous towards his sons than they deserved: he forgave them and presented the Young King and Prince Richard with castles and revenues. This gesture, he hoped, would prevent them from rebelling again.

But the family disputes were not over. King Louis of France died in 1180 and was succeeded by his much more capable and far more dangerous son, King Philip II Augustus. Together with his father's throne, Philip inherited his father's plans to poach the Angevin lands. The Young King and Geoffrey were ready-made stooges for Philip's wiles, but the French king's plans were stymied when both of them died prematurely. The Young King died of dysentery and fever in 1183. Geoffrey, who had a passion for tournaments, was killed in 1186 while fighting in the lists.

Only two of Henry's four legitimate sons were left. John remained faithful to his father, but Richard was

Henry II was heartbroken when he learned that his son John had betrayed him by joining his brother Richard in open rebellion. This picture shows the moment when the king, hand clutched to his heart, received the news.

nursing a new grudge: the king planned to give John certain castles in France which Richard claimed as his own. Even worse, King Henry refused to recognize Richard as heir to the English throne, even though, with the death of the Young King, he had become the eldest surviving son.

This was how Philip got a second chance in his bid to destroy the Plantagenets and their Angevin Empire. No one knows if Richard knew about Philip's secret agenda. But he made no bones about joining the French king in a last all-out assault on his father in 1189.

The king's premonition

King Henry had known all along that this was going to happen. Before the death of the Young King in 1183, he had commissioned a painting and ordered it to be displayed in the royal chamber of Winchester Palace. The painting showed four eaglets attacking a

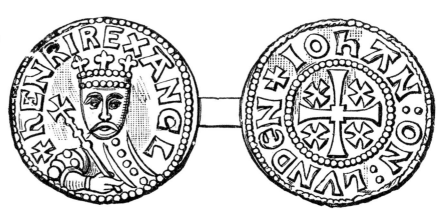

A silver penny minted in the reign of King Henry II. The king's portrait, together with his sceptre, the symbol of his power, is on the obverse (left). The lettering on the reverse (right), shows that the coin was minted in London.

Sick at heart and already ill with a fever, Henry died five days later. As he lay dying, he cursed his sons for their treachery. Only Geoffrey, his illegitimate son, was there at his bedside.

parent bird. The fourth eaglet was poised to peck out the parent's eyes.

The four eaglets', the king explained 'are my four sons who cease not to persecute me even unto death. The youngest of them, whom I now embrace with so much affection, will sometime in the end insult me more grievously and more dangerously than any of the others.'

The King's prediction came true when Prince John deserted his father and joined forces with Richard: the castles his father planned to give him were not grand enough for John's ambitions. The news broke Henry's

heart. After that, the end came quickly.

Richard and King Philip stormed across the territories of the Angevin Empire in northern France, capturing each of the king's strongholds, one after the other. At the same time, almost all the barons of Maine, Touraine and Anjou deserted Henry. Driven out of Le Mans, where he had been born, Henry fled to Chinon in Anjou and took refuge in his castle. His enemies pursued him even there. On 4 July 1189, they made humiliating demands on Henry. There was no way he could resist them.

Guillaume le Breton, King Philip's chaplain and biographer wrote:

'He resigned himself wholly to the counsel and will of Philip, King of France, in such a way that whatever the King of France should provide or adjudge, the King of England would carry out in every way and without contradiction.'

A broken man

Sick at heart and already ill with a fever, Henry died five days later. As he lay dying, he cursed his sons for their treachery. Only Geoffrey, his illegitimate son by Rosamund Clifford, was there at his bedside. This was how the chronicler Gerald of Wales described the last painful days of King Henry II:

'For as branches lopped from the stem of a tree cannot reunite,' he wrote 'so the tree stripped of its boughs, a treasonable outrage, is shorn both of its dignity and gracefulness.'

CRUSADING KINGS AND TROUBLESOME BARONS

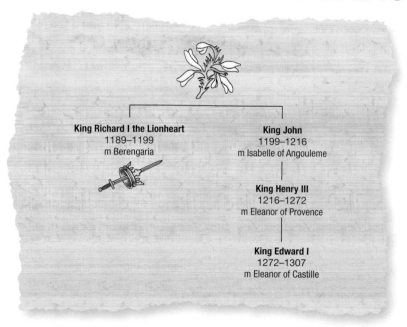

King Richard I the Lionheart
1189–1199
m Berengaria

King John
1199–1216
m Isabelle of Angouleme

King Henry III
1216–1272
m Eleanor of Provence

King Edward I
1272–1307
m Eleanor of Castille

When he learned of his father's death, the first thing the new king, Richard I, did was to go and pay his last respects to the parent he had betrayed. He didn't waste much time on it. Some said Richard knelt beside his father's body only for as long as it took to recite the Lord's Prayer.

◆

Next, Richard freed his mother, Queen Eleanor, from imprisonment at Winchester. Richard's coronation took place in September 1189. After that, he returned to Aquitaine. Leaving England set the pattern for Richard's reign.

Richard was already a celebrated warrior, so much

Although he shamefully neglected his kingdom of England, Richard the Lionheart has long been admired as a great and valiant warrior monarch. This statue stands in Old Palace Yard, close by the Houses of Parliament in London.

so that he was nicknamed the Lionheart. He certainly stands as the ultimate fighting king of medieval times. But he had no interest in fighting to defend England. Apart from crusades, Richard's main aim in life was defending his beloved Duchy of Aquitaine against the French king, Philip II.

Philip was not Richard's only dangerous enemy. Richard's younger brother, John, aimed to seize England during several of Richard's frequent absences. The chronicler Richard of Devizes once described John as 'a flighty, habitual traitor'. John had no

This picture, painted between 1475 and 1500, shows the coronation of King Richard I, which took place in London on 30 September 1189. Barons, bishops and monks took part in the coronation procession.

reservations about betraying his brother, just as he had betrayed his father.

Even so, Richard was fond of John. He arranged a marriage for him with a wealthy heiress, Isabel of Gloucester, and gave him huge estates in England. This, though, was not good enough for John, who had his heart set on becoming regent of England when

> **Largely victorious on crusade, Richard was hailed as an ever greater hero. But while in the Holy Land, he insulted a fellow crusader, Duke Leopold of Austria. Leopold swore vengeance...**

Richard left on a crusade. Instead, Richard chose his mother, Eleanor of Aquitaine, to look after his kingdom. John also expected to be named as Richard's heir. But that prize went instead to four-year-old Prince Arthur of Brittany, son of their late brother Geoffrey. As time would tell, John would deal with Prince Arthur in his own ruthless way.

Embarking on crusades to fight Muslims in the Holy Land was phenomenally expensive. To raise much-needed funds, King Richard virtually put England up for sale. He sold earldoms, lordships, sheriffdoms, castles, lands, estates, entire towns and anything else convertible into ready cash. He even planned to sell the capital, London. But, so he complained, he could not find anyone rich enough to buy it.

At last, in July of 1190, Richard set out for the Holy Land with a fleet of more than 100 ships and 8,000 men, intending to return within three years. But that was not to be.

Royal blunder

In military terms, the Third Crusade was a success. Richard gave the Muslims a thrashing and was hailed as an even greater hero than before. But while in the Holy Land, Richard made a crucial error. He insulted a fellow crusader, Duke Leopold of Austria. Leopold swore vengeance and spotted his chance when Richard was on his way home by sea in 1192. Richard's ship sank near Venice. From there, Richard was forced to complete his journey overland. In Vienna, Austria, Duke Leopold was waiting for him.

Many stories went around about how Richard slipped up, enabling Leopold to capture him. One had it that Richard tried to pass himself off as a kitchen

This picture, from the *Luttrell Psalter* (1300–1340) shows King Richard and Saladin jousting at a tournament. Saladin is portrayed with a fearsome blue face. The picture is fanciful: in real life, Richard and Saladin never met at a tournament.

A BITTER END

NO ONE KNOWS FOR CERTAIN what happened to Prince Arthur once he had been incarcerated in King John's castle in Rouen. But the annals of Margam Abbey in Glamorgan, Wales, contain a gruesome version of his final fate:

'... King John kept (Arthur) alive in prison for some time. At length, in the castle of Rouen, after dinner on the Thursday before Easter (3 April 1203) when he was drunk and possessed by the devil, he slew him with his own hand, and, tying a heavy stone to the body, cast it into the (River) Seine. It was discovered by a fisherman in his net... (and) taken for secret burial.'

Prince Arthur, who had a better claim to the English throne, was wasting his time pleading for his life with King John. John couldn't afford to let him live.

hand, but forgot to remove an expensive ring that no kitchen hand could possibly have owned.

The king's ransom

Once Leopold got his hands on Richard, he went for a quick profit. He 'sold' Richard to Emperor Henry VI of Germany. With this valuable 'property' in his possession, the emperor demanded a huge ransom. To make the most out of his rare acquisition, Henry put Richard up for auction. One of the main bidders was Richard himself. The others were King Philip and the faithless Prince John: John had allied himself to the French king as part of his latest scheme – to take Richard's lands in France.

This was an auction Richard had to win. If he had lost, King Philip would have had his wicked way with the Angevin lands in France. And Prince John would get his greedy hands on England. Fortunately, Richard was able to outbid his rivals. The ransom was set at 150,000 marks of silver.

Once again, England was milked dry to raise this immense sum of money. Every possible money-raising device was used. Church gold and silver plate were seized and sold. A whole year's wool crop was taken from ranches run by two Cistercian monasteries, and a hefty 25 per cent tax was levied on all incomes.

Big brother walks free

Richard was finally freed after 16 months, on 4 February 1194. He arrived in England about six weeks later.

Prince John had been informed that Richard was on his way. King Philip warned him: 'Look to yourself, the devil is loosed'. As soon as he heard Richard was coming home, John fled to Philip's court for protection. He was terrified of what would happen when his brother found him. Luckily for him, Richard did not punish John too severely. He took away John's lands for a time, but only to teach him a lesson, and they were soon restored.

A picture illustrating Richard's imprisonment in Austria, painted in 1200, the year after his death. Richard appears twice, in the middle holding a glove, and looking thoroughly fed up at a window, on the left.

FACT *or* FICTION

RUTHLESS REVENGE

MAYBE IT WAS NO COINCIDENCE that the de Briouze family were the patrons of Margam Abbey, where Arthur had disappeared. They soon found themselves next in line for John's revenge. William de Briouze had borrowed large sums of money from John, but he had failed to pay him back. Now John not only demanded immediate repayment, but ordered de Briouze and his wife, Matilda, to hand over their two sons as hostages for their father's debts. Matilda refused, courageously telling King John to his face that a man who had murdered his own nephew was not fit to have charge of her children.

From then on, the full weight of royal vengeance fell on the de Briouze family. William's castles were confiscated and his lands were seized. Worst of all, Matilda and her children were imprisoned in Windsor Castle: despite offers of ransom, John left them there to starve to death. After this, William de Briouze was a broken man. He fled to France, where he died in 1211.

'Think no more of it, John', Richard told him, 'You are only a child who has had evil counsel.' Yet John was no child – he was 27 years old at the time.

Although he forgave and indulged him, Richard did not trust his younger brother. He gave him no powers in England when Richard once more left for France on 12 May 1194. Richard never returned. King Philip was

> **John's second marriage was controversial from the start. Isabella had already set her heart on another man – Hugh de Lusignan.**

still preying on the Angevin lands, and Richard spent the last five years of his life fighting to keep him at bay. In 1199, he was badly wounded during the siege of Chalus Castle in Limousin. The wound became septic and killed him.

John's dream comes true

When news of his brother's death reached him, Prince John was in Brittany. He acted fast and returned to England at once. John spent the next few weeks gathering support from the barons and the clergy. That done, he had himself crowned king at Westminster Abbey on 27 May 1199. Next, John prepared to

provide his throne with heirs. He divorced his childless wife, Isabella of Gloucester, and married another Isabella, 12-year-old heiress to Angoulême in France.

A reluctant bride

John's second marriage was controversial from the start. Isabella had already set her heart on another man – Hugh de Lusignan. Hugh loved Isabella in return and the couple were betrothed. But Isabella's ambitious family had other ideas. They saw great advantage for themselves in having her as queen of England. If that meant Isabella had to give up the love of her life, well, so be it. Isabella dutifully married King John, who was 20 years her senior, at Bordeaux Cathedral on 24 August 1200.

Hugh de Lusignan was furious and complained to King Philip. Philip, of course, was only too pleased to beat the king of England with this particular stick. He demanded that the king explain himself. John, meanwhile, attempted his own solution. He tried to appease Hugh de Lusignan by offering his own illegitimate daughter, Joan. Hugh declined. In 1202, John refused to appear before Philip, as ordered. This gave the French king the excuse he needed to confiscate all John's lands in France. For the moment, though, Hugh de Lusignan had lost his Isabella.

John's luck holds

For John, there still remained the problem of his nephew, Prince Arthur of Brittany. As the son of

John's elder brother, the late Geoffrey, Arthur had a better claim to the English throne than John did. King Philip, always on the lookout for ways to cause trouble for John, supported Arthur's claim. So did the barons of Anjou, Maine and Touraine. This was pow-

King John is shown paying homage to King Philip of France for his French lands. Although he was King of England, John was the vassal of the French monarch, and regular homage reinforced his fealty to his lord.

erful opposition, but then John had a stroke of luck.

While in France in the summer of 1202, fighting to regain the lost Angevin lands, he managed to capture more than 250 knights during his siege of Mirabeau Castle in Aquitaine. One of them was Arthur of Brittany.

Arthur was imprisoned at a castle in Falaise belonging to John's chamberlain, Hubert de Burgh. John supposedly wanted Arthur blinded and castrated, but Hubert de Burgh would not hear of it. De Burgh

pres son regna Henry le terz sun fiz. lvi. aunz. si
fust de .ix. aunz de age quant fust corone. E en son
tens fust la bataylle de Euelsm. ou fust occys syr
Symund de munfort. e sun fiz Henry. e syre hugh le des
penser e muz des barons e des cheualers de Engle
tere. puis mourst cyl Henry le roy. e gist a Westmuster.

UNSCRUPULOUS AND IMMORAL

ALONG WITH NUMEROUS OTHER BAD HABITS, John also went in for sexual blackmail. He made a habit of seducing the wives, sisters and daughters of his barons, and then demanding hush money to keep the affairs quiet. The families of his victims had no choice but to pay up: if they refused, their family dignity was at stake. John's queen, Isabella of Angoulême, was naturally resentful. She tried paying her husband back in kind by taking lovers of her own. John soon brought her up short, however. He had her lovers killed and draped their bodies over her bed.

King John was the most reviled and detested monarch England ever had – the complete villain, in total contrast to his valiant brother Richard the Lionheart.

was not alone in his disdain for the king's plan. Another great magnate, William de Briouze, fourth Baron Briouze, also refused to countenance so callous a retribution.

John was not going to let the baron get away with such treachery. He marked down William de Briouze and his family for future punishment. As for Arthur, he was transferred to one of John's own castles, at Rouen. Once there, the king could do what he liked with him. Soon afterwards, Prince Arthur disappeared from history.

A slur on the king

By his ruthless and cruel treatment of the de Briouze family and others, John had fully alerted his barons to the fact that he was a dangerous tyrant. Even then,

In this illustration, King Henry III is flanked by two bishops who have just placed a crown on his head. This is possibly meant to illustrate Henry's coronation, although at the time, he was a young boy, not a grown man.

John might have saved himself had he proved to be that medieval ideal – a successful warrior king. Instead, he lost the Angevin lands in France to a triumphant King Philip in 1204. The magnificent Angevin Empire was gone forever. With this loss, the barons coined another nickname for John: 'Softsword'. It was the worst insult the barons could have dreamed up.

John, in turn, became intensely suspicious of anyone with power in the land. He even pursued barons who remained loyal to him, forcing some to become royal debtors by imposing huge sums in return for new titles. His victims, of course, could not refuse. Geoffrey de Mandeville, for example, was obliged to offer 20,000 marks for the earldom of Gloucester: part of the deal was that Geoffrey took John's former wife, Isabella of Gloucester, off the king's hands.

The king's bloodthirsty activities were taking a toll on his supporters. His treatment of the barons eventually became too much for them, and they rebelled. At Runnymede on 15 June 1215, the barons forced John to sign Magna Carta. This was not a declaration of democratic liberties, as is often thought, but a statement of the barons' rights and privileges.

Victory for France

However, breaking his word came all too easily for King John. He reneged almost at once. Civil war ensued. Surprisingly enough for 'Softsword', John was soon winning. In desperation, some barons turned traitor: they invited Louis Capet, the son of King Philip of France, to bring an army to England. Louis Capet was to remove King John from the throne and take his place.

Louis arrived at Dover, on the south coast of England, on 14 May 1216. Twelve days later he reached London, where his forces captured two important strongholds: the White Tower, at the Tower of London, and Westminster Palace. That done, Louis was hailed as King of England by his army. But in Rome, the Pope had other ideas. Louis had broken rules by attacking a rightful Christian king. As punishment, the Pope excommunicated Louis and placed his lands in France under interdict.

Meanwhile, John was gathering support all over England. If there was one thing the English detested, it

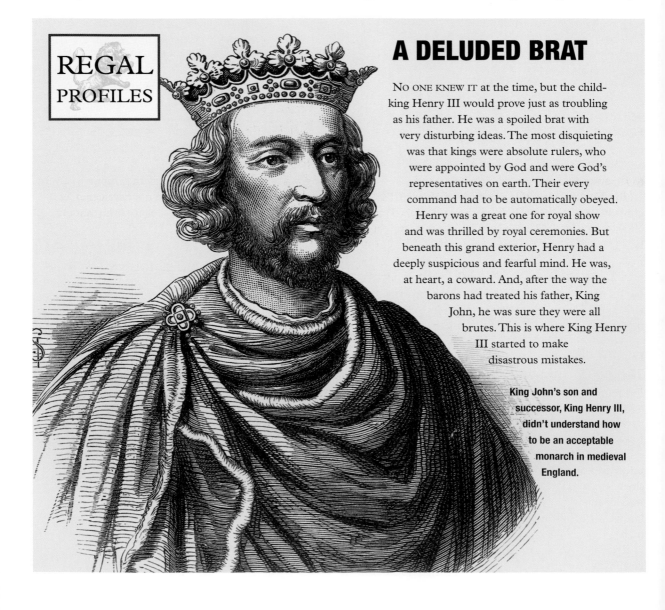

REGAL PROFILES

A DELUDED BRAT

NO ONE KNEW IT at the time, but the child-king Henry III would prove just as troubling as his father. He was a spoiled brat with very disturbing ideas. The most disquieting was that kings were absolute rulers, who were appointed by God and were God's representatives on earth. Their every command had to be automatically obeyed. Henry was a great one for royal show and was thrilled by royal ceremonies. But beneath this grand exterior, Henry had a deeply suspicious and fearful mind. He was, at heart, a coward. And, after the way the barons had treated his father, King John, he was sure they were all brutes. This is where King Henry III started to make disastrous mistakes.

King John's son and successor, King Henry III, didn't understand how to be an acceptable monarch in medieval England.

A charter issued by King John, dated 9 May 1215, carrying the royal seal. The same design was often used for seals in successive reigns. The royal seal validated the document to which it was attached and was therefore a protection against forgery and fraud.

was a foreigner attempting to snatch the throne. They would rather be ruled by a home-grown king like John, however unsatisfactory he was.

A child takes the throne

Then, quite suddenly, John died of dysentery on 18 October 1216. He was succeeded by his nine-year-old son, who became King Henry III. Now that the barons had a rightful king with no track record of dark deeds and dirty doings, their support for Louis Capet began to fall away.

But England was still in crisis, and Henry III's coronation was a hasty, hole-in-the-wall affair. The child-king, mother Queen Isabella and the royal family had fled to England's west country after Louis Capet reached London. This was why the ceremony took place in Gloucester Cathedral on 28 October 1216, ten days after John's death. It was a coronation without a crown: instead, Henry had to make do with his mother's torque, a small twisted gold necklace.

Regent saves the day

The situation in England was still very dangerous. Fortunately, William the Marshal, who was appointed King Henry's regent, was a splendid fighter. He soon dealt with Louis Capet. The French prince was forced to sign a peace agreement in London on 12 September 1217. By 1219, William the Marshal had the barons under control and order was restored. Only then, when she knew her son was safe on the throne, did Queen Isabella return to France. There, in 1220, she at long last married Hugh de Lusignan. Their long-delayed marriage was a happy one, and they had nine children.

Henry's views on the status of kings were ill-considered and unrealistic. He did not seem to understand that English kings had never been absolute rulers: there was always some assembly – the Anglo-Saxon Witangemot, the barons, ultimately Parliament – which took it as their right to 'advise' the monarch. Challenging such a right was something even kings could not get away with. As long as he remained under age, Henry's views on kingship did not matter too much. But he failed to outgrow them once he took on his full royal role in 1227.

Conflict of interest

There were serious differences between the interests of the king and those of his barons. Henry loved all things French. His barons had little interest beyond the shores of England. Henry dreamed of regaining the lost Angevin lands and even extending the empire eastward into Germany. The barons could not have cared less.

At court, where the barons believed they should

Des Roches, who had served King John, believed that royal power should be unrestricted and encouraged King Henry to become a despot.

---

have a major influence, they were vastly outnumbered by the French. Henry took a French wife, Eleanor of Provence, in 1236 and filled his court with her relatives. There was always a warm welcome, too, for the king's Lusignan half-brothers, the sons of his mother Isabella by her second marriage. But worst of all by far, King Henry ignored his barons and surrounded himself with French advisers.

One was Peter des Roches, who had served King John. Des Roches believed that royal power should be unrestricted and encouraged King Henry to become a despot. Another influential adviser was

William of Savoy, Queen Eleanor's uncle, who became important in the royal council. Even the Archbishop of Canterbury was a Frenchman – Boniface of Savoy, another of the Queen's uncles.

King hatches wild scheme

But then King Henry himself wrecked the whole situation, and gave the barons their chance to get their own back. The king was fond of ambitious, crazy schemes, and in 1254 he ran into big trouble. He had made a deal with the Pope to conquer the Mediterranean

> **De Montfort was a Frenchman who had inherited an English earldom through his mother. He was every inch a brutal, macho, self-seeking baron. But he possessed a personality that overwhelmed lesser men.**

island of Sicily: after that, Henry had planned to make his second son, Prince Edmund, king. To fund this plan, the Pope gave permission for King Henry to exact heavy taxes from his subjects. Henry's barons were furious. They had no interest in the King's mad plan. They refused to pay. The Church refused, too. The ordinary people were struggling with bad weather, failed harvests and famine, so they could not pay either.

Henry was unable to raise the funds agreed upon. There were rumblings from the Pope, and the king was threatened with excommunication. But with the king in trouble, a far greater threat came from a great council convened by the barons. In 1258, they drew up a long-term plan called the Provisions of Oxford. This was intended to banish French members from Henry's court.

Under the Provisions, the most important government posts were to go to Englishmen. The royal revenues were to be paid directly into the Exchequer: this was to prevent King Henry from frittering funds away on his French admirers. Among the most important provisions was the setting up of a 15-man baronial council to 'advise' the king. It was actually intended to control him.

The barons in this nineteenth-century engraving look respectful as they bow to King Henry, but what they're really doing is making their demands. This is why Henry, standing (left) with a crown on his head, looks so wary.

The king is captured

Henry was caught off guard. The royal treasury was almost empty. His subjects were starving. Their mood was turning ugly. He was left with only one course of action – give in. So Henry duly signed the Provisions of Oxford. This kept the barons happy for a time. But at once, Henry started to look for ways to renege.

Henry had to wait awhile for the chance to go back on his word. It came in 1264, when the barons, always vicious rivals, began to quarrel among themselves. But when Henry renounced the Provisions of Oxford, they set their rivalries aside. War followed, and extreme humiliation for King Henry. At the battle of Lewes in Sussex on 14 May 1264, the king and his son and heir, Prince Edward, were taken prisoner. They fell into the hands of the barons' charismatic leader, Simon de Montfort, Earl of Leicester.

Ironically, de Montfort was a Frenchman who had inherited an English earldom through his mother in 1230. He was every inch a brutal, macho, self-seeking baron. But he possessed a magnetic personality that overwhelmed lesser men. He was also a brilliant military leader of the Richard the Lionheart class.

Henry had been so impressed with Simon that in 1238 he had been allowed to marry the king's sister, Princess Eleanor. But Simon was not the sort of man to bow and scrape to his royal brother-in-law. Far from it. Simon had little time for the cowardly king. He once told Henry he should be locked up because of his feeble military abilities. Nor was Simon afraid to exploit his grand position to the fullest. He was impudent enough to use the king's name without permission to secure loans. He almost ended up in the Tower of London for such acts.

King's humiliation is complete

But when Henry reneged on the Provisions of Oxford, it was too much for Simon de Montfort. As far as he was concerned, breaking an oath was more than just blasphemy – it was an insult to God.

Thus Simon treated Henry III with even more contempt after the battle of Lewes. The king was not only Simon's prisoner, he was Simon's hostage and puppet.

Nor was Simon above intimidating Henry. He forced him to sign certain laws, orders and other documents. In 1265, he also convened a Parliament – something only the king could normally do – and made Henry submit to its demands. No king of England had ever suffered such humiliation, not even King John.

The son shines brightly

King Henry's son, Prince Edward, was kept prisoner along with his father. Edward, aged 25, was much more gutsy than Henry. He was not afraid of the mighty Simon de Montfort. Edward knew, too, that many barons were chafing under Simon's rule. They

DEEDS
of
POWER

MERCILESS UNTIL THE END

WHEN THE PAID KILLERS found Simon de Montfort, they showed him no mercy. They hacked him through the neck, and once on the ground, he was mutilated horribly. His body was torn to pieces. Having dealt with their leader, Edward was determined de Montfort's supporters should not get away. As they fled into a nearby church, they too were pursued and ruthlessly cut down by the same hit squad.

A monk who was hiding in the church at the time left an account of what he saw:

'The choir... and the inside walls and the cross and the statues and the altar were sprayed with the blood of the wounded and the dead, so that from the bodies that were around the high altar a stream of blood ran down into the crypt.'

Prince Edward (right), protects his aging father, King Henry III, during the battle of Evesham in which Simon de Montfort was killed.

He was watched by guards, including Simon's son, Henry de Montfort. Another of the guards, Thomas de Clare, seems to have been involved in the plot. Edward was riding side by side with Henry de Montfort when, by a given signal, he edged away. Then he spurred his horse and galloped off. Thomas de Clare followed. Though chased by other guards, they managed to make their escape.

Now that Edward was free, the discontented barons had a leader. A few weeks later, led by Edward, the forces of the king met Simon's army at Evesham in Worcestershire. Edward organized a hit squad to seek out Simon de Montfort and kill both him and his followers.

After this overwhelming and bloody victory, King Henry was restored to his throne. He immediately revoked all the documents Simon had forced him to sign. But at last he had learned his lesson. In the seven years until his death from a stroke in 1272, Henry concentrated on completing a new Westminster Abbey, leaving the government of England to Prince Edward.

The South Nave Aisle of London's Westminster Abbey, photographed in 1912. After he regained his throne in 1265, Henry III left political affairs to his son, Prince Edward. Instead, Henry spent the last seven years of his reign working on the restoration of the Abbey.

objected fiercely to the way he was feathering his family nest while the king was in his power.

First, though, Prince Edward had to escape. His opportunity came on 18 May 1265, while he was out riding near Hereford in the west of England.

As the Battle of Evesham demonstrated, Edward was not in the least like his father. Forceful and brutal, he was willing to shed blood in buckets to get his own way. But as King Edward I after 1272, he was also the strong, dominant royal leader England had been lacking for more than 80 years. The downside was that Edward I was a hard act to follow. The son who had to follow him in 1307 was not up to the job. Yet another scandalous reign loomed over England. And the new king, Edward II, was going to suffer for it in the most ghastly way his enemies could devise.

LOVERS, LAND AND TREASON

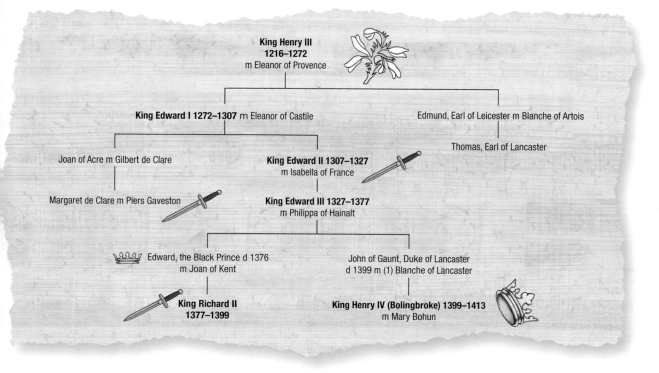

King Henry III
1216–1272
m Eleanor of Provence

King Edward I 1272–1307 m Eleanor of Castile

Edmund, Earl of Leicester m Blanche of Artois

Thomas, Earl of Lancaster

Joan of Acre m Gilbert de Clare

King Edward II 1307–1327
m Isabella of France

Margaret de Clare m Piers Gaveston

King Edward III 1327–1377
m Philippa of Hainalt

Edward, the Black Prince d 1376
m Joan of Kent

John of Gaunt, Duke of Lancaster
d 1399 m (1) Blanche of Lancaster

King Richard II
1377–1399

King Henry IV (Bolingbroke) 1399–1413
m Mary Bohun

Edward II was undoubtedly a disaster on two legs. Long before he became king in 1307, his courtiers and officials knew all about his curious habits and strange interests.

✦

Edward enjoyed menial pursuits. He liked nothing better than digging and thatching, very undignified work for an heir to the throne. The barons were thoroughly scandalized. For them, it was bad enough that Edward was no good at proper royal activities – like jousting in tournaments and making war. But a king who enjoyed grubbing around in the earth like a peasant was just too much.

On 28 February 1308, Edward II and his wife Isabella were crowned king and queen at Westminster by the Bishop of Winchester.

The king in love

This was not the worst of it. Edward II was a blatant homosexual. Except for his wife, Queen Isabella and her ladies-in-waiting, Edward banned women from his court. He was much more interested in beautiful young men like his beloved 'Perot' – Piers Gaveston, a Gascon knight who became his closest companion. No one doubted that Edward and Gaveston were lovers. They had known each other since they were children. Gaveston was good looking and physically attractive. Unlike Edward, he excelled at jousting tournaments. He made a habit of challenging barons to matches and beat them all. What's more, he insulted them by poking fun and assigning them rude nicknames. They hated him.

While King Edward I was still alive, father and son had violent public quarrels over Gaveston. Twice, the old king threw Gaveston out of England, and forbade him to return. But once his father was dead and he became king, there was no holding back King Edward II. He immediately recalled Gaveston to England and showered him with gifts. He made him Earl of Cornwall and lord of the rich estates that went with the title.

Marriages a sham

Gaveston married Edward's niece, Margaret Clare, a rich heiress in her own right. But Margaret's marriage was no more fulfilling than Isabella's. Their husbands were besotted with each other and the wives had to take a back seat.

King Edward was warned often enough that he was playing a dangerous game. But he was stubborn, always wanted his own way, and paid no attention. Secure, so he thought, in the love of the king, Gaveston himself became unbearable.

'He lorded it over (the barons) like a second king,

Brute force and threats came naturally to Thomas of Lancaster and his fellow barons. In 1308, they resorted to both. Like his grandfather, Henry III, Edward was at heart a coward.

---

to whom all were subject and none equal ', wrote the monk of Malmesbury. 'For Piers accounted no one his fellow, save the king alone…. His arrogance was intolerable to the barons and a prime cause of hatred and rancour.'

King and lover delight to shock

Edward took every opportunity to show off his lover. The greatest performance of all was at his coronation in 1308, where a major role was bestowed upon Gaveston: he carried the crown and another precious piece of regalia, the sword of Saint Edward. So splendidly dressed was he that it was said he appeared more like the Roman god Mars than a mere mortal.

At the feast that followed, Gaveston sat next to the king in the place Isabella should have occupied. Even more shocking, the king and his lover repeatedly fondled each other at the table while the guests watched, open-mouthed.

Isabella was only 12 years old when she came to England to marry King Edward II. It was a dynastic marriage, meant to ally England with France. But for Isabella, a homosexual husband was not part of the deal. Nor did she expect to see Gaveston wearing rings and jewels that her father had given Edward as wedding presents. So it wasn't long before the child bride was writing to her father complaining she was 'the most miserable wife in the world'.

Barons demand Gaveston's exile

Queen Isabella was too young to do anything about her wretched situation. But the barons had no intention of sitting helplessly on the sidelines. They planned to get rid of Gaveston. Fortunately, the barons had among them the leader they needed to oppose King Edward and bring Gaveston down: Thomas, Earl of Lancaster, Leicester, Derby, Lincoln and Salisbury, and lord of extensive lands in the north of England. Thomas was King Edward's first cousin. He was vicious, greedy, ambitious and self-serving. And he hated Edward with a passion.

Brute force and threats came naturally to Thomas of Lancaster and his fellow barons. In 1308, they resorted to both. Like his grandfather, Henry III, Edward was at heart a coward. He caved in to the barons' demands.

Gaveston was again forced to leave England. But he soon returned, and the barons had to turn up the pressure. On 27 September 1311, the barons warned Edward that if he did not get rid of Gaveston the result would be civil war. Once again, Edward caved in. Gaveston left for France, but again he came back, this time within three months, at Christmas, 1311.

The end of the affair

Eventually the barons acknowledged that exile was not working. Gaveston would always find some way to sneak back to his lover. And the infatuated king would always welcome him, quite literally, with open arms.

The English barons were sick of Piers Gaveston, who was stopping them from exerting influence over Edward II. Once they made Gaveston their prisoner, he was doomed. He was summarily killed, without trial.

The barons knew what they must do. On 9 June 1312, they had Gaveston kidnapped and imprisoned in Warwick Castle. The castle belonged to Thomas of Lancaster. Ten days later, Gaveston was marched out, barefoot, to nearby Blacklow Hill. There, two of Thomas's men impaled him on their swords and hacked off his head.

King Edward was distraught. He wept and lamented over his murdered lover. But killing Gaveston was not the barons' only intention. They were determined to grab top positions in the king's government. So, in 1311, they forced Edward to agree to a set of ordinances. Edward was forbidden to leave England without the barons' permission. He must stop appointing ministers and officials. He had to summon Parliament at least once a year. Parliament would control the king's finances. It was a straitjacket: the purpose was to prevent another Piers Gaveston from monopolizing the king.

Two new companions

Edward chafed and fumed over these restraints. All the same, for nine or ten years, he more or less behaved himself. He had had to. Thomas of Lancaster, now the real ruler of England, was watching everything he did. Then, in about 1320, the king's love life started to heat up again. He managed to sneak two new close friends into his court – a father and son, both named Hugh Despenser.

It was the Gaveston business all over again. The Despensers snapped up gifts, estates and money. Hugh

Thomas of Lancaster wanted to ensure that Piers Gaveston was dead and ordered one of the Welshmen who had killed him to show him Gaveston's severed head. After this, a Dominican friar took it to show the king.

Despenser the son acquired a rich wife who was one of the heiresses to the earldom of Gloucester. Between them, the Despensers kept the king to themselves. Presumably, both were his new homosexual lovers.

Just how damaging these men's power over the king became was revealed by the French chronicler, Jean Froissart:

'...Hugh Despenser told King Edward that the barons had formed an alliance against him and would remove him from the throne if he was not careful. Swayed by [Despenser's] subtle arguments, the king had all these barons seized at a Parliament at which they were assembled. Twenty-two of the greatest...were beheaded, immediately and without trial.... '

But the barons who survived this slaughter were undaunted. They were still gunning for the Despensers. They went to the king and in July 1321, demanded that father and son be exiled. King Edward was thoroughly cowed. The barons got their way, only to find history repeating itself. Within a few months, Hugh Despenser the son was back in the arms of the king. Hugh Despenser the father also returned to England. Edward welcomed him back with a great gift: he made him Earl of Winchester.

This portrait of Queen Isabella, wife of Edward II, is very deceptive. Here, she looks sweet, good natured and gracious. In real life, Isabella was the vicious mastermind behind the downfall and death of her husband.

DEEDS *of* POWER

HARSH JUSTICE

THE ELDER DESPENSER was first to be captured. He was taken to Bristol in southwest England. There, he was stripped naked and a crown of nettles placed on his head.

Next, on 24 November 1326, in front of a large crowd, Despenser was dragged by four horses to a gallows 50 feet (15m) high. Queen Isabella was there, watching, as her arch-enemy was strung up and a fire lit in front of the gallows. Then, as the mob roared, Despenser's genitals were cut off as punishment for 'unnatural practices with the king'.

His suffering was not over yet. Despenser was disemboweled while still alive. He had to watch his innards being burned in the fire. Finally, mercifully, he was beheaded and his body cut into four pieces. This was the grisly death accorded traitors – hanging, drawing and quartering. Despenser's son was well aware that the same horrific fate awaited him.

King Edward, too, realized the game was up. Accompanied by the younger Hugh Despenser, he tried to escape to Ireland by sea. They never reached their destination. They were ambushed at Llantrisant in Wales on 16 November. Hugh Despenser, as he had expected, suffered the same gruesome traitor's death as his father. His head was sent to London, where it was stuck on a pike on London Bridge. The four quarters of his body were displayed the same way in four other English towns. They remained on pikes until they rotted away, a terrible warning to anyone else with treason in mind.

Edward's punishment was to be even more ghastly. Edward II was made to listen as a long list of his misdeeds and errors was read to him. He burst into tears as the list was read out. At one point he

This 14th century manuscript illustration shows the fires being lit. Sir Hugh Despenser is mutilated, hung, drawn and quartered.

even fainted. When he recovered, he sobbed that he 'was aware that for his many sins he was thus punished, and grieved for having incurred the hatred of his people, therefore (he) besought those present to have compassion on him in his adversity.'

Compassion for the ex-king, however, was in very short supply. He was locked up in a secure dungeon and systematically tortured. Then, on the night of 22 September 1327, his jailers prepared a fire and placed a plumber's soldering iron in it until it was red hot. Edward was held down, with cushions placed over his head. Then, the soldering

A detail from the tomb of Edward II in Gloucester Cathedral showing a portrait sculpture of the king. The king's tomb rapidly became a popular site for visitors.

iron was pushed up his back passage and into his bowels – or, as one chronicler phrased it, through 'those parts in which he had been wont to take his vicious pleasure.' Edward's cries of agony could be heard all over the castle and even in the nearby town of Berkeley. The barbaric punishment was carried out – according to hearsay – on the direct orders of Queen Isabella.

The she-wolf bares her teeth

When the Despensers were exiled, the barons described them as 'evil counselors.' It was a surprisingly mild term for leeches who were taking King Edward for everything they could get. But for Queen Isabella, the Despensers were much more than that: they were symbols of her years of humiliation and neglect.

Isabella also had a personal reason for wanting revenge on the Despensers. In 1324, they had seized her lands in France. They had also taken her four children from her. They planted spies in her household to keep an eye on her. By this time, Isabella was no longer the helpless little girl who had married the king in 1308. Now a mature 28, she had become the so-called She-Wolf of France and she was about to show just how terrible the fury of a woman scorned could be.

> ## Isabella plundered the royal treasury. She made huge grants to herself and her lover. She used Parliament to rubber stamp any laws that she wanted. It was clear that Isabella would have to go, and Mortimer with her.

Although he had neglected her shamefully, King Edward trusted Isabella's political abilities. In 1325, he sent her to France to negotiate a dispute between himself and her brother, the French King Charles IV.

While she was in Paris, Isabella met Roger Mortimer, the wealthy and ambitious seventh Baron Wigmore. Mortimer was just the sort of man to appeal to a new, vengeful Isabella – a man's man, rough, tough, brutal and arrogant. Mortimer became Isabella's lover and the two openly lived together. And together, they plotted the downfall of King Edward II.

Mortimer and Isabella raised an army and on 24 September 1326, they invaded England. The immediate targets were the Despensers, who were rounded up and duly murdered, brutally. The king, too, was ambushed and taken to Berkeley Castle, near Bristol Channel in southwest England. There, he was forced

Edward III styled his court on the stories of King Arthur and the Knights of the Round Table that became very popular during his long reign. In 1348, Edward founded the Order of the Garter, an order of chivalry that still exists today.

to abdicate on 24 January 1327. The next day, his son, 14-year-old Prince Edward, was proclaimed King Edward III. Later that year, Edward II also met an almost inconceivably cruel end.

Insatiable greed

Isabella and Roger Mortimer, who was made the Earl of March in 1328, were now the rulers of England. Mortimer's main concern was to enrich himself and his family, and he did not care how he did it. He seized lordships, castles and estates and any other treasure he could lay his hands on.

Isabella was no better. She plundered the royal treasury. She made huge grants to herself and her lover. She used Parliament to rubber-stamp any laws and orders she wanted. The situation could not continue. Isabella would have to go – and Mortimer with her.

At first, though, the underage King Edward III had no authority to act against the regal pair. Not until he turned 16, in 1330, was he able to take on the full powers of king. One of his first acts was to destroy Roger Mortimer.

In October 1330, Mortimer and Isabella were staying at Nottingham Castle. They knew they were in danger and had ordered the gates locked. Guards were set to patrol the castle walls. But there was a secret passageway into the castle which led to Mortimer's bedroom. Together with a small band of men, the young king entered by the passageway, unseen.

The band cut down the two knights on guard and seized Mortimer. Isabella heard the scuffle and rushed into the room. When she saw what was happening, she screamed: 'Have pity on gentle Mortimer!' Regardless of her pleas Mortimer was taken to London, where he was hung, drawn and quartered on 29 November. Isabella's days of power and revenge were over. But she was not executed. Instead, she was retired to Castle Rising, in Norfolk.

A fresh start, but a sorry end

Now, in Edward III, England could look forward to a respectable king for the first time in 20 years. The third Edward knew just how to keep his barons happy. He

THE DEMISE OF A HERO

IN THE LAST YEARS before his death, Edward spent long hours alone in his apartments, refusing to see members of his family or his household. In this pitiful state, Edward fell into the clutches of his mistress, Alice Perrers, the mother of at least two of his illegitimate children.

King Edward first met Alice Perrers when she became a maid-of-the-bedchamber to his wife, Queen Philippa of Hainault, in 1364. She became his mistress soon afterward. The Queen died in 1369. From then on, the greedy Alice could do anything she wanted with the king. He gave her manors, money and

Alice Perrers, Edward III's mistress, was a very greedy woman. In 1377, the senile King lay dying. Alice, realizing that this was her last opportunity to enrich herself, stole the rings from his fingers.

jewels. He even gave her some of Queen Philippa's jewels.

Gossip circulated that Alice was a witch, and that she made wax images of Edward and herself to keep him in her power. Parliament tried hard to get rid of Alice, but the king was always there to rescue her. In 1376, when she was impeached by Parliament, he simply quashed the sentence passed on her.

But that same year, tragedy struck the king. Edward's heir, Edward the Black Prince, died. The prince had been a fearless warrior. The king never got over his son's death. He suffered a stroke and spent the rest of his life in mourning. After his stroke the king did not live long. When Edward III died on 21 June 1377, Alice Perrers was with him. Greedy and grasping to the last, she quickly removed Edward's rings.

allowed them what they most wanted – to act as his advisers. He satisfied them even more by the splendid victories he and his son, Edward, the Black Prince, won over the French. The reign of Edward III was regarded as a glorious time in English history, despite the horrific Black Death, or bubonic plague, of 1349–1350, which killed a quarter of his subjects.

But Edward III lived too long. He became senile in the seven years before his death in 1377, aged 64, a sad shadow of the great warrior king he had once been.

A new king and a peasant uprising

Three weeks later, King Richard II, Edward's grandson and son of the Black Prince, was crowned at Westminster Abbey. He was 10 years old and at first seemed likely to be a good king. Four years later, Richard became a national hero when he rode out in person to confront the leader of the Peasants' Revolt, Wat Tyler. Tyler had 60,000 followers with him. They were protesting about a poll tax of a shilling, which had to be paid by all adults aged 14 and over. It was far more than many poor peasants could afford, So they rebelled, and three days and nights of anarchy and bloodshed followed.

The young king must have known how violent and dangerous the rebels were. But he showed no signs of flinching. He calmed the situation by offering to withdraw the poll tax and give the rebels a pardon. But Wat Tyler approached Richard in such a menacing way that, fearful for the king's safety, the Mayor of London, William Walworth, stabbed him with a sword. Tyler's head ended up on a pike on London Bridge.

As Tyler fell to the ground, menacing murmurs came from the crowd. They moved forward, as if to attack the king and his officials. But young Richard kept his cool.

'Sirs,' he cried, 'will you shoot your king? I am your captain, follow me!'

That was the end of the Peasants' Revolt. Many people came to believe that England now had a brave young king who would one day match the great deeds of his father, the Black Prince. Or so it appeared on the face of it. But the face was deceptive. The fact that Richard had given in to the rebels, and had offered to grant them pardons after all the killing, destruction and chaos they had caused, was not a promising sign. It suggested that basically he was timid and would crack under pressure.

Call me Your Majesty

Added to that, Richard lacked the temperament of a traditional medieval king. He was not interested in military matters; he was over-emotional and hot-tempered. And, like King Henry III before him, he thought royal commands should be instantly obeyed without question.

Because Richard was underage when he came to the throne, a regency council ruled for him. Meanwhile, he stayed at home with his mother, Joan of Kent. But at every opportunity, he demonstrated what a thoroughly spoiled brat he was.

In 1382, he dismissed his chancellor, the Earl of Suffolk, for failing to obey his commands. The following year he told Parliament that he would choose any adviser he wanted and insisted that Parliament accept his wishes without question.

Before long, Richard had made rather too many enemies – powerful ones. He surrounded himself with advisers, making it clear that any opposition to his will would be regarded as treason. He invented new, more exalted terms of address: anyone speaking to him had to call him Your Majesty instead of the usual Your Grace.

Richard was obviously a tyrant. But English nobles had seen it all before. They knew what had to be done. In 1387, five so-called Lords Appellant – the Dukes

They persuaded Parliament to charge Richard's most important supporters with treason. Richard was forced to watch as four of them were hung, drawn and quartered.

of Gloucester and Hereford, the Earls of Arundel and Warwick, and Thomas Mowbray, Earl of Nottingham, took a stand. They persuaded Parliament to charge Richard's most important supporters with treason. Richard was frightened. He gave in. He was forced to stand by and watch as four of his supporters, including his aged tutor Sir Robert Burley, were hung, drawn and quartered.

After this, Richard laid low. He did nothing to upset Parliament. He created a magnificent court

Though only 14 years old, Richard II faced up bravely to Wat Tyler, leader of the Peasants' Revolt in 1381. Tyler moved toward the young king in a threatening manner, and for this he was killed by William Walworth, Mayor of London.

and filled it with artists, writers and other harmless, non-military, types. But it was a smokescreen. All the while, Richard had been plotting his revenge.

By 1397, he was ready. Suddenly, without warning, the king ordered the arrest of the Lords Appellant. Three of them – the Duke of Gloucester and the Earls of Arundel and Warwick – were charged with treason. They were found guilty and executed. The Duke of Gloucester was arrested in Calais. He was smothered to death with a mattress.

Cousins at war

King Richard had a special punishment in mind for the fifth Lord Appellant, Thomas Mowbray. It was one that would also get rid of Richard's first cousin, Henry Bolingbroke. Richard had always been jealous of Henry, who was the epitome of a chivalrous knight. He was well educated and spoke several languages. He was admired at royal courts throughout Europe. And he was heir to the magnificent Duchy of Lancaster.

But Henry was far too trusting. He did not realize how devious Richard could be. Henry fell straight into Richard's trap after Thomas Mowbray warned him that the king was plotting the downfall of the House of Lancaster. Bolingbroke accused Mowbray of speaking treason against Richard. Richard ordered that the dispute be settled the old-fashioned way: in a trial by battle.

On 26 September 1398, a huge crowd gathered to watch the combat. But as soon as Bolingbroke and Mowbray came out dressed for battle, Richard suddenly forbade them to fight. He exiled Thomas Mowbray for life. Henry Bolingbroke was exiled for 10 years.

Bolingbroke's bitter chalice

Five months later, on 3 February 1399, Henry Bolingbroke's father, John of Gaunt, died. The exiled

Bolingbroke succeeded him as Duke of Lancaster. But he was a duke without rights or lands. As soon as John of Gaunt was dead, Richard announced that Bolingbroke would be banished for life. He ordered that lands belonging to the Duchy of Lancaster be handed over to the Crown.

Henry Bolingbroke soon struck back. Within a few weeks, he sailed home from France. He landed at Ravenspur in Yorkshire, in the north of England, on 30 June 1399. Bolingbroke claimed he had returned only to reclaim the Duchy of Lancaster. But there

was a lot more at stake than that. Richard had finally gone too far. He had made too many enemies. And his enemies believed he was no longer fit to be King of England.

When Henry Bolingbroke landed in England, King Richard was in Ireland. He rushed back and shut

In this 15th century painting, the youthful Richard II sits with members of the Royal Council beneath an ornately decorated canopy. Richard was one of those kings who wanted absolute power – and paid the penalty for it.

himself up in Conway Castle, in Wales. But everyone had deserted him. He might have held out for a time inside the castle but for Thomas Arundel, brother of the executed Earl of Arundel, who assured him that if he came out he could make peace with Bolingbroke and still be allowed to remain king. It was a trap. On 20 August 1399, as soon as King Richard set foot outside Conway Castle, he was ambushed and taken prisoner.

Richard was taken to London, and imprisoned in the Tower. At the end of September, Parliament forced him to abdicate. Henry Bolingbroke claimed the throne of England.

After that, Richard did not have long to live. He was taken to Pontefract Castle, in west Yorkshire. There, it was said, he was slowly starved to death. But his end

This formidable fortress is Conway Castle, where Richard II attempted to hide from the forces of his cousin Henry Bolingbroke. The castle was fairly new in Richard's time, having been built in the 13th century.

This picture shows Richard II abdicating his throne, surrounded by knights and courtiers. It was painted at some time between 1400 and 1425 and comes from *The History of the Kings of England* by French chronicler Jean Creton.

might have been much more violent. It seems that on 14 February, eight men armed with axes burst into Richard's cell in the castle. Richard was eating dinner at the time. He immediately overturned the table and grabbed an axe. He set about his attackers and managed to kill four of them. But there was no doubt about the outcome. The remaining four assassins overwhelmed the ex-king and hacked him to death.

By this time, Henry Bolingbroke had already been crowned King Henry IV on 13 October 1399. But Henry was not happy. He was a usurper and had stolen the crown from its rightful owner, King Richard.

Henry was well aware of it. 'God knows by what right I took the Crown,' he said later. Strictly speaking, Henry had no right, and he was tortured by guilt for the rest of his life.

INSANITY, CIVIL WAR AND CHILD MURDER

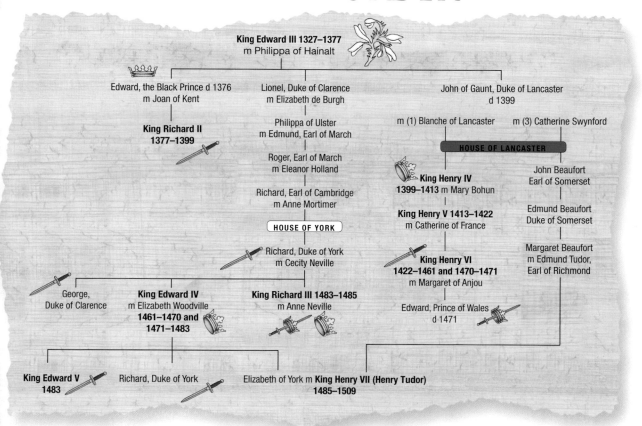

King Edward III 1327–1377
m Philippa of Hainalt

Edward, the Black Prince d 1376
m Joan of Kent

**King Richard II
1377–1399**

Lionel, Duke of Clarence
m Elizabeth de Burgh

Philippa of Ulster
m Edmund, Earl of March

Roger, Earl of March
m Eleanor Holland

Richard, Earl of Cambridge
m Anne Mortimer

HOUSE OF YORK

Richard, Duke of York
m Cecity Neville

George,
Duke of Clarence

King Edward IV
m Elizabeth Woodville
**1461–1470 and
1471–1483**

King Richard III 1483–1485
m Anne Neville

John of Gaunt, Duke of Lancaster
d 1399

m (1) Blanche of Lancaster   m (3) Catherine Swynford

HOUSE OF LANCASTER

King Henry IV
1399–1413 m Mary Bohun

John Beaufort
Earl of Somerset

King Henry V 1413–1422
m Catherine of France

Edmund Beaufort
Duke of Somerset

**King Henry VI
1422–1461 and 1470–1471**
m Margaret of Anjou

Margaret Beaufort
m Edmund Tudor,
Earl of Richmond

Edward, Prince of Wales
d 1471

**King Edward V
1483**

Richard, Duke of York

Elizabeth of York m **King Henry VII (Henry Tudor)
1485–1509**

> **King Henry IV was always nervous, constantly watching his back. He could never be sure how long he would be able to hang on to his stolen throne.**

✦

There were enemies lurking in the wings, many of whom had better claims to the throne. There was troublesome gossip, too. Henry had based his claim to the throne on the fact that he

The coronation of Henry IV in 1399 was overshadowed by guilt and tragedy. Henry had usurped the English throne from his cousin, Richard II. The ex-king did not have long to live.

was the grandson of King Edward III. But according to hearsay, when King Edward's wife, Philippa, lay dying in 1369, she made a confession. She revealed that in 1340, she had given birth to a daughter while in Ghent, in present-day Belgium. But by accident, Philippa had killed the young princess. Philippa was terrified the king would find out. So she had a boy, the son of a porter, smuggled into her apartments.

THE BLUSHING KING

As WELL AS LOATHING WAR, fighting and executions, the timorous King Henry VI was also a prude. Nudity made him blush and run. One Christmas, a guest of the king tried to please him by providing entertainment. Or so he thought. This guest brought along a troupe of topless dancing girls. Henry was shocked and stormed out of the room in a huff.

Nevertheless, like all sovereigns before him, Henry had a duty to provide at least one heir to the throne, so he was married, in 1445, to the fiery Margaret of Anjou. However, no children came along for eight years. Gossip provided the truth of the matter: one of Henry's advisers, William Ayscough, Bishop of Salisbury, had turned him off sex. For reasons known only to himself Ayscough advised the king not to have his sport with the queen. The bashful king was not hard to persuade.

Philippa passed this boy off as the child born to her in Ghent. King Edward was delighted with his new 'son'. But the child's real background was kept a secret. The boy grew up to become John of Gaunt, Duke of Lancaster. John of Gaunt was Henry IV's father.

Consumed with guilt and plagued by illness

If Henry IV had known the truth about his father, he kept it quiet. But there were other pressures. He was consumed by guilt over the murder of King Richard II. He tried to make up for it by paying monks to say prayers for Richard's soul. But it did not make him

---

When Edward was brought to him on New Year's Day, the king didn't know why. He'd forgotten he was the child's father. Instead, he thought the father was the Holy Ghost.

---

feel any better. Having stolen the English crown, he had laid himself open to conspiracies. There were several plots to kill him. There were many rebellions against him. King Henry survived them all. But the strain showed. Henry suffered the first of several strokes in 1406. Tales spread that he was suffering from leprosy, though he more probably had eczema.

He had epileptic fits. Henry IV was a physical and mental wreck when he died in 1413, aged 47.

Other Plantagenets had not forgotten their own claims to the throne. But they had to wait awhile to make their bids. There was no chance during the reign of Henry IV's son and successor, King Henry V. Henry V was one of England's greatest and most successful warrior monarchs and remains one of England's national heroes. But when he died suddenly in 1422, aged 35, his son and successor was just the sort of king his rivals had been waiting for.

Henry VI was still in his cradle when he became king. He grew up weak and timid. Anyone could push him around. He had no military skills and hated bloodshed. Sometimes, he stopped the executions of criminals or traitors – he could not bear to see them die. But Henry was very religious. When he had to wear his crown on feast days, he felt he had committed the sin of pride. So he wore a hairshirt next to his skin to make up for it.

The king loses his mind

By rights, Henry should have been a monk, or better yet, a hermit. He found being king very hard going, so much so that in August 1453, he went mad. He no longer knew where he was, what year it was or even who he was. But somehow Henry had escaped from Ayscough's influence long enough to conceive a child – Prince Edward, born in 1453. But when Edward was brought to him on New Year's Day 1454, the king did not know why. He had forgotten he was the child's father. Instead, he thought the father was the Holy Ghost.

Rival for the throne

All this was icing on the cake for King Henry's rivals. A mentally unbalanced king with an infant heir was a double gift to anyone who wanted to seize power. As a mad king, Henry had to have a protector. So up stepped Richard, Duke of York. Ten years older than Henry, Richard was everything Henry was not – proud, warlike, ambitious and greedy.

Richard of York had his own claim to the English throne, a better one than either King Henry's or Prince Edward's. King Henry VI was descended from John of Gaunt, Duke of Lancaster, the fourth surviving son of King Edward III. Richard of York was descended from Lionel, Duke of Clarence, King Edward's third surviving son and John of Gaunt's elder brother.

Richard's first move was to have himself appointed the mad king's protector, in March 1454. His next was to arrest Edmund Beaufort, Duke of Somerset. Somerset was King Henry's most powerful supporter. He was sent to the Tower of London.

Richard was also gunning for Queen Margaret. But he had to be careful. The bold, proud Margaret dominated her spineless husband. And beside being Queen Consort of England, she was also the mother of the heir to the throne. So however much Richard of York wanted to pack her off to the Tower of London, he did not dare.

Henry VI was as unlike his father, Henry V, as it was possible to be. Timid and weak-minded where Henry V was valiant and strong, Henry VI was more like his maternal grandfather, Charles VI of France – insane.

Richard could remain protector only as long as King Henry's madness lasted. It did not last very long. By Christmas 1454 he was better and Richard lost his job. But by now, the power struggle had gone too far. The Plantagenet royal family had already split into two rival factions: King Henry's House of Lancaster and Richard's House of York. The only way to settle their rivalry was by civil war.

Their struggle was called the War of the Roses. This was because the badge of Lancaster was a red rose and the badge of York was a white one.

The war

This formidable-looking woman was Queen Margaret, wife of Henry VI, who was completely dominated by her. Margaret was the driving force behind the resistance of the House of Lancaster to the claims of the House of York.

began with the battle of Saint Albans, Hertfordshire, on 22 May 1455. The House of York won. Henry VI was such a weakling that he even forgave Richard. Afterwards, Richard's supporters were even given prestigious posts in the government. Richard could afford to let the harmless Henry VI remain king. As long as he did what he was told, that is. Henry VI was very good at doing what he was told. Even so, Richard took the precaution of imprisoning the king in the Tower of London.

But Richard had reckoned without Queen Margaret. Unlike her husband, she had never dreamed of giving in. Margaret raised an army and confronted the Yorkists at Wakefield, in Yorkshire. She won a great victory. Richard of York was killed in the fighting. Later, his skull was displayed from the walls of York, wearing a paper crown. Now the House of Lancaster had the upper hand – but not for long.

The Duke of York's son Edward, aged 18, took over his father's claim to the English crown. Of the two – Richard and Edward – Edward was by far the better man. He was handsome, charming and a fine military commander. Edward made far more headway than Richard had. He twice defeated the Lancastrian army. Afterwards, he was crowned King Edward IV of England on 28 June 1461.

Royals reduced to begging

King Henry, Queen Margaret and Prince Edward managed to escape to Scotland. But they arrived like beggars. On the way, Margaret was robbed of everything she had — her plate, jewels and gowns. At one point, she was reduced to borrowing money. A chronicler wrote of how 'the king her husband, her son and she had...only one herring and not one day's supply of bread. And that on a holy day, she found herself at Mass without a brass farthing to offer; wherefore, in beggary and need, she prayed a Scottish archer to lend her something, who half loath and regretfully, drew a Scots groat from his purse and lent it to her.'

While the royal fugitives were in this terrible state, King Edward IV was living it up in London. He was very popular and women adored him. They did not have much trouble attracting Edward's attention. He was a good-looking, lusty six-footer with a roving eye for beautiful women. Soon, everyone was gossiping about the number of women he had bedded. But before long, his roving eye got him into trouble.

A secret marriage

Edward IV's most powerful supporter was Richard Neville, Earl of Warwick. Warwick fancied himself as a 'kingmaker'. Edward owed much of his success to Warwick. So, when Edward became king, this was payback time as far as Warwick was concerned. Warwick decided he was going to control the king. He planned a brilliant marriage for him, to a French princess. But Edward had other ideas. He had set his heart on an Englishwoman: Elizabeth Woodville, a 27-year-old widow with children. Edward wanted her badly. At first, he tried to seduce her, but she refused him. The gossips said Edward put a dagger to her throat, but she still resisted him. There was only solution: the king had to marry her.

> **Queen Margaret and Prince Edward managed to escape to France. The deposed King Henry VI was left behind. He had to wander from one safe house to the next. Often, he disguised himself as a monk.**

But Edward was still very young and afraid of Warwick. So he married Elizabeth Woodville in secret on 1 May 1464. Edward managed to prevent Warwick from learning about his marriage for four months. When Warwick found out, at the end of September 1464, he was furious. The king had made him look like a fool. But that was not all. Elizabeth Woodville's many relatives – including her seven unmarried sisters – were soon taking advantage and leeching off the king. They were given titles, grants of money, grants of lands – all of which Warwick had wanted for himself. Even more infuriating, King Edward preferred to go to the Woodville family for advice rather than to Warwick.

Meanwhile, in 1463, Queen Margaret and Prince Edward managed to escape to France. The deposed King Henry VI was left behind. He had to wander from one safe house to the next. Often, he disguised himself as a monk. But Edward IV's spies were after him. They found him at Waddington Hall in Lancashire in July 1465. True to form, Henry did not put up a struggle. He was taken to London, and made a prisoner in the Tower for a second time.

Richard Neville, Earl of Warwick – 'Warwick the Kingmaker' – was the most powerful English noble during the Wars of the Roses. In 1470, Warwick had the Yorkist king, Edward IV, imprisoned and the Lancastrian Henry VI locked up in the Tower.

The kingmaker and the queen

Now, King Edward had Henry in his power. But he still had to deal with the Earl of Warwick, who was a dangerous man. So, in March 1470, King Edward accused the earl of treason. Warwick fled for his life to France. There, he contacted the woman who had once been his greatest enemy, Queen Margaret. Six months after Warwick and the Queen had joined forces, Warwick brought an army to England. Margaret was to follow on with another army. Warwick was determined to topple Edward IV and pay him back for insulting him. Warwick pulled it off. King Edward was captured after a battle at Northampton, in central England.

Now, Warwick really was a kingmaker. He had King Edward IV imprisoned in his castle of Middleham in northern England. King Henry VI was in the Tower of London. Warwick could do what he liked with both. Warwick chose to put Henry VI back on the throne. He was easier to control than Edward IV. After all, he was called Henry the Hopeless, the king who would do as he was told.

But King Edward escaped from Middleham Castle and managed to reach France. He did not stay there long. Soon Edward was back in England, this time with a new army of his own. Edward's forces met Warwick's at the battle of Barnet, just north of London, on 14 April 1471. Warwick had brought King Henry from the Tower and sat him by a tree to watch the fighting. What Henry saw, however, was Warwick's defeat. Warwick fled from the battlefield. But the triumphant Edward IV was not about to let him get away. The earl was pursued and killed. Poor King Henry was then seized and sent back to the Tower for the third and last time.

Warwick the Kingmaker was killed at the Battle of Barnet when Edward IV's forces defeated the Lancastrians. Warwick began the Wars of the Roses fighting for the Yorkists, but he changed sides because of a quarrel with Edward IV.

The same day, Queen Margaret and Prince Edward returned to England. But Edward made short work of Margaret and her army. At Tewkesbury in Gloucestershire on 4 May 1471, Queen Margaret was defeated. Seventeen-year-old Prince Edward ran away from the battle, but was pursued and killed.

Margaret was devastated. But for her, worse was to come. The victorious King Edward IV could not afford to let Henry VI live any longer. On the night of 21 May 1471, around midnight, Henry was stabbed to death in his cell at the Tower of London. One of the killers was Richard, Duke of Gloucester, Edward IV's youngest brother.

Later, Henry's body was publicly displayed so everyone would know he was dead. According to the official story he had died naturally, 'of pure displeasure and melancholy'. But there was also talk that blood had spurted from his wounds, signifying what had really happened to him.

This was the end for Queen Margaret. She had lost everything – her husband, her son and her crown. Her father, King René of Sicily, ransomed her and she lived in France until her death in 1482.

The following year, Edward IV's days of enjoying high living and his scores of mistresses caught up with him. He suffered a stroke and died on 9 April. He was only 42. He left his throne to his 12-year-old son, who became King Edward V.

Queen Margaret was taken prisoner after the Battle of Tewkesbury in 1471 and her son, Prince Edward, was killed. Later Margaret's husband, Henry VI, was murdered in the Tower of London.

> **Richard of Gloucester would go down in English history as the evil uncle, a deformed monster and just about everything else bad.**

Edward V was an invitation for trouble. With a civil war simmering, the last thing England needed was a boy king. No king could actually rule until he grew up. A royal council ruled for him. And this gave ambitious men ideas about seizing power for themselves. The most ambitious of them was Richard of Gloucester.

'Woe to the land that's governed by a child!' Shakespeare wrote in *Richard III*. This was certainly true for Edward V. Robbed of his throne by his uncle, Richard III, Edward became the third English king to be murdered in the 15th century.

Tudors demonize Uncle Richard

Richard of Gloucester would go down in English history as the evil uncle, a deformed monster and just about everything else bad. This picture of Richard was pure propaganda. It was dreamed up by the Tudor royal family, which took over from the Plantagenets after the Wars of the Roses ended in 1485.

Like all propaganda, it was more powerful than true. The Tudors did a very thorough job in creating Richard's demonic image. They turned him into a hunchback. They said he had been born with teeth and born breech – legs first – which was considered extremely bad luck in highly superstitious times when anything 'unnatural' was seen as the work of the devil. And by the time the Tudors had finished with him, no one doubted Richard was one of the devil's own.

But Richard was not a hunchback. His portraits show there was nothing wrong with him. During the Wars of the Roses, he had stuck loyally by his brother King Edward IV. Edward trusted Richard so completely that he sent him to rule the troublesome north of England. He ruled it well and became very popular. Even today, more than five centuries later, people in the north of England look back on Richard of Gloucester with affection.

Elsewhere, however, the Tudor smears about Richard stuck – firmly. So did the idea, encouraged by the Tudors, that Richard had murdered his way to the throne. The list of accusations was a long one. To begin with, he allegedly had murdered King Henry VI in the Tower of London in 1471. The same year,

so the story went, Richard killed Henry VI's son, 17-year-old Prince Edward, at the battle of Tewkesbury. Seven years later, Richard was blamed for the death of his own elder brother, George, Duke of Clarence, also in the Tower of London. It is a well-known story that Richard drowned George in a butt of Malmsey wine. The simple truth was that George was a habitual traitor, and Edward IV had had him executed.

After George, only two people stood in Richard's way: the boy king Edward V and his 10-year-old brother, Richard, the Duke of York.

On 1 May 1483, Richard of Gloucester abducted Edward V while the boy was on his way to London.

FACT *or* FICTION

THE LOST BOYS

RICHARD HAD PLACED the two young boys, Edward V and the Duke of York, in the Tower of London. There was nothing particularly suspicious about this. In the

This sinister looking passage is in the White Tower of the Tower of London where Edward V was lodged before his planned coronation.

fifteenth century, the Tower was a palace as well as a prison. English kings normally stayed there before their coronations. The difference was that King Edward V never came out. And he never had a coronation.

In 1513, Sir Thomas More published his *History of King Richard III*. This book contained More's account of what happened in the Tower on the night of 3 September. In the fifteenth century, it was easy to hire assassins. For a fee, they would quietly kill a victim, conceal the body and hide the evidence. According to More, Richard III had paid a Yorkist knight named Sir James Tyrell to do away with The Little Princes in the Tower.

'SMOTHERED AND STIFLED'

'For Sir James Tyrell,' wrote More, 'devised that they should be murdered in their beds. To the execution whereof, he appointed Miles Forest, one of the four that kept them, a fellow fleshed in murder before time. To him he joined one John Dighton, his own horsekeeper, a big broad, square, strong knave.

'Then, all the others being removed from them, this Miles Forest and John Dighton, about midnight (the innocent children lying in their beds) came into the chamber and suddenly lapped them up among the clothes, so bewrapped them and entangled them, keeping down by force the feather bed

This romantic portrait, painted in 1878 by pre-Raphaelite painter Sir John Millais, shows the 'Little Princes in the Tower' – King Edward V and his brother Richard, Duke of York.

and pillows hard unto their mouths, that within a while, smothered and stifled, their breath failing, they gave up to God their innocent souls into the joys of heaven, leaving to the tormentors their bodies dead in the bed.

'After that the wretches perceived, first by the struggling with the pains of death, and after lying still, to be thoroughly dead: they laid their bodies naked out upon the bed, and fetched Sir James to see them. Which, upon the sight of them, caused those murderers to bury them at the stair foot, meetly (suitably) deep in the ground, under a great heap of stones.'

AN ENDURING MYSTERY

Nearly two centuries later, in 1674, workmen rebuilding the stairs to the Tower's Royal Chapel came upon a wooden chest buried 10 feet below the stairs. Inside was an assortment of bones. Sir John Knight, chief surgeon to the then king, Charles II, decided they were the bones of 'two striplings' – in other words, Edward V and his little brother.

But in 1933, the bones were reexamined. The results were not so certain. There had been many deaths in the Tower over the centuries and the bones could have been anybody's. So, the mystery remains. Currently, the King Richard III Foundation Inc., which seeks to clear the king's name of murder, has asked for DNA tests to be made on the bones. If that happens, the riddle may be solved once and for all.

Richard had always hated Queen Elizabeth Woodville and her family. When the queen heard the boy king was in Richard's clutches she took fright and bolted, taking her younger son, Richard, Duke of York with her to the safety of Westminster Cathedral. There, under the protection of the Church, Richard could not get at her. Or so the queen thought. But Richard found a way. On June 16, he threatened the Queen so fiercely that she let him take the young Duke of York away. That was the last she saw of him. She never again saw her elder son, Edward V, either. From time to time, the boy king and his brother were seen playing in the gardens of the Tower. But by July 1483, the sightings had stopped. They were never seen alive again. There was no funeral. The boys had simply vanished. Later, they became known as the tragic Little Princes in the Tower.

Richard claims the crown

Meanwhile, Richard of Gloucester made preparations to seize the throne. He propagandized that Edward V and the Duke of York were illegitimate. This was because when their father married their mother, he was already betrothed to another woman. In other words, the marriage was illegal. It was a terrible smear on the boys, but Londoners just about believed the story. Richard was proclaimed King Richard III. His coronation took place on 6 July 1483.

It is possible that just then the boy king and his brother had still been alive. But once their uncle had

Shakespeare's Richard III is one of the great tragic parts in British theatre. Ian McKellen (below) played the role on film in 1995. Forty years earlier, Laurence Olivier starred in and directed another film version.

usurped the throne, they were not going to be permitted to remain alive for long. The boy king and his
brother were killed, possibly on 3 September 1483.

As a usurper, Richard III had many enemies. After
the deaths of the Princes in the Tower, people found
it easy to believe he would do anything to retain the
stolen throne. When his wife, Anne Neville, died in
1484, people said that Richard had poisoned her so he

**During a propaganda campaign against him, the Tudors
presented Richard III as an evil hunchbacked monster who
was born unnaturally, with teeth. This portrait shows there
to be nothing wrong with Richard.**

could marry his niece Elizabeth, daughter of Edward
IV. That marriage would have strengthened Richard's
hold on the throne.

But that was just gossip. Richard's real enemy was Henry Tudor. Henry was the chief claimant to the throne from the House of Lancaster. He had spent most of his life in exile. For years, Henry moved from one secret place to another, dodging the thugs that Yorkists had sent to kill him. He escaped them all. And in 1485, he set out to remove Richard from his stolen throne.

It is told that during the battle Richard's crown fell from his head and rolled in the dirt. Supposedly, it was later found hanging from a bush, where Lord Stanley picked it up and then placed it on Henry Tudor's head.

Betrayal and suicide

On 7 August, Henry Tudor arrived with an army of 4,000 to 5,000 men at Milford Haven in south Wales. It was not a large force. So, on 22 August, when Henry Tudor confronted Richard and his army of 12,000 men at the battle of Bosworth, in Leicestershire, his chances did not look good. But what neither Richard nor Henry knew was that three of

The seal of Henry VII, the first Tudor monarch. It shows King Henry with the royal coat of arms on either side. An official document was only valid if it bore this seal.

At the battle of Bosworth Field in 1485, two of Richard III's most powerful supporters changed sides. Richard was doomed. He then staked everything on a desperate attempt to reach his rival, Henry Tudor, and kill him, but he failed.

Richard's commanders were about to desert him. One, Henry Percy, Earl of Northumberland, refused to move his troops when ordered. Two others, Sir William Stanley and his brother Lord Stanley, planned to switch sides. Richard was doomed.

All he could do in the circumstances was make a desperate attack. It proved to be suicidal. With a small force of men, Richard spurred his horse through the front line of Henry Tudor's army. His aim was to reach Henry and kill him. Richard never got that far. He managed to kill Henry's standard bearer, but Henry's soldiers closed in and trapped him. Before long, Richard was pulled from his horse and killed. Afterwards, his naked body was slung over the back of a packhorse. Then it was taken to Leicester, where it was buried in Greyfriars Friary Church. Rediscovered in 2012, the king's remains were reinterred in Leicester Cathedral.

Richard III was indeed the unlucky 13th Plantagenet king of England. With his death, the Wars of the Roses came to an end. One story recounts that, during the battle, Richard's crown fell from his head and rolled in the dirt. It was later found hanging from a bush. Supposedly, Lord Stanley picked it up and placed it ceremoniously on Henry Tudor's head.

After 330 years, Plantagenet rule in England had finally come to an end. As Henry VII, Henry Tudor became the first king of a new dynasty.

6

CONSPIRACY AND BLOODSHED

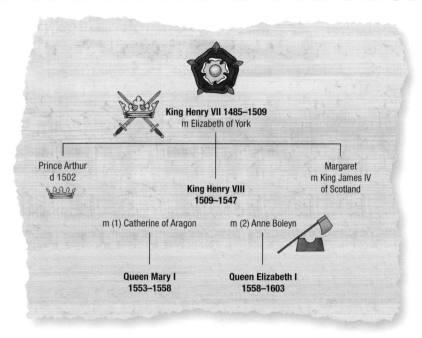

King Henry VII 1485–1509
m Elizabeth of York

Prince Arthur
d 1502

King Henry VIII
1509–1547

Margaret
m King James IV
of Scotland

m (1) Catherine of Aragon

m (2) Anne Boleyn

Queen Mary I
1553–1558

Queen Elizabeth I
1558–1603

The Plantagenet dynasty was gone. Now, the Tudors were in charge. But the Plantagenet family was still around. Henry VII, first king of the new Tudor dynasty, tried to heal the rift that had led to the Wars of the Roses.

After the battle of Bosworth, he married Elizabeth of York, daughter of King Edward IV. This, King Henry hoped, would finally reunite the rival houses of York and Lancaster. But there was not a chance. The Yorkists were still out for revenge, and would try any trick in the book to dislodge the Tudors.

A 'king' with no crown

In 1487, a young man arrived in Ireland claiming to be Edward Plantagenet, Earl of Warwick. His real name

Cardinal Wolsey was Henry VIII's chief minister. The two were friends for the first 20 years of the king's reign, but Wolsey's relationship with Henry was soured by his failure to persuade the Pope to grant Henry a divorce.

was Lambert Simnel, son of a joiner in Oxford. The true earl was the son of George, Duke of Clarence, brother of King Edward IV. That gave Simnel a putative claim to the throne of England. He staked this claim on 24 May 1487: that day, he was crowned 'King Edward VI' in Dublin Cathedral. For a crown, the 'king' had to use a gold circlet 'borrowed' from a statue of the Virgin Mary.

The 'king's' humble end

When Henry VII heard about it, he responded vehemently. He knew this 'King Edward VI' was an impostor because he had the real Earl of Warwick imprisoned in the Tower. To prove Simnel was a sham, Henry brought the real Earl of Warwick out of the

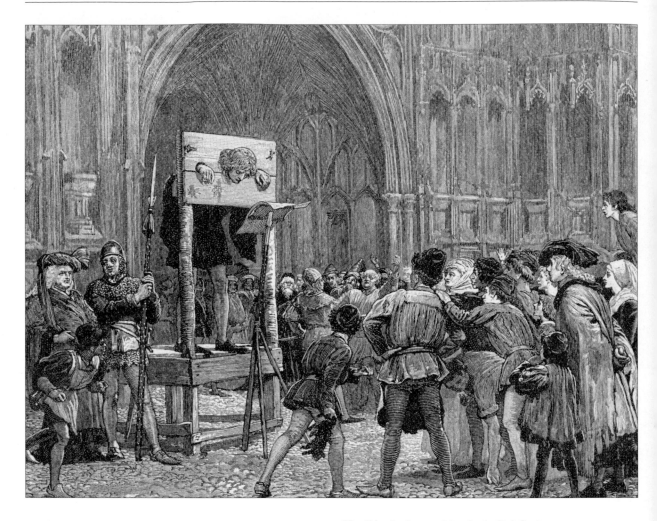

Perkin Warbeck, the second royal impostor of Henry VII's reign, is seen being put in the pillory where anyone was free to abuse him or throw missiles. Unlike the first impostor, Lambert Simnel, Warbeck was eventually executed.

Tower. He made a big show of parading him through the streets of London so everyone would know who he was. But this did not deter Simnel and his supporters. They landed an invasion force in Lancashire, in the north of England, on 4 June 1487, then marched south toward London.

King Henry was waiting for them at Stoke in Nottinghamshire, and won the battle that ensued. He also captured Lambert Simnel. Arguably, Simnel deserved to be executed for treason, but Henry decided to shame him instead. So he made Simnel a servant in the royal kitchens.

The 'king' who would not admit defeat

Lambert Simnel was not the only false claimant to the crown. In 1491, another young man turned up in Cork, Ireland, claiming to be the Earl of Warwick. Then he changed his story and said he was an illegitimate son of King Richard III. Finally, he settled for pretending to be Richard, Duke of York, one of the Princes in the Tower. The young Duke of York, so he declared, had not died in 1483; he had escaped and somehow made his way to safety. And here he was, in Ireland, ready to claim the throne of England that was rightfully his.

The young King Henry VIII was handsome and personable, with a flair for dancing. It was only later that he became a bitter, overweight, cruel and much feared despot with a reputation as a wife killer.

MARCI · 10
ITE IN MVDVM VNIVERSV ET PREDICATE
EVANGELIVM OMNI CREATVRE

The Byward Tower at the Tower of London was meant to be the last in a series of strongholds for the complex. Even today, nighttime visitors have to give the right password to the sentry on guard before they can enter the Byward Tower.

The 'Duke of York' was, of course, another impostor. His real name was Perkin Warbeck. He was son of a customs official in the Netherlands. Warbeck was 19, about the same age the real duke would have been if he were still alive.

For Henry VII, this impostor was even more dangerous than Lambert Simnel. Henry sent agents to scour Europe and find him. Henry need not have bothered, for Warbeck fell straight into his hands. In 1497, he landed in Cornwall, in southwest England, with a force of 120 men. He gathered support and before long had raised an army of 8,000. Now, he felt secure enough to declare himself King Richard IV.

But Warbeck was no military leader. His followers were a rabble, with no idea how to fight a battle. Most of them fled when they encountered Henry's army at Taunton in Somerset. After that, Warbeck was easily captured and forced to confess that he was not really Richard IV. At first King Henry was kind to him. He made him one of his courtiers. It was only when Warbeck tried to escape that he was dispatched to the Tower of London.

> ### King Henry VIII was obsessed with the Plantagenets. He set out to get rid of every Plantagenet he could lay his hands on.

That did not cure him. In 1499, King Henry's spies discovered that Warbeck and the real Earl of Warwick were planning to escape. It was the end for both of them. Warbeck was hanged. Warwick was beheaded.

There were no more impostors during the reign of King Henry VII, which ended with his death in 1509.

But his successor, King Henry VIII, was obsessed with the Plantagenets and their conspiracies. As king he set out to get rid of every Plantagenet he could lay his hands on.

Henry VIII's chief target was the De la Pole family. They were descended from George, Duke of Clarence, the brother of Edward IV and Richard III. Their claim to the throne was somewhat distant, but legitimate all the same.

During Henry's reign, the senior member of the family was Margaret Pole, Countess of Salisbury. Cardinal Reginald Pole, son of the countess, managed to escape into exile in Europe. But his brother Geoffrey Pole was arrested. He gave evidence against his mother the countess, another of his brothers, Henry Pole, Lord Montague and two other relatives, Henry Courtenay, Marquis of Exeter, and Sir Edward Neville. All were executed.

By this time, Henry had gained a very bloodthirsty reputation. Much later, he was given the nickname 'Bluff King Hal' – jolly, friendly, kindly and always

KING WITH A LUST FOR BLOOD

THERE WAS LITTLE DOUBT how the evidence against the Poles and their relatives was obtained. Geoffrey Pole was tortured. When the agony became too much for him, he 'confessed'. But he did not have to confess to much. Any excuse was enough for King Henry to order an execution.

Lord Montague was condemned to death for letting slip a piece of gossip about the king and his father: When Henry VIII was a boy, Montague said, his father did not like him. Sir Edward Neville was condemned because he once opined: 'the king is a beast and worse than a beast'. It was careless talk, nothing more. But both Montague and Neville were executed on Tower Hill on 9 December 1538. Henry Courtenay died with them.

By this time, Margaret, Countess of Salisbury was in prison. She was a harmless lady in her late sixties. As with Montague and Neville, the evidence against her was trivial. Her crimes? She forbade her servants to read the Bible in English, and was once seen burning a letter. The truth was that her death sentence owed to her Plantagenet blood alone.

She, too, was executed on Tower Hill, outside the Tower of London, on 28 May 1541. Her death was grotesque. The countess was senile. When led out to the execution block, she did not know where she was or what was happening. She was told to lay her head on the block. Instead, she wandered around Tower Hill.

She was grabbed and forced back to where the block stood. Her head was pushed into place. Unfortunately, the executioner was young and inexperienced. The axe was probably blunt. He had to hack away at the countess's head three or four times before it fell off.

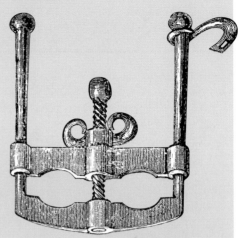

A common instrument of torture, the thumbscrew was designed to extract information and confessions from prisoners.

Margaret, Countess of Salisbury, a senior member of the Plantagenet royal family, was beheaded for treason in 1541.

good for a laugh. The real King Henry VIII hardly matched that description. In truth he was terrifying. By 1541, Henry had married four wives, and each had had time to discover what he really was: a cruel despot who would not hesitate to torture and execute anyone in his way.

Blissfully wedded

Henry VIII's first wife was Catherine of Aragon, daughter of King Ferdinand and Queen Isabella of Spain. Catherine had been married before, to Henry's elder brother Arthur. But Arthur died in 1502, soon after the wedding. Little did Catherine know that

> **Henry loved his daughter Mary and was very proud of her. But England was not yet ready for a reigning queen. Henry needed a new, young wife who could give him the son he so desperately craved.**

this first marriage would later provide Henry with ammunition against her. Catherine was six years older than Henry. She had to wait for him to grow up before he could marry her. He was 18 and already King of England, and she was 24 when the ceremony took place on 11 June 1509.

At first, Henry and Catherine were very happy. 'My wife and I be in good and perfect love as any two creatures can be,' Henry wrote to Catherine's father, King Ferdinand. Their first child, a son, was born on New Year's Day, 1510. His delighted father held a tournament in celebration at Richmond Palace. Then, tragedy struck. The baby prince lived for only seven weeks. Henry and Catherine were devastated. But things would only get worse.

Dark clouds on the horizon

Catherine had several more children. All except one died in infancy or were born dead. The only survivor was a daughter, Princess Mary, born in 1516. Catherine had been a beautiful woman. But all those deaths had worn her down. By age 30 she had lost her

Catherine of Aragon, the first wife of King Henry VIII, was born a Spanish princess in 1485. She was trained and educated for her role as a Queen Consort and was capable of taking over from the king when he was absent abroad.

looks and her figure. Even her hair had turned silver. She became intensely religious. Most of her time was spent at prayer. She even wore a hair shirt under her gowns, in the manner of an ascetic or saint.

None of this appealed much to Henry. He liked young, lively women and Catherine was no longer young nor lively. But most of all, he longed for a son to succeed him.

Henry loved his daughter Princess Mary and was very proud of her. He also spoiled her. But England was not yet ready for a reigning queen. Henry needed a new, young wife who could give him the son he so desperately craved.

New flesh for the king

In 1522 Anne Boleyn came to court as one of Queen Catherine's ladies-in-waiting. She was 21, stylish, sexy and sophisticated. Although not beautiful, Anne knew how to attract men. She was a tremendous flirt with a few tricks up her sleeve. Even King Henry was taken aback by how much she knew about the arts of love.

Anne Boleyn was also ambitious. Once she arrived at the royal court, she aimed for the top prize: Henry VIII himself. But she was not going to make the same mistake as her sister Mary, who had once been Henry's mistress. Mary had learned a great deal at the royal court in France, which was in fact little more than an upscale brothel. She joined in the fun with such zest that even the French king, Francis I, considered Mary little more than a common prostitute. When Henry took her over, he thought he could benefit from such an experienced mistress. But maybe he hadn't been able to keep up with her: Anne Boleyn said later that he was not a very good lover. Even so, Henry had tired of Mary Boleyn after two years and thrown her out. Anne was not going to let that happen to her.

All or nothing

In 1526, Henry asked Anne to become his mistress. He was flabbergasted when she turned him down. He kept on trying, but the more he tried, the more Anne refused. He wrote her passionate love letters. She took her time answering, just to keep him on the hook. But

Catherine, seen in the foreground, knew about Henry VIII's romance with her lady-in-waiting, Anne Boleyn. In this 20th century illustration, Henry and Anne are seen chatting in the background while a tearful Catherine walks alone in tears.

she would not budge. She knew she had driven the King of England into a frenzy of desire – just where she wanted him.

Meanwhile, Henry was having big trouble with Catherine. She had always been a great lady; calm, modest and gracious. It would not be difficult to get around her, or so Henry believed. Then, he could have Anne Boleyn. But in June 1527, when he told Catherine he wanted a divorce, he found out differently.

Henry had discovered a good reason for divorcing Catherine, a religious reason that should have done the trick. The 'Prohibition of Leviticus' in the Bible forbade marriage between a man and his brother's widow. King Henry could always persuade himself that whatever he wanted he should have. And the

Prohibition of Leviticus persuaded him that his marriage to Catherine had been cursed. That was why all their sons had died.

The queen digs her heels in

Catherine burst into tears when he told her. But that did not mean she was giving in – far from it. When she stopped crying, Catherine told Henry that he could not have a divorce. She claimed that her brief marriage to Prince Arthur had never been consummated and therefore had not been a marriage at all. The Prohibition of Leviticus did not, therefore, apply. This was the start of one of the most ferocious marital contests in English history.

Now that it was war, husband and wife lined up their ammunition. Henry tried to gather evidence that Catherine and Prince Arthur had slept together. He did not get far with that line of inquiry. Some courtiers said they had, others said they had not.

Henry was furious. But he tried to get around

the problem by sending his chief minister, Cardinal Thomas Wolsey, to Rome. Wolsey's orders were to obtain permission from the Pope for Henry to marry Anne Boleyn. But Catherine had better firepower. She had powerful relatives in Europe. The mightiest was her nephew, King Charles I of Spain, who had the Pope, Clement VII, in his pocket. There was no way Henry was going to get what he wanted from him.

When Catherine told King Charles what was happening, he sent a stern warning to Henry to forget about the divorce or prepare for the consequences. But Charles had other things on his mind, such as French invasions of Spain and his own lands in Italy. These problems distracted the Spanish king long enough for Pope Clement to slip his leash. Clement agreed to send a legate, Cardinal Lorenzo Campeggio, to England to judge the royal divorce case.

The pope steps in…diplomatically

Pope Clement was a cautious man. He told Campeggio to waste time by taking the longest route to England. When he arrived, Campeggio was told, he should start by trying to patch up the royal marriage. Above all, Campeggio was to delay, delay again, and make no decision.

Until 1529, Cardinal Thomas Wolsey was a very powerful man. He is shown here receiving petitions and requests from people who treat him with extreme deference, bowing and kneeling as he passes by.

In this 19th century illustration, Cardinal Campeggio, the papal legate, questions Queen Catherine at the inquiry into the divorce while her husband, Henry VIII, glowers in the background.

The Pope need not have taken the trouble. When Campeggio reached England after a journey of four months, he found that Henry and Catherine were still at odds. Neither would back down. Catherine fought Campeggio all the way. No, she told him, she would not enter a nunnery. No, she would not leave the court. And she would rather die twice than admit her marriage to Henry was invalid.

Campeggio had no better luck with King Henry. He wanted Anne Boleyn and that was that. Clearly, it would be a fight to the finish. All the same, the cardinal convened a special court on 21 June 1529. He ordered King Henry and Queen Catherine to attend. But after they arrived, it was Catherine who captured all the attention.

In her speech to the court, she asked for justice as Henry's 'true and obedient wife.' Then, she asked – in all innocence – how she had offended him. It was a great performance. At the end, Catherine swept out of the court. Henry commanded her to return. She refused.

…a friend indeed

Henry exploded. In his fury, he turned on Cardinal Wolsey, his faithful minister since the beginning of his reign. But Wolsey's devotion did not matter now. What mattered was that he had failed to persuade the Pope to let Henry marry Anne Boleyn. Anne had already been running a slander campaign against Wolsey. She had Henry spellbound, and it was only a matter of time before he accused Wolsey of high treason. Wolsey was so upset he became seriously ill. In 1530, he died on his way to London where the treason trial was to have taken place. Anne Boleyn celebrated his death with a court entertainment called *The Going to Hell of Cardinal Wolsey*. Henry was disgusted. But he was so scared of Anne and her sharp tongue that he let her get away with it.

By now he had gone too far with the divorce to walk away from it. Meanwhile, Charles of Spain had thrashed the French invaders. So the Pope was in his power again and Henry would have no joy there. He was also thoroughly bedeviled by his women. Catherine still defied him. So did their daughter, Princess Mary. And Anne Boleyn continually nagged him to marry her.

In 1531, egged on by Anne Boleyn, Henry separated Catherine from their daughter Mary. Anne believed that the two had conspired against the king. Splitting them up might weaken their resistance. The king ordered Catherine to More House in Hertfordshire. Mary was sent to the royal palace at Richmond, Surrey. Mother and daughter would never see each other again.

After that, Catherine was moved from one house to the next. Each was more decrepit and unhealthy than the last. Wherever she was, Henry sent counsellors and other officials to crack her resistance. They tried threatening her. They terrorized her. They told her terrible things would happen to Princess Mary if she did not change her mind. They got nowhere.

Anne throws her weight around

Meanwhile, Anne Boleyn was showing off in London. She said she would rather see Catherine hanged than acknowledge her as Queen of England. Henry demanded that Catherine hand over her jewels. When she did so, he gave them to Anne.

Anne was already living in the royal apartments that had once belonged to Catherine. She had her own ladies-in-waiting. It was as if she were Queen Anne already. She was constantly with the king. They dined together, danced together, went hunting together. They did everything except sleep together. This stoked up Henry's passion even more. In addition to jewels, he sent Anne other luxurious gifts, such as hangings in cloth of gold and silver, and lengths of embroidered crimson satin. Henry also gave her a title – Marquess of Pembroke: lands worth £1,000 a year went with it. Anne Boleyn was riding high.

But she did not intend to hold off Henry forever. Around November or December 1532, she at last let the king take her to bed. A month or so later, she was pregnant. This was probably no accident. Anne was determined to be queen.

Her pregnancy was a warning

Born to a poor family in Ipswich, the son of a butcher, Thomas Wolsey rose to the greatest heights possible: he effectively governed England for the first 20 years of Henry VIII's reign. He also had ambitions to become Pope.

This gold medal was minted in 1545 to commemorate Henry VIII's new role as head of the English church in place of the Pope. Henry appears on the medal wearing an ermine robe and a cap and collar studded with jewels.

to Henry to put his foot down and get that divorce. Henry's response to Anne's demands was to change England and the lives of its people forever.

A milestone in history

Elsewhere in Europe, the Reformation was already underway. Protestants, challenging papal authority and criticising the Church's sale of indulgences to lessen a person's sins, were breaking away from the Pope and Roman Catholicism. Henry was a sincere Roman Catholic, but, when the Pope would not give him the divorce he desired, he broke with Rome just the same. He made himself Supreme Head of the Church of England and granted himself the divorce that he wanted.

Anne finally gets her way

Henry VIII and Anne Boleyn were married in secret on 25 January 1533. Henry had given Catherine one last chance to give up her rights and title as queen. She had still refused. The outlook was bad for Catherine. After the break with Rome, the English church no longer needed the Pope's agreement for anything. So it was easy for Thomas Cranmer, Archbishop of Canterbury, to declare that Catherine's marriage was at an end. At the same time, he decreed that Anne's marriage was legal.

Catherine was ordered to stop calling herself 'Queen of England'. She had to use the title 'Princess Dowager' instead. It was a terrible insult. Once more, Catherine refused. When Henry sent her a document changing her title to Princess Dowager, she returned it with the new title crossed out. The furious Henry threatened her. Still Catherine held out.

By now, the struggle between Henry and Catherine had gone beyond a marital spat. Catherine's nephew, Charles of Spain, threatened to invade England. Moreover, Henry's subjects did not like Anne Boleyn, but loved Catherine. Whenever Catherine had to move from one house to the next, people gathered by the thousands to cheer her. Anne was often booed in public. There were public demonstrations against Anne. She was called a 'whore' and a 'witch'. A huge crowd gathered when she rode through the streets of London on the way to her coronation on 1 June 1533. The crowd had been ordered to cheer. Instead, they yelled: 'Nan Bullen shall not be our Queen!'

His Majesty regrets

By this time, the King had become desperate. Catherine and Mary were still defying him. As for Anne, she was giving her husband a hard time.

After the downfall of Cardinal Wolsey, Henry took over his magnificent palace, Hampton Court, by the River Thames. He was astounded and also infuriated at the luxurious fittings and decorations, like those seen here in the Great Hall.

A LOVE TEMPERED BY DIGNITY

IN HER LAST HOURS, Catherine dictated a letter to the king. Even in the face of his great cruelty, as the last line clearly shows, she had always loved the king.

'My most dear lord, king and husband: the hour of my death drawing on, the tender love I owe you forceth me…to commend myself to you and to put you in remembrance…of the health and safeguard of your soul, which you ought to prefer before all wordly matters…for which you have cast me into many calamities and yourself into many troubles. For my part, I pardon you everything and I wish devoutly to pray God that He will pardon you also. For the rest, I commend unto you our daughter Mary, beseeching you to be a good father to her…. Lastly, I make this vow, that mine eyes desire you above all things. Farewell.'

Catherine needed help to hold the pen as she signed the letter. Her signature was shaky. It read 'Catherine, Queen of England.' She had defied King Henry to the last.

Anne was a real tartar, demanding and vengeful. She threw one tantrum after another. Her child, born on 7 September 1533, turned out to be another girl – the future Queen Elizabeth I. There were no celebrations.

Henry felt that he had been made the laughing-stock of Europe. In England, he had to face fearful slanders. It was said that the king was living in sin with Anne, that she was no more than a wicked woman with loose morals who deserved to be burned at the

> **Catherine did not have much longer to live. By 1534, it was said she had dropsy. In fact, she was suffering from cancer. 'So much the better', retorted the king when he heard about it.**

stake. Princess Elizabeth was condemned as illegitimate. Before long, Henry decided it was Anne's fault that their child was not the son he wanted. He began to refer to his second marriage as his 'great folly'.

It certainly looked that way. Henry had no control over Anne. She would insult him in front of his courtiers. She never apologized. All Henry could do was to complain to Anne's father, Sir Thomas Boleyn, that

Queen Catherine had never used such language to him. The pressure brought out Henry's natural cruelty. He began to mull over the idea of getting rid of Anne. But, as long as Catherine lived, he was stuck with her.

Catherine, however, had not much longer to live. By 1534, it was said that she had dropsy. In fact, she was suffering from cancer. 'So much the better', retorted the king when he heard about it. Catherine was then shortening whatever life she had left by refusing to eat. She was afraid that her ex-husband was going to poison her.

Meanwhile, there was opposition to his second marriage. Henry's answer was to execute anyone who spoke out against it. One of the condemned was Sir Thomas More, scholar and author, who had once been Henry's chancellor. More was beheaded on Tower Hill on 6 July 1535.

By that time Catherine was dying. Somehow she hung on over Christmas 1535 and into 1536. But she was in a terrible state. She was so wasted, wrote ambassador Chapys, 'that she could hard sit up in bed. She couldn't sleep. She threw up what food she managed to swallow.' Finally, she passed away on 9 January 1536.

Sir Thomas More, Henry's former chancellor, refused to acknowledge Henry as the head of the English church. Found guilty at his trial for high treason, More was executed in 1535. Here he is, saying goodbye to his daughter, Margaret Roper.

7
DECAPITATION AND DIVORCE

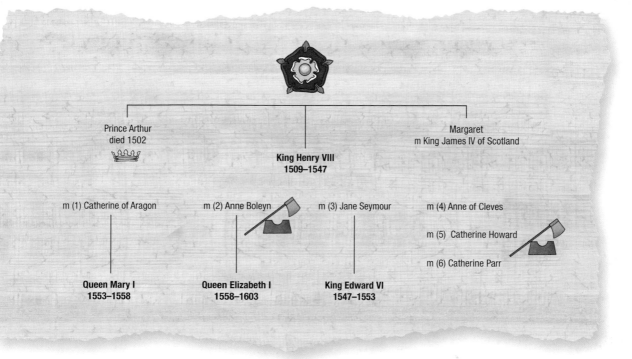

Prince Arthur
died 1502

Margaret
m King James IV of Scotland

King Henry VIII
1509–1547

m (1) Catherine of Aragon

m (2) Anne Boleyn

m (3) Jane Seymour

m (4) Anne of Cleves

m (5) Catherine Howard

m (6) Catherine Parr

Queen Mary I
1553–1558

Queen Elizabeth I
1558–1603

King Edward VI
1547–1553

Free of Catherine at last, King Henry VIII began to think of ways to get rid of Anne. He was tired of clever, educated women like his first two wives. What he wanted now was a nice, placid girl who would not argue with him.

◆

enry found his new wife in the same place he had found Anne Boleyn: among the queen's ladies-in-waiting.

The perfect partner

Jane Seymour, daughter of Sir John Seymour, appeared to fit the bill perfectly. She seemed quiet and modest with a nondescript personality. Nor was she very pretty: she had a long chin, a tight mouth and a

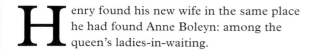

The Tower of London had been used as a palace, a prison and a place of execution since Norman times. Here Henry's second wife, Anne Boleyn, would meet her end.

large nose. She could hardly read and write, beyond signing her own name. Yes, dull, plain Jane Seymour was just what Henry wanted.

But Jane Seymour was much more calculating than Henry could have known. She quickly gathered that Anne Boleyn was on the way out. This was Jane's cue to step in smartly. She played the game perfectly. She accepted gifts Henry sent her. But she would not open his letters or accept money. Once, she kissed a letter sent to her on the king's behalf. Then she handed it back to Sir Nicholas Carew, who had brought it to her. She also gave back the purse of gold that came with it. Jane asked Sir Nicholas to tell the king she would only accept money when God sent her a husband. Subtle hints were not Jane's style.

Poor fool Henry was taken in again. He was delighted that Jane had proven so virtuous and demure. But Anne Boleyn was not so easy to deceive. She knew exactly what was going on.

A minx at court

Jane heartlessly rubbed Anne's nose in the dirt. Henry sent Jane a portrait of himself in a locket. In front of Anne, she toyed with it. She opened and closed it and cooed over it. Anne was so furious that she tore the locket from Jane's neck. Several times she slapped Jane's face when gifts and messages from Henry arrived. Jane made no secret of where they had come from.

Now that Henry had found a new love, there was only one hope for Anne: to produce the longed-for son. She became pregnant three more times. She lost two of the babies, but near the end of 1535, she was pregnant again. Henry began to hope, but still carried on with Jane. Then, on the afternoon of 29 January the day Queen Catherine was buried, something happened to push Anne over the edge: she found her rival sitting on the king's knee.

Anne flew into such a wild fury that Henry began

Torture was used to obtain Smeaton's confession. Henry knew perfectly well that Anne was being framed. But he was satisfied.

---

to fear for the child she was carrying. He tried to calm her down. But she raged on and on. A few hours later, the inevitable happened. Anne miscarried. When it was examined, her child appeared to be a son. For Anne, it was the end. She had a violent argument with the king. Each of them blamed the other for the miscarriage. Eventually, the king stormed out, vowing Anne would have no more sons by him.

This time, Henry did not have divorce in mind. Anne, he knew, would plague him for as long as she lived. There was only one answer: Queen Anne Boleyn had to die.

Anne Boleyn was the fiery, sexy and ambitious second wife of Henry VIII. She got away with treating him with little respect, but fell foul of fate when, instead of the longed-for son, her child born in 1533 turned out to be a girl.

Henry chose his weapons. He would accuse Anne of witchcraft, adultery and plotting his death. All these charges carried the death penalty. Henry set his chancellor, Thomas Cromwell, to gather the 'evidence' together. Thomas Cromwell was a highly inventive man. Gossip and reports from spies formed part of his dossier against Queen Anne. The rest he made up. Henry now learned that Anne supposedly had had four lovers: three courtiers and a court musician, Mark Smeaton. Cromwell also 'discovered' that Anne had committed incest with her brother, Lord Rochford.

As per usual in Tudor times, torture was used to obtain Smeaton's confession. The others all denied the charges. Henry knew perfectly well that Anne was being framed. But he was satisfied. He ordered Anne's arrest on the evening of 2 May 1536. She was taken to the Tower of London in a paroxysm of fear. She had to be helped out of the barge that took her to the Tower. By the time she stepped inside she was hysterical and sobbing wretchedly. In mid-May, her 'lovers' went on trial. The evidence given was full of holes. Anne and her 'lovers' could prove they were all in different places when the alleged adulteries had taken place.

No place for truth

It did not matter. Henry could always fall back on the supposed plot to kill him. It was 'guilt by accusation', but it did the trick. The four 'lovers' were all found guilty. They escaped the penalty for traitors: hanging, drawing and quartering. Instead, they were beheaded on Tower Hill on 17 May 1536. The same afternoon, Anne's marriage to Henry was annulled.

At her own trial, Anne was calm and dignified. She denied everything. But it did her no good. She was found guilty and condemned to death. From her apartments at the Tower, she watched workmen constructing her scaffold. They worked all night and by 9:00 A.M. the next morning, 18 May, the scaffold was ready. The queen was executed the following day.

While Anne's trial was going on, Henry was making arrangements to marry Jane. Their engagement was announced on the same day Anne Boleyn died. Eleven

A DEATH WITH DIGNITY

HENRY DID ANNE one last good turn. Instead of being beheaded with an axe, like a common criminal, she was given a more dignified execution: her head was cut off with a sword. On 19 May 1536, a swordsman was waiting as she walked out across Tower Green and climbed the scaffold steps. He had tactfully hidden his sword underneath straw.

With a priest, Anne knelt and prayed. In these last moments of her life, she was calm. She took off her hood and necklace. A blindfold was tied over her eyes. As she prayed again, the executioner swiftly sliced off her head. Her last words had been: 'Mother of God! Pray for me. Lord Jesus! Receive my soul!'

Thereafter, Anne Boleyn was wiped off the royal map. In the royal palaces, her portraits were removed from the walls. Masons, carpenters and seamstresses stripped her initials from sheets and cushions and everywhere else they had been applied.

Anne Boleyn bids farewell to her ladies-in-waiting in this illustration. Her executioner, a French swordsman, waits in the background (right), beside the execution block.

This picture shows the inside of Traitor's Gate, one of the entrances to the Tower of London. Traitor's Gate was close by the Thames and prisoners were rowed along the river to disembark at the bottom of the steps leading up to it.

days later, on 30 May 1536, Jane became Henry's third wife and queen in a ceremony at Whitehall Palace. Jane was also Henry's third chance to have the son he so greatly desired.

But by now, King Henry was no longer the handsome young man he had been in his youth. He was 45, nearly 20 years older than Jane. He had grown fat and had a troublesome ulcer on his leg. His temper was worse than ever. But Jane played the submissive wife, which made Henry feel a bit better. It is likely, however, that the king's bad health prevented Jane from conceiving quickly. It was January, 1537, before she could tell Henry she was expecting.

Henry became almost mad with joy. He was sure that the child would be a son. This time, he was right.

Ecstasy gives way to agony

Jane gave birth to Prince Edward on 12 October 1547. Henry's joy knew no bounds. Church bells pealed in celebration. Bonfires blazed. Twenty thousand rounds of ammunition were fired off at the Tower of London. Doors were decorated with garlands. Banquets were held throughout England. The party went on for 24 hours.

But something had gone wrong. Jane seemed to recover quite well from the birth. But four days later, she fell ill. It was soon clear that Jane had childbed fever. Her doctors were helpless. All they could conclude was that Jane's servants had given her too much rich food. After three days, Jane was delirious. Another three days passed, and she was dying. She hung on for a while, but passed away on 24 October.

Henry was demented with grief. He bolted to Windsor Castle and shut himself up, unwilling to see or speak to anyone. His ministers were, in any case, terrified of him. None dared come near him for some

German artist Hans Holbein came to England in 1526 and again in 1532 to paint a series of magnificent portraits of prominent men and women, including the original version of this picture of Henry VIII.

time. Particularly not with the plans they had already laid for his fourth marriage.

Duty comes first

Henry's ministers were practical men. With his second and third marriages, the king had failed to do his dynastic duty: to make a marriage for political advantage. Also, one infant son as heir to the Tudor throne was not enough: babies and children died all too easily and far too early in the 16th century. Henry had to marry again.

But Henry had a terrible track record. One wife hounded to death; another executed. A third, Jane Seymour, had survived mainly because she knew how to keep her mouth shut. The remnants of the

Plantagenet family, and several high profile victims such as Thomas More, had all been beheaded. This King of England, it seemed, was dangerous. To marry him looked very much like a prescription for suicide.

The search for a willing bride

Likely brides in Europe were thoroughly alerted. Two were daughters of King Francis I of France. He refused to let them even think of marrying Henry. Another French princess, Mary of Guise, hastily married someone else – King James V of Scotland – upon hearing that Henry had been after her. Another, Duchess Christina of Milan, agreed to marry the king – as long as she could have two heads, one for the axeman and one for herself.

It was not just the risk of disgrace and death that put these women off. Nearly 50 years old, Henry was not much of a catch. He needed a nurse, not a wife. His health was poor, his temper worse than ever. He could no longer ride or joust in the lists, once his best-loved sport. All in all, he was a wreck.

Fortunately for Henry, there was still political advantage in marrying the King of England. In Europe, small Protestant states were under threat from the prominent Roman Catholic powers, Spain and France. One such state was Cleves, in Germany. For England, the Duchy of Cleves would be a useful ally against the French and the Spaniards. The ruling Duke of Cleves, John III, had two unmarried daughters. In 1538, Duke John offered the elder, Anne, as a bride for King Henry.

The nightmare bride

Anne of Cleves was ugly, skinny and loud-mouthed. Neither was she much concerned about personal hygiene. Anne was a problem. Henry liked his wives well-covered, good-natured and retiring. He had had enough of clever women with opinions of their own. But Henry's ministers, who approved of the match, got around this by lying to Henry about Anne. They

Jane Seymour, Henry VIII's third queen, was quiet, demure and ill-educated – just the sort of wife he wanted. Though pale-faced and plain, Jane looks magnificent in this portrait, which emphasizes her rich robes and jeweled headdress.

SVÆ · 21

described her as 'moderately beautiful'. They said she was tall, but did not mention she was skinny. To back this up, they commissioned a leading artist, Hans Holbein, to paint a portrait of Anne. It showed her as a dumpy young woman with dreamy eyes, but that was not all it showed. Most of the portrait was taken up with Anne's magnificent jewel-encrusted gown and headdress.

Henry fell for it. He soon was madly in love, and demanded to meet Anne as soon as possible.

A date with disappointment

The meeting was a disaster. Anne and her entourage arrived at Deal in Kent on 26 December 1539. She set out for London at once and arrived four days later. In a tizzy of love, King Henry rushed to see her. What he beheld was not the beautiful bride he anticipated, but an absolute fright. She was badly dressed and gawky. And she smelled awful. Henry was repelled. 'I like her not, I like her not,' he kept repeating. Henry was enraged.

Cromwell takes it on the chin

Henry summoned Thomas Cromwell, his chancellor, who had made the marital arrangements. The king habitually thrashed Cromwell, who was of low birth. Cromwell was often witnessed staggering out of meetings with Henry, his clothes awry and his hair askew. He also had at least one –more frequently two – black eyes. At their meeting to discuss Anne of Cleves, Henry was more violent than ever. But Cromwell kept his cool. He knew the alliance with Cleves was important and managed to convince the king that he was sincerely committed to this marriage. Henry, no fool, understood the significance of the alliance, too. So he gritted his teeth and married his ugly, foul-smelling bride on 6 January 1540.

But already, the king was trying to think of a way out. He had his lawyers look for loopholes in the marriage contract. The contract proved to be watertight. Next, Henry suggested that Anne was not a virgin when she married him. If she had been with other men, the marriage could have been annulled.

Catherine Howard looks a lot older than her 15 years in this portrait, based on a painting by Holbein. Catherine managed to ruin herself within two years of her marriage and suffered the same fate – execution – as her cousin Anne.

A marriage made in hell

Henry knew perfectly well that Anne was a virgin. He kept her that way by refusing to sleep with her. Poor Anne spoke little English and knew nothing of the 'facts of life'. She was bemused by the jokes that went around Henry's court about the virgin bride who did not know how to do 'it'. But Anne soon learned that she had failed to please. Her coronation as queen had been set for February 1540. Henry called it off without giving a reason.

> **Catherine Howard, a cousin of Anne Boleyn, was about 15 years old, but she was very beautiful and knew how to please men. She had had at least two lovers since the age of 12.**

Then Anne's ladies-in-waiting explained to her what should happen when a husband and wife get into bed together. Anne could then hardly fail to realize that what was meant to happen was most definitely not happening. At last, it dawned on her that Henry was trying hard to get rid of her. And, as everyone knew, when Henry VIII got rid of a wife, she usually ended up in a grave.

Dumb but alluring

Alarm bells began to ring loudly for Anne when Henry started paying too much attention to one of her ladies-in waiting. Catherine Howard, a cousin of Anne Boleyn, was about 15 years old, but was very beautiful and knew how to please men. She had had at least two lovers since the age of 12. Although she could not read or write, and was interested in nothing but her own pleasure, Catherine was lovely to look at, young, flirtatious and ignorant – for King Henry, Catherine Howard filled the bill perfectly.

Anne was not jealous, it seemed, but was terribly frightened. Henry began to complain that she 'waxed wilful and stubborn with him'. Thomas Cromwell, just as scared, had to tell Anne not to antagonize the king or both of them would suffer.

JOY AT LAST FOR ANNE

AFTER THE DIVORCE ANNE remained in Britain. Henry gave her an allowance of £4,000 a year, a stupendous sum for the time. He also gave Anne two manors and a castle of her own. It was a wonderful ending for Anne; she was rich and independent for the first time in her life. Best of all, she was out of danger.

For the next 17 years, until her death in 1557, Anne led the life of a great lady. She staged huge banquets for her friends. She chose a different gown every day from her vast new wardrobe. She enjoyed every minute of it.

Holbein's portrait of the plain Anne of Cleves was meant to convince Henry of her 'beauty'. It succeeded – until the King met her in person.

Cromwell was the first to suffer. Six months after Henry married Anne, Cromwell had done nothing to get Henry off the hook. In the summer of 1540, Henry ran out of patience and set the dogs on him. On 10 June 1540, Cromwell was arrested and taken to the Tower of London. The same day, he was accused of treason and heresy. It was a trumped-up charge, but having framed Cromwell, Henry pursued it to the end. On 28 July, Cromwell was duly executed on Tower Hill.

Henry had already taken charge of ending his hated fourth marriage. He sent Anne to Richmond Palace, promising to join her in two days. He never showed up. Meanwhile, he pursued Catherine Howard. Every evening, the king could be seen sailing by barge along the River Thames to Lambeth, where Catherine had been given apartments.

At Richmond, Anne became more and more agitated. So it was a tremendous relief to her when, on July 6, Henry's counsellors arrived to ask if she would agree to a divorce. Anne had feared much worse. She grabbed the divorce with both hands. Her marriage to Henry ended three days later.

Just under three weeks after his divorce from Anne, on 28 July 1540, King Henry married Catherine Howard. He thought he had achieved bliss at last, but he was wrong, mainly because he had failed to read the tell-tale signs at the start. Catherine Howard had been on the 'good-time-girl circuit' – always looking for wild fun and not minding how she got it. She had lost her virginity long before Henry married her and her worldliness stood her in good stead when it came to seducing the aging, sickly king.

Catherine pretended to ignore Henry's huge bulk: he had a 54-inch waist. She also overlooked the oozing ulcer on his leg. Once, Henry had been able to dance

This document, dated 9 July 1540, set out the annulment of Henry's marriage to Anne of Cleves. Henry had not been able to bring himself to consummate the marriage, but he was fond of Anne and often visited her after their union ended.

Excellentissimo

illustrissimo et potentissimo in Christo principi
et domino nostro domino Henrico octavo dei gratia
Anglie et Francie Regi, fidei defensori et domino
Hybernie ac in terra immediate sub Christo
supremo capiti ecclesie Anglicane. Thomas
Cantuariensis et Edowardus Eboracensis Archi-
episcopi ceterique episcopi ac reliqui totius regni
clerus auctoritate litterarum commissionalium de stre-
nue auctoritatis congregati et Synodum universale
representantes cum obsequio reverentie et honore debitis. Salutem
et felicitatem. QUUM Nos humillimi et Maiestatis vestre devo-
tissimi subditi convocati et congregati sumus virtute commissionis
vestre magno sigillo vestro consignate date septimo die July Anno
felicissimi regni vestri tricesimo secundo, quam accepimus in hec
que sequuntur verba. HENRICUS octavus dei gratia Rex Anglie
et Francie, fidei defensor. Dominus Hybernie ac in terra immediate
sub Christo supremum caput ecclesie Anglicane. Archiepiscopis Cant-
et Ebor ac ceteris regni nostri Anglie Episcopis. Decanis, Archi-
diaconis et universo clero. Salutem. Egerunt apud nos regni
nostri proceres et populus, ut cum nuper quedam emerserint, que,
ut illi putant, ad nos regnique nostri successionem pertineant, inter
que precipua est causa et conditio unionis quod in illustri et nobili femina Domina Anna Clevensi, propter externam quandam coniugii
speciem perplexam aliamque etiam, multis ac varijs modis ambi-
guum, videt. Nos ad eandem unionis dispensationem ita procedere dig-
naremur, et opinionem vestram, qui in ecclesia nostra Anglicana etiam
verbi dei et doctrinam profitemini, requiramus. Vobis igitur disqui-
rendi licentiam ita demandamus, ut si animus vester fuerit, persuasu
unionem cum prefata Domina Anna minime consistere aut cohere
debere. Nos ad unionem contrahend cum alia liberos esse vestro
primum ac reliqua deinde ecclesie suffragio pronuncietur et confirmet.
Nos autem qui versi in reliquis ecclesie huius Anglicane negocijs
gravioribus, que ecclesiasticam economiam et religionem spectent

all night and ride all day. Now, he could barely walk. Catherine paid no attention to that, either. Instead, she flattered him. She appealed to his vanity. He was hooked. He made a spectacle of himself in public, kissing and fondling her no matter who was watching. He called Catherine his 'rose without a thorn'. He pampered her, showering her with sumptuous gifts. In 1541 he presented her with jewels – 52 diamonds, 756 pearls and 18 rubies – to say nothing of furs, velvets, brocades and other finery.

Henry loved to show Catherine off. In July 1541, he took her on a 'progress', or tour, though the eastern and northern counties of Britain. But Catherine was

Catherine Howard was barely 17 years old when she was accused of adultery and beheaded in 1542. This illustration shows Catherine being rowed in some luxury to her imprisonment in the Tower of London.

in for a shock. When the 'progress' reached Pontefract in Yorkshire, Francis Dereham, one of her former lovers, showed up. Dereham knew far too much about Catherine, things that she did not want King Henry to discover. When Dereham asked to be allowed to join Catherine's household she had to agree. On August 27 Dereham became Catherine's private secretary.

If Catherine had hoped that would satisfy him, she was mistaken. Francis Dereham was the sort of young buck who could not keep his mouth shut. Dereham began to boast that he had known Catherine before King Henry. Everybody realized what he meant by 'known'. Sooner or later, the truth about Catherine's past was bound to come out.

Love is blind

It was sooner. In October 1541, Thomas Cranmer, Archbishop of Canterbury, received information about

A BRUTAL END FOR THE MOST BELOVED

CATHERINE WAS NOT GIVEN A TRIAL. That would have been too much for Henry, since his own folly would have been revealed in court. He would have looked like an old fool for having fallen for the wiles of a scheming harlot. Instead, charges were brought against Catherine in Parliament on 16 January 1542. She was presumed guilty and condemned to death.

Catherine was paralyzed with fear. When guards came to take her to the Tower of London, she refused to go. She had to be carried struggling to the barge that was to take her along the River Thames to the dreaded prison. By the time the barge reached there, Catherine was in a state of collapse.

Three days later, on 13 February 1542, she was led out to Tower Green. She could barely walk. Somehow, the executioner managed to get her to lay her head on the block. Then he swiftly chopped off her head with an axe.

An axe was normally used for executions by beheading, the fate of Catherine Howard in 1542.

Catherine's life before marriage. The information came from Mary Lascelles, who had lived in the same household as Catherine in Norfolk. Cranmer decided to investigate. He had a heart-to-heart talk with Mary Lascelles. She told him everything.

Cranmer turned pale as Mary described Catherine's noisy lovemaking sessions with Francis Dereham. He heard of how another lover, musician Henry Manox, boasted that he knew of a mark on Catherine's body where no man but her husband had a right to look. When Cranmer told King Henry, he refused to believe a word of it. It was just wicked gossip, he said. But just in case, he asked Cranmer to make further investigations. Meanwhile, Henry ordered Catherine to remain in her apartments. The allegations, he was sure, would soon be disproven.

They were not. Cranmer's new investigations backed up everything the Archbishop already knew. Henry was devastated. He sat on his throne in the Council chamber and wept openly. He shut himself away in his palace at Oatlands in Surrey. He was eaten away with grief for his shattered happiness.

When Catherine was charged with 'misconduct', she became hysterical. She wept and wailed and threw herself about so violently that her attendants feared she was going to kill herself. When she calmed down, Catherine knew she had only one hope: she would have to beg Henry to forgive her.

Catherine waited until Henry passed close by her apartments on his way to prayers. She dashed past her

This elegant portrait features Henry's sixth and last wife, Catherine Parr, who married the king in 1543. It is based on a painting by Hans Holbein, who died during an epidemic of bubonic plague in London the same year.

guards and ran towards the king. But she was unable get near him. The guards grabbed her before she could speak to him. Catherine was taken back to her apartments, screaming and struggling. She never saw Henry again.

Now Catherine and her lovers were quizzed relentlessly for evidence. Cranmer did not get much information out of Catherine. Whenever he tried to question her, she wept and became hysterical. However, she did mention another man she had known before marriage – Thomas Culpepper, now at Henry's court as a gentleman of the King's Privy Chamber. Culpepper was immediately arrested. His rooms were searched and a love letter from Catherine was found.

Cranmer was now hot on the trail. When he questioned Lady Rochford, one of Catherine's attendants, she told him everything about the love affair between Catherine and Culpepper. Lady Rochford disclosed how she had stood guard outside the bedroom door while the pair made love at Pontefract and elsewhere. Having sex before marriage was bad enough. But lovemaking at Pontefract meant that Catherine had committed adultery. And for that, there was only one penalty: death.

On 10 December 1541, Thomas Culpepper and Francis Dereham were executed. Afterwards, their heads were stuck atop pikes on London Bridge. The queen was executed two months later.

Finally, an enduring love

At long last, King Henry had learned his lesson. He would never find happiness by marrying young girls. The next time he chose a wife, in 1543, he chose well. Catherine Parr was a mature woman who had had two previous husbands. Thirty-one years old, she was more than 20 years younger than Henry. But she was level-headed, pleasant and kind-hearted. Henry married for the sixth and last time on 12 July 1543. During the next four years, Catherine Parr made a happy home for him and his three children. This was something none of them had ever known before.

But four years were all they would have. By the end of 1546, King Henry was in a worse state than

ever. He found it difficult to walk. He had to be winched up and down stairs by a mechanical hoist. He was dying.

Gone, but never forgotten

Catherine stayed with him as he lay on his deathbed. So did his daughter by Catherine of Aragon, Princess Mary. But both became so upset that Henry told them to go away. For Catherine, it was a good thing. Before King Henry died on 28 January 1547, it was not her name that he cried out as he lay dying. Instead, he called for Jane Seymour, whom he had loved and lost ten years before. After his death, Henry was buried next to Jane at St. George's Chapel, Windsor.

This letter from Catherine Howard to Thomas Culpepper – probably dictated since she was almost illiterate – was open and affectionate, and became a vital piece of evidence against her when she was accused of adultery.

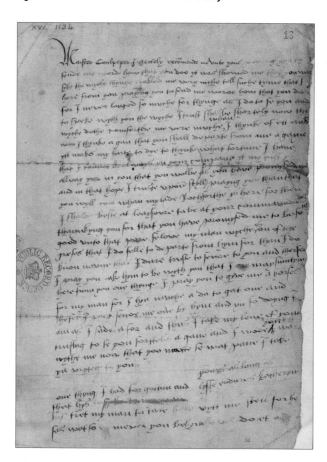

TURMOIL, TERROR AND FATAL ILLNESS

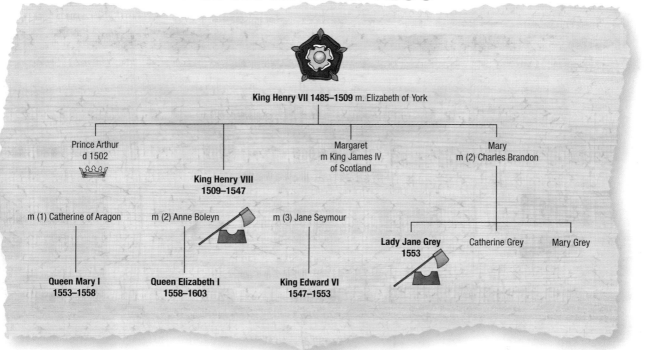

King Henry VII 1485–1509 m. Elizabeth of York

Prince Arthur
d 1502

Margaret
m King James IV
of Scotland

Mary
m (2) Charles Brandon

King Henry VIII
1509–1547

m (1) Catherine of Aragon   m (2) Anne Boleyn   m (3) Jane Seymour

Lady Jane Grey
1553   Catherine Grey   Mary Grey

Queen Mary I
1553–1558

Queen Elizabeth I
1558–1603

King Edward VI
1547–1553

The new king, Edward VI, was a boy of nine. His heirs were his half-sisters, Mary, daughter of Catherine of Aragon, aged 31, and Elizabeth, aged 13, daughter of Anne Boleyn.

This was just the situation King Henry VIII had wanted to avoid. He had destroyed two wives in his search for a son to succeed him. Now, the Tudor throne was in the hands of a boy, a woman and a girl. And though it was not yet apparent, the last two had been badly affected by the turmoil of Henry's first two marriages.

This painting illustrates the scene at the execution of the unfortunate Lady Jane Grey, a victim of the plot that surrounded the succession to the English throne in 1553.

Princesses with a legacy of pain

Princess Mary had once been a bright, beautiful child, adored by her father. But she had suffered badly during her father's battle with her mother, Catherine of Aragon. Mary, aged 31 when Henry died, was left mentally scarred. Deprived of love, she craved it badly. Roman Catholicism was outlawed in England by this time. But Mary remained a devout Catholic. It all led to terrible mistakes and a sad, lonely end.

Princess Elizabeth could have gone the same way. But years of turmoil had hardened rather than

weakened her. She was unusually shrewd, even at 13. She was also very wary. She had been less than three years old when her father killed her mother. When Elizabeth was only eight, there was another execution: Catherine Howard, who had befriended Elizabeth, had her head chopped off. After that, Elizabeth came to believe that marriage was dangerous. Men were dangerous. These fears were to affect Elizabeth for the rest of her life.

Schemers 'protect' the boy-king

King Edward VI also had a problem: he was too young to rule on his own. He had to have a protector. This was the cue for two very ambitious men to seize the power they had always wanted: the boy-king's uncles, Edward and Thomas Seymour.

Edward Seymour was a fast mover. Two days after the death of King Henry VIII, he filled the Royal Council with his cronies. Then, with their help, he had himself proclaimed the boy-king's Protector. Next, Seymour gave himself a grand title – Duke of Somerset.

Meanwhile, Seymour's younger brother, Thomas, was plotting his own way to power. He planned to get it by the back door: if he could marry into the royal family, he would gain riches and a say in government.

There were three ways Thomas Seymour could ally himself to the royal family – he could marry Princess Mary, Princess Elizabeth or Henry VIII's widow, Catherine Parr. Mary and Elizabeth turned him down flat. They were princesses. Marriage to an upstart like Thomas Seymour would have been beneath their royal dignity. So Thomas fell back on Catherine Parr, who had in fact been betrothed to him before she married King Henry. Now he charmed her again. They married in secret in May 1547. Thomas Seymour had reached first base.

Not that his marriage stopped him from playing around. Seymour was particularly keen on Elizabeth. Seymour often went to her bedroom, wearing scanty clothes. He played suggestive games with Elizabeth. Seymour did not attempt to hide his activities. At court, he paid Elizabeth so much attention that Catherine, who was pregnant, became jealous.

Another Tudor family portrait by Holbein, this time of Edward VI, who succeeded his father, Henry VIII, in 1547. There was something wrong with the Tudor line – Edward was the third Tudor boy to die young, at just 15.

The unfortunate Catherine died in childbirth on 5 September 1548. This robbed Thomas Seymour of his precious royal connection. He became desperate. One night in January 1549, he was found outside King Edward's bedroom. He held a smoking pistol in his hand. The young king's pet dog lay dead at his feet. The only explanation offered was that Thomas had meant to kill the king.

Edward Seymour was a fast mover. Two days after King Henry VIII's death, he filled the Royal Council with his cronies.

Protector Edward Seymour had never trusted his scheming brother. This was a chance to get rid of him. Thomas was accused of treason, and on his brother's orders, was executed on 20 March 1549.

No love lost between brothers

But Edward Seymour had himself made many enemies. He was hated for the way he grabbed power in 1547. The most deadly of his enemies was John Dudley, Earl of Warwick. Dudley was a cool customer. He was cunning, clever and much more ruthless than Edward Seymour. He had been planning the Protector's downfall for some time. On 6 October 1549, he struck.

Dudley arrived with a small armed force at Hampton Court Palace, near the River Thames. King Edward and Seymour were there at the time. The Protector hustled the boy-king onto a barge and ordered the bargemen to row downriver for Windsor – fast. Edward got there safely. But Seymour knew the writing was on the wall. Eight days later, he gave himself up and was sent to the Tower of London.

Subsequently, Seymour was charged with embezzlement and unlawful seizure of power. He was fined, and sacked from his role as Protector. He was released, and Dudley allowed Seymour to live a while longer, safe in the knowledge that sooner or later the former Protector would slip up. Then he could be accused of more serious crimes – crimes that carried the death penalty.

Seymour
gave Dudley the
chance he wanted in 1552.
The Catholic Princess Mary had refused to have anything to do with Protestant church services. The Royal
Council tried to bully her, but she would not give in.

Unfortunately for Edward Seymour, he had a fond-
ness for Mary and supported her. With that, John
Dudley pounced. He accused Seymour of wanting to
restore the Roman Catholic Church in England. To
back that up, Seymour was also charged with conspir-
ing against the Royal Council.

It was a lethal package. Seymour was found guilty
and sentenced to death. King Edward was horrified.
He begged Dudley to spare Seymour's life. Dudley
ignored his pleas and Edward Seymour was executed
on 22 January 1552.

John Dudley, Duke of Northumberland, plotted to supplant
Princess Mary, the rightful heir to the throne. His scheming
ended in disaster and death for himself, his son Guildford Dudley and Dudley's wife Lady Jane Grey: all of
them were executed.

England on the verge of bankruptcy

With both the Seymour brothers dead,
John Dudley had a free hand to do as
he pleased. He gave himself and his
supporters grand titles. He became
Duke of Northumberland. Dudley
and his cronies plundered the
monasteries and university libraries
of their treasures. They grabbed royal
estates worth a phenomenal £30,000
a year. By the time they had finished,
England was almost bankrupt.

Meanwhile King Edward, now
14, was feeling the strain. The
Seymour brothers had pressured
him and torn his loyalties back and
forth. But John Dudley was much
worse. He was a pure brute. He treated
the boy-king like a puppet, bullying
him mercilessly. He nagged him to sign
documents and laws. Edward had no say in
anything: Dudley was all powerful.

Then, at the end of January 1553, Edward
became seriously ill. He had a high fever, his
lungs were congested, he could barely breathe.
When Princess Mary came to visit him, he failed to
recognize her. Edward, aged 15, was clearly dying.
Alarm bells rang for John Dudley. If Edward died,
Catholic Mary would become reigning queen. That
would be the end of Dudley's power. He had no
intention of letting that happen.

Swift marriages to aid plans

The plot he laid to hang on to power was truly das-
tardly. Dudley arranged three marriages. Sisters Lady
Jane Grey, Catherine and Mary were members of the
Tudor royal family, descended from Henry VIII's sister

Jane Seymour's brother Edward made himself Protector to
her son, King Edward VI, but was outmanoeuvred by the more
brutal and ambitious John Dudley. Accused of treason, Edward
Seymour was sent to the Tower and executed in 1552.

Mary. Jane Grey was considered most important of the three. Dudley married her off to his own son, Guildford Dudley. Catherine and Mary married powerful nobles, both Dudley's allies. That done, Dudley went to King Edward and bullied him into agreeing that if Princess Mary became Queen it would be a disaster for England. Poor Edward was too ill to resist. On Dudley's orders, the young king changed the succession to the throne. Now, his successor was to be Lady Jane Grey.

But Dudley had not finished with Edward. The boy was now a ghastly figure. He looked like a skeleton. His lungs had been eroded by tuberculosis. There were running sores all over his body. Dudley decided that he had to be kept alive. He called in a quack doctor who dosed Edward with arsenic. This drastic treatment revived the boy for a time. It was just long enough, Dudley thought, to trap Mary and Elizabeth. He invited both to Greenwich, in London, to see their dying half-brother.

Elizabeth immediately suspected a trap and refused to come. She guessed, correctly, that Dudley meant to imprison her and Mary. Mary was not quite so astute. She set out for London. But when she reached Hoddesdon, 25

The order for the execution of Lady Jane Grey that took place in 1554. Queen Mary shrank from executing her after the failure of Northumberland's plot, but the rebellion against Mary's planned marriage to Philip of Spain meant Jane had to die.

The escape of Elizabeth and Mary foiled Dudley's plan. But there was nothing he could do about it. Late in the evening of 6 July 1553, Edward VI died. At the end, he had been too weak to speak, or even cough.

Subjects loyal to Mary

John Dudley was in a fix. In Norfolk, nobles rushed to support Princess Mary, escorted by their armies. Soon, Mary's forces numbered 30,000 men. On 9 July Dudley had Lady Jane Grey declared Queen. But Mary's support kept growing.

Mary was now safeguarded in the fortress at Framlingham. Dudley set out from London to capture her. With Dudley gone, his supporters became so frightened they shut themselves up in the Tower of London. Lady Jane Grey and her husband were among them.

'Long live the queen!'

On his march to Framlingham, things went from bad to worse for Dudley. His troops started to desert. He heard that Londoners had declared their support for Mary. He himself was branded a rebel and realized his plan was hopeless. Overnight, his power had vanished. Dudley became hysterical. He tossed his cap into the air and shouted: 'Long live Queen Mary!' Tears ran down his cheeks as he said it. Against the odds, Mary was queen, the first reigning queen England had known.

John Dudley was arrested on 21 July, accused of high treason. Guarded by 4,000 soldiers, he was taken back to London. The people of England had come to hate Dudley. All the way, people lined his route to the capital. They jeered at him. They cursed him. They threw stones, shook their fists, shouted insults. When he reached London, he was imprisoned in the Tower.

John Dudley was arrested on 21 July, accused of high treason. Guarded by 4,000 soldiers, he was taken back to London.

---

miles (40km) from the capital, she received a warning that Dudley was up to no good. Mary fled to Kenninghall, her house in Norfolk. It was a much safer 85 miles (136km) from London.

Although she has since acquired the nickname 'Bloody Mary', Mary I began as England's first ever reigning queen with an act of mercy: she pardoned five prisoners incarcerated in the Tower of London.

Mary's triumph

Meanwhile, on 3 August 1553, Queen Mary entered London. It was a triumph all the way. Huge crowds gathered to cheer her. Some were so happy they wept. The noise was deafening. No monarch of England had ever received such a greeting.

Mary dressed for the occasion. Her gown was of royal purple. Her neck was circled with jewels. Even her horse had trappings made of cloth of gold. But she was now 37 and looked even older. All her sufferings now showed on her lined, pale face. Mary was not a cruel woman. She tried to see good in everyone. She was remarkably forgiving. But she could not forget what she had endured during the reigns of her father and brother.

As the cheering Londoners would soon learn, Mary's reign would be payback time for those sufferings. Her subjects would suffer in turn.

Queen of hearts

Queen Mary was on a high. And it was typical of her to begin her reign with an act of mercy. She pardoned five prisoners from the Tower of London. Mary's ministers expected her to punish the conspirators who had tried to cheat her of her throne. Mary confounded their expectations by pardoning all but three. Only John Dudley and two cronies were executed, on 22 August 1553.

But what to do with Lady Jane Grey, who had been 'queen' for only nine days? What about her husband, Guildford Dudley? People expected that they, too, would soon lose their heads. But Mary would not execute them, though they did remain imprisoned in the Tower.

Mary's primary aim was to restore England to the Roman Catholic Church. Unfortunately, she did not understand that her subjects were solidly Protestant. They wanted nothing to do with Catholics or with the Pope. With this, the stage was set for a major clash between the queen and her people. It became even bigger when news leaked out of Mary's marriage plans. Mary had chosen Philip, the son of King Charles of Spain – a Catholic, and a foreigner.

Wyatt's rebellion, which protested against the planned marriage of Queen Mary and Philip of Spain, was a terrifying experience for Londoners. Wyatt's army was massing, ready to march on the beleaguered city.

Mary was not as free to choose her own husband as she thought. Reaction against the 'Spanish Marriage', as it was called, was violent. Parliament was against it. Mary's ministers were opposed. Protestant bishops of the English church disapproved. Most of all, the people were against it. But foolishly, Queen Mary ignored them all. On 29 October 1553, she announced that she was betrothed to Philip. She would 'never change,' she said, 'but love him perfectly...'

Panic spreads

A wave of alarm spread through England. There were fearful stories doing the rounds that a Spanish army

DEATH OF AN INNOCENT

MARY HAD WANTED to let Lady Jane Grey and Guildford Dudley live. But the queen was not a soft touch any longer. The day after Wyatt surrendered, she signed death warrants for both. They were led out to execution on 12 February 1554. Guildford Dudley died first.

Later a chronicler wrote: 'His carcase thrown into a cart, and his head in a cloth, he was brought to the chapel within the Tower, where the Lady Jane...did see his dead carcase taken out of the cart....'

The seventeen-year-old Lady Jane Grey died bravely and with dignity. The chronicler continued: 'She gave...(her attendants) her gloves and handkerchief, and her book...she untied her gown. The hangman went to her to help her therewith...giving to her a fair handkerchief to (tie) about her eyes.

'Then feeling for the block she said, "What shall I do? Where is it?" One of the standers-by guiding her thereto, she laid her head down upon the block, and stretched forth her body and said: "Lord, into thy hands I commend my spirit!" And so she ended.'

A fanciful illustration of the execution of Lady Jane Grey: the blow of the axe was normally administered to the back, not the side of the neck.

8,000 strong was en route to England. The Spaniards sought to take over the Tower of London, ships of the English Navy and England's ports.

None of these stories were true, of course. But rebellions were being planned all over the country. The rebels' leader, Sir Thomas Wyatt, was ready to march on London. Once there, Wyatt planned to use his military might to force Queen Mary to put a stop to the Spanish Marriage.

Wyatt and his followers set out for the capital on 25 January 1554. There was panic in London. Watchers were posted at every gate into the city. Mary ordered the bridges over the River Thames destroyed. Soldiers guarded the streets. Lawyers,

priests and tradesmen wore shirts of mail beneath their robes for protection.

About the only one who did not panic was Queen Mary herself. She refused to leave London. She told Londoners: 'Good subjects, pluck up your hearts and like true men, stand fast against. . . our enemies and yours, and fear them not, for I assure you I fear them nothing at all!'

That cheered up Londoners for a while. But panic soon returned. The bridges had been destroyed, as Mary had ordered. But on the night of February 6, Thomas Wyatt swam across the icy River Thames. He found a boat and used it as a floating platform to repair one of the bridges.

Battle in the heart of London

That done, some 7,000 rebels marched across and on to London once again. On 17 February they reached the gates of the city. There, waiting for them, stood 10,000 soldiers, 1,500 cavalry and row upon row of heavy cannon.

Despite her bravery, Mary was badly shaken by Wyatt's rebellion. She realized that she could no longer afford to be merciful. There would be no pardon for the rebels this time.

As the rebels advanced, the lines of soldiers parted. Wyatt rushed through with his vanguard of about 400 men. But it was a trap. The soldiers closed in behind

him. Now Wyatt had to fight it out in the streets of London with only a small force to help him. At first, he met no resistance. But when he reached Charing Cross, he came up against a force of the Queen's Guards. But they did not fight. They ran for safety to the nearby Palace of Whitehall. Wyatt and his force followed. They peppered the windows of the palace with arrows.

Queen Mary, inside, heard the noise. One of her senior commanders, Edward Courtenay, was quivering with fear.

'Well then, fall to prayer', the queen told him scornfully. 'And I warrant you, we shall hear better news anon.'

Better news soon arrived. A troop of Mary's cavalry attacked Wyatt and his followers. Before long, Wyatt's men were cut down. The streets were stained with their blood. At last, with only a handful of men left standing, Thomas Wyatt surrendered.

Despite her bravery, Mary had been badly shaken by Wyatt's rebellion. She realized that she could no longer afford to be merciful. There would be no pardon for the rebels this time. Nearly 200 were condemned to death. Forty-six were hanged in London in a single day. Lady Jane Grey and Guildford Dudley were executed soon thereafter.

The unfortunate Lady Jane had had to die, but she was an innocent victim. The same could not be said of Princess Elizabeth, Queen Mary's half-sister. At least, Mary did not think so. What made Mary suspicious was the way Elizabeth avoided contact with her. She would not come to court. She would not attend Catholic Mass. Mary was sure Elizabeth had conspired with Thomas Wyatt and the rebels.

Today, the Tower of London is no longer a place of terror and death. It is one of London's most popular tourist attractions: the spot where the scaffold once stood is marked out for visitors to see the place where so many people were beheaded.

Queen Mary I was an attractive young woman before frustration, disappointment and a failed marriage embittered her and aged her before her time. She was particularly fond of jewels, fine brocaded fabrics and delicate lace ruffs and collars.

Surprising support for Elizabeth

Then, on 17 March 1554, Elizabeth was arrested and taken to the Tower of London. But she denied knowing anything about Wyatt's rebellion. There was no real evidence against her. After two months, she was released, and taken under guard by barge to be kept in a lodge house in Woodstock, Oxfordshire.

Queen Mary was alarmed to see how popular Elizabeth was. All the way, people lined the banks of the river. They cheered her loudly. Church bells rang out. Guns were fired in celebration. Women baked special cakes for Elizabeth. Before long, her barge was piled high with gifts.

Meanwhile, the leaders of Wyatt's rebellion were heavily punished. One of them, the Duke of Suffolk, was beheaded on February 23. Wyatt himself was hung, drawn and quartered.

Members of Parliament had protested violently against the Spanish Marriage. But the day that Wyatt died, they gave in. The Royal Marriage Bill became law. Gritting their teeth in fury, Parliament told Mary that Philip would be welcome in England.

Reluctant groom

But Philip was not too happy about the marriage, either. The last thing he wanted was to marry a scrawny, ageing queen 11 years his senior. But he had to go along because his father, King Charles, wanted to ally Spain with England. That way, Charles could get his hands on English money and troops for his war with France.

Mary knew nothing of all this. She imagined her marriage was going to be a great romance. She longed to be loved. She looked forward to showing off her handsome young husband. Philip, Mary thought, had been given to her by God. Poor Mary. It was all a dream.

DEEDS *of* POWER

THE REMORSEFUL COWARD

IN ALL, SOME 300 PEOPLE WERE BURNED at the stake during Mary's reign. Most were ordinary men and women. Some were very high profile. Thomas Cranmer, Archbishop of Canterbury during the reigns of Henry VIII and Edward VI, was burned on 16 October 1555. Cranmer had been terrified of burning to death.

To avoid it, he admitted he had been wrong to become a Protestant, even signing a confession saying so. But he was condemned to burn just the same. When he realized what a coward he had been, he decided to make up for it. When the fire was lit, he thrust his hand into the flames. He held it there until it completely burned away. It was the hand he had used to sign his confession.

Thomas Cranmer, Henry VIII's Archbishop of Canterbury, seen here at Traitor's Gate at the Tower of London, later died bravely at the stake.

Philip left Spain for England on 4 May. He took his time getting there. It was not until 21 July that he met Mary for the first time. It was not a happy meeting. Philip found Mary repulsive and could not stand being near her. But he endured it and didn't let his real feelings show.

Philip and Mary were married in Winchester Cathedral on 25 July 1554. Within days, Mary became pregnant – or at least she thought so. Great preparations were made for the birth. A religious service was held to give thanks for the queen's quickening, the moment when her baby showed its first signs of life. Mary sat there, proud and happy.

A devout Catholic, Queen Mary I longed to return the English church to the jurisdiction of the Pope in Rome, and during her reign some 300 Protestants were burned at the stake for resisting her demands.

PHILIPPE II. CATHOLIQVE ROY D'ESPAGNE,
DES INDES, ET MONARQVE DV NOVVEAV MONDE

Moncornet ex.

Philip of Spain was 11 years younger than Queen Mary when, very reluctantly, he agreed to make a political marriage with her. Later, as King Philip II, he became the sworn enemy of Mary's Protestant half-sister, Queen Elizabeth I.

She let her swelling belly show, so that 'all men might see she was with child'.

'Bloody' Mary

But Mary's plans to return England to the Catholic faith were not going well. There was a lot of resistance, so much that Mary resorted to burning the resisters in public. That was a mistake. The watching crowd howled with anger. Each burning inspired more ugly scenes than the last. Hatred for Queen Mary increased. Now, she had a new name – 'Bloody Mary'.

Philip tried to put a stop to the burnings. Unlike Mary, he realized the more people she burned, the more she was hated. Even for his sake, however, she would not stop. The burnings went on.

A blow for the queen

But a terrible humiliation awaited her. The birth of her baby had been expected on or near 23 May 1555. But the date passed and there was no sign of a baby. There had been nothing by the end of June. There were suggestions that the Queen was not pregnant at all, that she had imagined the whole thing.

At first, Mary refused to believe it. But months passed. Still nothing happened. In the end, Mary had to admit she had been wrong. There was no baby. She became deeply depressed. At this point, just when she needed him most, Philip decided to leave England. Mary begged him not to go. But Philip had had enough of England, the English and their queen. On 22 August 1555, he left for his own territory, the Spanish Netherlands. Mary wept bitterly as she watched him leave.

Happy husband on the loose

Soon, gossip reached England that Philip was having a great time in the Netherlands. He was going to parties, attending weddings and dancing until dawn. He was also playing around with other women – all in all, acting as if he had been freed from prison. No one dared tell Mary what was going on. But that was not all they dared not tell her. Mary's doctors had now discovered the truth of her 'pregnancy': she had a tumor in her womb.

Philip kept promising Mary that he would soon return to England. But he had no intention of returning. Mary became more and more depressed. She could not perform her duties as queen. She shut herself away and mourned for Philip as if he were dead.

Joy for the queen

Time passed, and Philip showed no signs of coming back. Then, in 1556, his father, King Charles, gave up the throne of Spain. Philip was now king in his own right, King Philip II of Spain and of its huge, rich empire in America.

> **For hours, Mary lay in a coma. When she spoke, she talked of seeing little children in her dreams. A priest came to give her last rites. While he was saying the prayers, she died. When news got out that 'Bloody Mary' was dead, England celebrated.**

To defend his vast territories, Philip needed money. And for money, he needed England. Philip returned at last in 1557. Mary greeted him with joy. But joy soon faded. Once Philip had the money, troops and ships he needed, he was gone. Mary never saw him again. All she had for comfort was the belief that she was pregnant again. But it was another phantom pregnancy. Philip had not gone near his wife while he was in England. The truth was that Mary's tumor had returned.

The end of a hated sovereign

By November 1558, Mary was dying. For hours, she lay in a coma. When she spoke, she talked of seeing little children in her dreams. A priest came to give her last rites. While he was saying the prayers, she died.

When news got out that hated 'Bloody Mary' was dead, people all over England celebrated. They sang and danced in the streets. They rang bells. For many years thereafter, the day Mary died, 17 November, was celebrated in England as a public holiday.

GLORIANA AND GORE

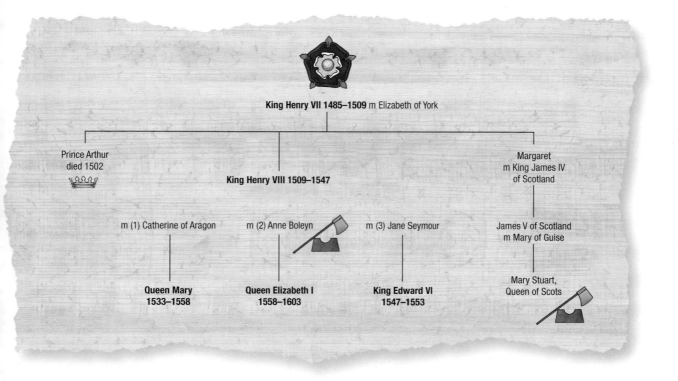

King Henry VII 1485–1509 m Elizabeth of York

Prince Arthur
died 1502

King Henry VIII 1509–1547

Margaret
m King James IV
of Scotland

m (1) Catherine of Aragon   m (2) Anne Boleyn   m (3) Jane Seymour

James V of Scotland
m Mary of Guise

Queen Mary
1533–1558

Queen Elizabeth I
1558–1603

King Edward VI
1547–1553

Mary Stuart,
Queen of Scots

Now Elizabeth was Queen of England, at only 25. The journey to the throne had been a hazardous one. Queen Mary had hounded Elizabeth and imprisoned her in the Tower of London.

King Charles of Spain wanted her executed. English Catholics believed that she was Protestant and hated her. To them, she was illegitimate, not only by birth, but also as queen.

But if Elizabeth's life was in peril before she came to the throne, it was far more dangerous for her afterwards. More enemies were lying in wait. On

Elizabeth I's richly embroidered robes and magnificent jewels disguised the weakness of her realm and made her appear more powerful.

England's northern border, Scots were making trouble. The Catholic kings of France and Spain wanted to invade England and remove Elizabeth from the throne. Pope Pius V was Elizabeth's avowed enemy, too. He excommunicated her in 1570.

Tolerance wins over the people

But Catholics at home and abroad were not Elizabeth's only problems. England was a small, poor country. Its armed forces were below par. Its people were exhausted and confused by 25 years of religious

(continued on page 135)

GLORIANA, THE VIRGIN QUEEN

WATCHING ELIZABETH'S 'PROGRESSES', her travels through her realm, no one would ever have guessed that the royal treasury was bankrupt. The courtiers who accompanied the queen were richly dressed. Their horses were magnificently attired. And there in the midst of it all, was Elizabeth herself. She rode in a splendid litter, swathed in sumptuous brocade gowns, covered with the finest ornaments and dazzling jewels.

Wherever she went, people rushed to see her. They were thrilled by the splendid sight of Elizabeth riding by. They began to look upon their queen as more of an icon than a human being. This was exactly what Elizabeth wanted.

Furthermore, playwrights, artists and balladeers endorsed Elizabeth's magical image. Edmund Spenser, for example, turned her into 'Gloriana', the heroine of his fantasy The Faerie Queene. Artists produced dazzling portraits of her – smothered in jewels and richly dressed. Elizabeth was also an inspiration to famous seamen, including Sir Francis Drake and Sir John Hawkins. They sailed across the Atlantic to raid and rob Spanish colonies in America. The Spaniards called them pirates. The English welcomed them home as heroes.

Elizabeth's image as a glorious queen, surrounded by pomp and glory, was a great propaganda job. But there was one thing Elizabeth would not do for her people. She refused to get married. Her ministers nagged her constantly. They told her a monarch had to have heirs to the throne. She told them she was 'married' to England. She preferred to remain the 'virgin queen'.

Opposite: The scene in 1580, when Elizabeth knighted Sir Francis Drake on the deck of his ship *Golden Hind* after his voyage around the world.
Below: This scene from a manuscript dedicated to Elizabeth I shows the queen in a procession.

dispute. Hundreds had been executed for their beliefs. Now, they looked to Queen Elizabeth I to find a cure for their years of trouble.

Fortunately, Elizabeth was just the package that they needed. In matters of religion, she did not make the mistakes of Protestant Edward VI or Catholic Mary I. Instead, she sat on the fence. Personally, she was not all that interested in religion. Certainly, she did not intend to persecute anyone because of it.

Religious tolerance was part of Elizabeth's plan to make herself attractive to her subjects. She put on a magnificent show. No monarch had ever made so many public appearances.

'We princes', Elizabeth told the English Parliament 'are set as it were upon stages in the sight and view of the world.'

The Queen's fears of marriage

In spite of Elizabeth's refusal to consider marriage, several betrothals were arranged for her. But she kept all her suitors dangling. One, François, Duke of Alençon, tried for years to persuade the queen to marry him. Alençon, 21 years younger than Elizabeth, was not a pretty sight. He was squat and ugly. His face was covered with scars and his nose was misshapen. All the same, he seemed to imagine that Elizabeth, who called him her 'frog', was indeed willing to marry him. But she would not say 'yes' and she would not say 'no'. She just kept putting Alençon off. In the end, the poor man was still trying to marry Elizabeth when she was in her forties. He never succeeded. No one did. Elizabeth gave all her suitors the brushoff.

She had several reasons for doing so. First, she was frightened of marriage. And she was scared of childbirth. Childbirth was still very dangerous for women in the 16th century. Elizabeth had seen Jane Seymour die after giving birth in 1537. In 1548, Catherine Parr had died the same way.

But that was not all that Elizabeth was afraid of. Her father, King Henry VIII, had executed two of his wives. The first was her own mother, Anne Boleyn. The other was the king's fifth wife, Catherine Howard, who had befriended Elizabeth as a child. Elizabeth's half-sister, Queen Mary, had made enemies among

Amy Robsart, wife of the Earl of Leicester, lies dead at the foot of the stairs. It was said by some that Amy was murdered so that her husband could marry the queen.

her subjects by marrying Philip of Spain. No wonder Elizabeth thought that marriage was dangerous.

Unrequited love

Another reason was that Elizabeth had already been in love long before she became queen. Robert Dudley had known Elizabeth since both were children. They might have been in love even at that early age. But Dudley had a terrible family history. His father had been John Dudley, Duke of Northumberland, who was executed for plotting to cheat Queen Mary of her throne. His grandfather, Edmund Dudley, had also been executed, in 1510. His crime was treason.

Amy Robsart died in suspicious circumstances. Her servants returned from a day out and found her dead at the bottom of the stairs. Her neck was broken. It might have been suicide....

With such a family background, Robert Dudley didn't have a chance of marrying Elizabeth. She did make him her closest companion at court, showering him with gifts and a title, Earl of Leicester. But that was as far as Robert Dudley got. There was something else, too. In 1550, Dudley had married Amy Robsart. He kept Amy hidden away in Oxford while he spent most of his time at court. It is possible that Elizabeth did not even know about her.

A scandal that ruled out marriage

But, on 8 September 1560, Amy Robsart died in suspicious circumstances. Her servants returned from a day out and found her dead at the bottom of the stairs. Her neck was broken. It might have been suicide; Amy had been suffering from breast cancer. But gossip soon went around. It was said Amy had been murdered so that Robert Dudley could marry the queen. Dudley was known to visit his wife from time to time. Just before she died, Amy had ordered a new dress, maybe because she was expecting to

(continued on page 138)

DEEDS *of* POWER

LOVE, JEALOUSY, REVENGE AND MURDER

MARY, QUEEN OF SCOTS is often pictured as a beautiful, desirable young woman. It was not true. Mary was no romantic heroine. She was an ignorant, foolish, indiscreet airhead. She managed to do almost everything wrong and was certainly not the queen 16th century Scotland needed. The country was in constant turmoil. Scottish lords were out of control. All Mary did was make a bad situation worse. In 1565, for example, she married Henry Stuart, Lord Darnley. The lords hated him. But Mary went further. She made court 'pets' out of men the lords detested, resulting in at least one untimely end.

One of Queen Mary's 'pets' was her Italian secretary, David Rizzio. Lord Darnley, Mary's husband, was jealous of him. He believed Rizzio was Mary's lover. So Darnley plotted, with others, to have Rizzio killed. The murder took place at Holyrood House in Edinburgh on the evening of 9 March 1566. The Queen, six months pregnant, was dining with Rizzio and one of her ladies-in-waiting when Lord Darnley and other conspirators burst into the room. They seized David Rizzio. As they dragged him away, the Italian tried to grab Mary's skirts, screaming 'save me, my lady, save me!'. Mary was helpless. One of the murderers kept a pistol pointed at her as Rizzio was pulled into the room next door.

The daggers came out and Rizzio was stabbed 56 times, dying in a spreading pool of blood. Later, the conspirators kept Mary a prisoner, but she managed to keep her head. She calmed them by promising a pardon. Two days after the murder, she managed to escape from Holyrood through underground passages in the chapel where the Scots' royal tombs were situated. From there she rode 20 miles to Dunbar – and safety.

Soon there was gossip that Mary wanted revenge for Rizzio's death by having Darnley killed. The truth was worse than that, Mary had fallen in love with

Mary, Queen of Scots was the focus of plots to depose and kill Elizabeth and replace her on the throne of England.

This 19th century illustration depicts the murder in 1560 of David Rizzio by Mary's jealous husband, Lord Darnley, and her unruly nobles.

a Scottish noble, James Hepburn, Earl Bothwell. Another reason for getting rid of Lord Darnley.

Bothwell, it seems, made arrangements for Darnley to die. On the night of 10 February 1567, Mary left Kirk o'Field, her house near Edinburgh, to attend a wedding. Darnley, who was ill, remained at home.

Sometime during the night, there was a huge explosion at Kirk o'Field. The building was flattened. Darnley was not killed in the explosion. He tried to escape.

But conspirators were waiting for him. Later, Darnley was found dead outside the house. He had been strangled. Three months later, Mary married Bothwell. He had already made her pregnant – with twins. But the Scottish lords hated Bothwell. The marriage was the last straw. Mary had to go – and Bothwell with her.

On 24 July 1567, at Loch Leven Castle, Mary was forced to abdicate. Later, she suffered a miscarriage. Scotland was now a dangerous place to be. So Mary headed for England. She arrived there on 16 May 1568. Bothwell fled to Denmark. They never saw each other again. Bothwell went mad and died in a Danish prison in 1578.

see her husband. But during his visit, so the gossips said, Dudley killed her. Nothing was proven. But the scandal had been too great. Elizabeth had to send Dudley away from her court. After a time he returned and became Elizabeth's pet once again. But marriage was out of the question.

Even so, it seems that Dudley still wanted to marry the queen. In 1563, Elizabeth suggested he marry her cousin, Mary, Queen of Scots. At that time, Mary was heir to Elizabeth's throne. So Dudley could have become King of England had he played his cards right. But he hadn't. He refused to marry Mary, preferring to stay in London, close to Elizabeth...and hope.

In 1568, Mary, Queen of Scots was imprisoned in Loch Leven Castle, where she was forced to abdicate. She managed to escape, but there was nowhere safe for her to go but England, where she became Elizabeth's prisoner.

The Trouble with Mary

Mary, Queen of Scots became a major problem. She was Catholic. The French and the Spanish wanted her to become Queen of England once they had removed Elizabeth from the throne. Catholics in England wanted the same thing. But in 1568, the problem grew bigger. Mary was forced to abdicate and fled south, where she placed herself under Elizabeth's protection.

Elizabeth granted Mary the protection that she sought. Mary wanted Elizabeth to help her to get back her Scottish throne. Elizabeth agreed to consider it. But she did not like the idea. Mary on the loose in Scotland would be more trouble than Mary in England. So Elizabeth stalled, and went on stalling.

Mary pushed her plan several times. In the end, it was foiled by her son, King James VI of Scotland. He grew up cold-hearted and cunning. He did not want his mother around. James was, after all, the second

William Cecil, Lord Burghley, served both Mary I and Elizabeth, who appointed him Secretary of State when she became Queen in 1558. Burghley was the principal architect of Elizabeth's policies for the next 40 years, until his death.

heir to the throne of England after Mary. If he played his cards right, he could have two crowns instead of one.

Safe, but never free

If Mary was not about to return to Scotland, what was Elizabeth to do with her? Elizabeth decided that Mary must be kept under house arrest. She would be comfortable and have servants. But she would be watched. English spies planted in Mary's household could read letters and messages she received. Even more important, they could find out who sent them.

Of course, Catholics and other sympathizers might try to rescue Mary. As a precaution, from time to time Elizabeth had Mary moved from one house to another. Catholics were not fooled. Several attempts to rescue Mary were made. All were unsuccessful.

Fending off rescuers was largely the work of Sir Francis Walsingham, Elizabeth's Secretary of State. Walsingham was really a secret agent, and a very good one, too. He had 53 agents planted in foreign courts. Another 18 worked for him in Europe. Between them, Walsingham's spies kept him well fed with information from 42 European towns and cities. Thus he was always one step ahead of conspirators who wanted Mary free and Elizabeth dead. Walsingham hated Mary. He called her 'that devilish woman'. His aim in life was to destroy her.

Mary always claimed that she knew nothing of the plots against Elizabeth. The truth was that she was involved up to her neck. The first serious plot against Elizabeth occurred in 1571. It was hatched by Robert Ridolfi, a Catholic banker from Florence, Italy. Ridolfi wanted to see Mary on the throne of England. So did his supporters in Europe. They included Philip II of Spain and the Pope himself.

Elizabeth's enemies hatch a plot

Ridolfi planned to invade England with a force of around 6,000 men. Meanwhile, rebels in Norfolk, in eastern England, would kidnap Elizabeth and hold her hostage. It was also planned that Mary should marry a

Catholic, Thomas Howard, Duke of Norfolk. Together, they would rule England and Scotland.

But Ridolfi ruined his own plot. He could not keep his mouth shut. He talked of his plans to the

---

One day, Babington received a letter from Mary. He was immensely flattered. But it was a ploy and Babington fell for it.

---

wrong people. The plot thereby reached the ears of Elizabeth's Chief Minister, William Cecil, Lord Burghley, who put a tail on Ridolfi. Burghley's spies got their hands on messages that he sent and letters he wrote. The letters were in code, but the code was broken and all was revealed.

Soft-heartened queen saves Mary

The Ridolfi Plot, as it was called, never got off the ground. Subsequently, the Duke of Norfolk was accused of treason. He was executed in 1572. But Ridolfi got away scot-free. So did Mary. Elizabeth's ministers begged her to have the Queen of Scots executed. But she refused. The English queen did not like spilling blood – especially royal blood. She simply could not bring herself to sign a death warrant for another queen.

This might not have been wise, however. As long as Mary lived, plots against Elizabeth would go on. But Sir Francis Walsingham had plans of his own. It has been said that he turned double agent and hatched his own 'plot' against the English queen. Walsingham's plan was to involve Mary. He knew Mary was vain and empty-headed and loved being the focus of intrigue. Walsingham was sure she would fall for his plot. Then, he could trap her. And when her guilt was revealed, Elizabeth would have to execute her.

But this scheme was to be unlike other secret agent operations. Walsingham's plans for getting rid of Mary

Reputedly very beautiful, Mary, Queen of Scots, became a tragic heroine after her execution in 1587. In reality, Mary was foolish, lacked royal dignity, and had a fatal penchant for political conspiracies.

coincided with Spanish preparations for invading England. Philip of Spain had wanted to invade England ever since Elizabeth became queen. Now, the time had come.

What Philip did not know was that his security screen had already been broken. English spies in Spain knew all about Philip's huge fleet, the Armada. But combined with Walsingham's plot against Elizabeth, this put England in double peril.

A fool for love

Walsingham needed a fall guy to head his plot. Sir Anthony Babington was just the man for it. He was only 25 and a secret Catholic. Among 'young bloods' of his kind, it was fashionable to be in love with the Queen of Scots. Babington was head-over-heels about her.

One day, Babington received a letter from Mary. He was immensely flattered at such attention from the beautiful Mary; it quite turned his head. But it was a ploy, and Babington fell for it. He started smuggling letters and packages to and from the Queen of Scots. These letters contained news of secret Catholic activities in England.

At the end of May 1586, one of Mary's agents, John Ballard, told Babington of the secret plot. Catholics in England would revolt. England would be invaded. Elizabeth would be murdered. Mary would be released from house arrest and placed on Elizabeth's throne.

At first, Babington was frightened by all this. He decided to get out of England. Better to plot against Elizabeth from outside the country, he thought. But in order to leave England, Babington needed to get special travel papers from Walsingham.

A certain Robert Poley volunteered to help Babington get his documents. Poley was one of Walsingham's agents. He made friends with Babington, who came to trust him. This proved most unwise, for Poley managed to get details of the plot out of Babington and passed the information to Walsingham.

Babington, meanwhile, wrote to Mary, and told her about the plot. Walsingham, of course, had read it before it was delivered to the Scottish queen. Walsingham had devised a foolproof method of delivering letters to and from Mary: they were hidden in a cask of beer. When Mary replied to Babington, her letter was thereby smuggled out. And when

In 1586, Mary was put on trial at Fotheringhay Castle in Northamptonshire for plotting against Elizabeth. Questioning the court's authority over her, she pleaded innocence, but was nevertheless condemned to death.

Walsingham read it, he knew that at last he had Mary where he wanted her. He sketched a gallows on the letter.

Babington went into hiding in St. John's Wood, near London. But Walsingham's agents soon found him. Babington was taken to the Tower of London. The young man was scared witless. It soon turned out that he would say anything, betray anybody, to save himself.

At their trial for treason, Babington put all the blame on John Ballard. It did him no good. Babington was sentenced to be hanged, drawn and quartered. So was Ballard. Terrified at this gruesome prospect, Babington begged Elizabeth for mercy. He offered the huge sum of £1000 to a friend if the friend could get him off the charge. This did not work either.

On 20 September 1586, Babington and Ballard were dragged through the streets of London to where a huge gallows had been specially built. Babington was forced to watch as Ballard suffered the tortures of a traitor's death. Somehow, during this ghastly procedure, Babington found courage. Instead of praying on his knees as Ballard died, he stood upright,

The Palace of Holyroodhouse in Edinburgh was the official residence of Mary, Queen of Scots. Building began in the reign of King James IV (1473–1514), and later the palace was improved and enlarged several times.

hat in hand. When his turn came, he died bravely. When Elizabeth heard of the great cruelty that the executioners had employed, she was horrified. Seven other conspirators awaited execution. Elizabeth ordered that, unlike Ballard and Babington, they should not be taken down from the gallows while still alive. Only once they were dead could the drawing and quartering proceed.

Mary, Queen of Scots went on trial at Fotheringhay Castle in Northamptonshire the following 14 October. She was defiant from beginning to end. The court had no right to try her, Mary protested.

'I came into this kingdom under promise of assistance, and aid, against my enemies and not as a subject,' she said. 'Can I be responsible for the criminal projects of a few desperate men, which they planned without my knowledge or participation?'

She was, of course, lying through her teeth. The judges were not impressed. Mary was found guilty of treason and sentenced to death. William Davison, Elizabeth's secretary, drew up the death warrant. Predictably, Elizabeth refused to sign it. But Walsingham, Burghley and other ministers were not going to let her off the hook.

REGAL PROFILES

BRAVERY AT THE BLOCK

ON 8 FEBRUARY 1587, Mary entered the Great Hall at Fotheringhay Castle, in procession with her groom holding a large crucifix in front of her. She was wearing a black dress with a red petticoat underneath and a veil around her head and shoulders. Three hundred people were there to watch her die.

One of them, Robert Wynfielde described what happened.

'She (knelt) down upon the cushion most resolutely, and without any token or fear of death.... Groping for the block, she laid down her head, putting her chin over the block with both her hands.... Lying upon the block most quietly, and stretching out her arms cried, *In manus tuas, Domine* (Into your hands, Oh God, I give myself), three or four times.

'Lying very still upon the block, one of the executioners holding her slightly with one of his hands.... She endured two strokes...of the axe...and so the executioner cut off her head...which being cut asunder, he lifted up her head to the view of all.... Her lips stirred up and down a quarter of an hour after her head was cut off.

'...One of the executioners...espied her little dog which had crept under her clothes, which could not be gotten forth but by force, yet afterward would not depart from the dead corpse, but came and lay between her head and her shoulders, which (were) soaked with her blood.'

They nagged and pleaded with Elizabeth. They argued that if Mary were allowed to live, other potential traitors would believe they too could get away with treason. They reminded the queen that before long Spaniards were going to invade her realm. If the invasion succeeded, Mary would become Queen of England.

That finally did it. The idea of Mary on her throne, as a puppet of Philip II of Spain, was too much for Elizabeth. She signed the warrant and on 8 February 1587, Mary, Queen of Scots was duly executed.

In London, bells rang and bonfires were lit to celebrate the execution. But when Queen Elizabeth learned that Mary was dead, she had a fit of hysterics. She wept, she wailed, she threw herself about dramatically. She blamed her ministers, calling them 'criminals'. But Lord Burghley told the queen to stop play-acting. No one, he said, was going to be convinced by her antics. Everyone knew that she had hated Mary and was glad to be rid of her at last.

Spain defeated, thousands killed

The following year, 132 ships of the Spanish Armada left Spain for the invasion of England. King Philip was sure that his 'Enterprise of England' would succeed. But he was wrong. The English navy had a secret weapon. When the Armada entered the English Channel on 31 July, the English fleet kept its distance and raked the Spanish vessels with gunfire. Several were wrecked. Many were set on fire. Thousands of Spaniards were killed.

Then the weather in the English Channel turned stormy and violent. Ferocious winds drove the Spaniards to the eastern end of the Channel. From there they limped back to Spain around the tip of Scotland. Of the Armada's 132 ships, only 60 made it home. Of the Armada's 30,000 crew, more than a third perished.

The English had scored a tremendous and unexpected victory. They celebrated with dancing in the streets, bonfires and fireworks. Elizabeth celebrated more quietly. On 24 November she held a service of thanksgiving in St. Paul's Cathedral in London.

Despite her misgivings, Elizabeth I finally assented to the execution of Mary, Queen of Scots at Fotheringhay Castle in 1587. It was a violent end to nearly 20 years of exile and imprisonment in England.

10

ROUNDHEADS AND REGICIDE

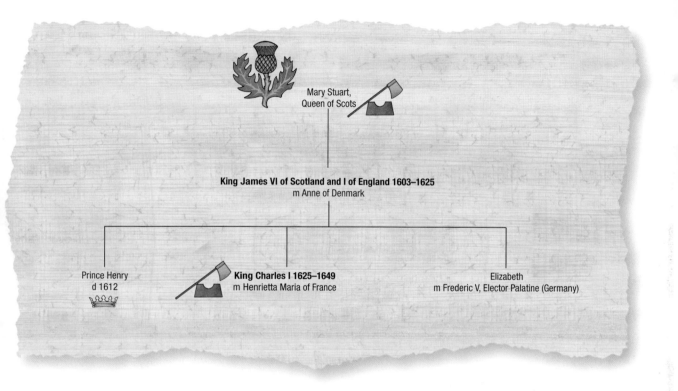

Mary Stuart,
Queen of Scots

King James VI of Scotland and I of England 1603–1625
m Anne of Denmark

Prince Henry
d 1612

King Charles I 1625–1649
m Henrietta Maria of France

Elizabeth
m Frederic V, Elector Palatine (Germany)

Queen Elizabeth I lived longer than any other Tudor monarch. She lost her hair and her teeth, but she kept her guts. In 1601, when she was 67, her beloved Robert Devereux, the Earl of Essex, rebelled against her.

◆

She was furious…so furious that she declared she would step out onto the streets of London to see if any rebels dared to shoot her. Her ministers barely prevented her from doing it.

But by late in 1602, Elizabeth was not well. She refused to eat. She would not take any medicines. She even refused to go to bed. She thought if she went

to bed, she would die. There was not long to go until the end. Elizabeth died sitting in a chair on 24 March 1603, the last of the Tudor monarchs. It was only at the very last moment that she named her heir – King James VI of Scotland. In a historic event which united the monarchies of England and Scotland, he then became James I of England, first of the Stuart kings.

Rapturous welcome for the new king

James set out for London in May 1603. He was so eager to get there that he rode 40 miles in less than

Charles I was the first and only king of England to be publicly beheaded. A special scaffold was built at London's Whitehall for the execution that took place on 30 January 1649.

A GROTESQUE ODDITY
WITH REPULSIVE HABITS

THE ENGLISH DISCOVERED that King James was extremely strange. He looked creepy. He had spindly legs. His tongue was too big for his mouth. It slopped about when he ate or talked. He drooled. He did not wash very often. His hands were always black with dirt. He looked scruffy because he dressed so badly.

James was terrified of being assassinated. Many Scottish kings in the century or two before had been murdered. So he always wore dagger-proof padded clothes, giving him an

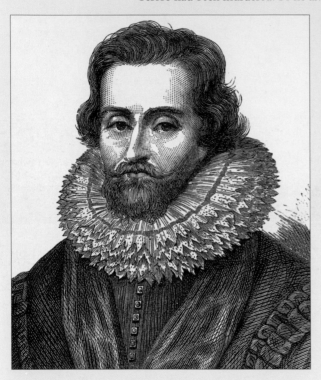

alarmingly lumpy shape. As if this were not enough, King James I had some shocking habits. He played with himself in public. He loved crude jokes. In front of his courtiers, he would make statements such as 'God's wounds! I will pull down my breeches and they shall also see my arse.' When he went hunting, he would jump feet first into the innards of animals he had killed and mingle in their blood and gore.

But his unpleasant appearance and habits aside, and idiosyncratically for his time, James I was tolerant about religion. Many contemporaries were not. English Protestants detested Roman Catholics. Catholics feared persecution. Many had gone into hiding. James decided to put an end to all this. He decreed that Catholics should be allowed to follow their faith openly. But so many Roman Catholics came out into the open that James became frightened. Hastily, he withdrew his decree. It was back to square one.

In this illustration, King James I looks neater and cleaner than he actually was. He hardly ever washed, was always itching and scratching and smelled bad.

four hours. That was fast going for the time, but too fast. On the way to London, James fell off his horse, injuring himself. His doctors thought he had broken his collarbone.

When James reached London at last, he received a great welcome. Thousands turned out to see their new king enter the city. Celebrations went on far into the night. But the excitement soon wore off when the public discovered its new monarch not only looked weird, but that his personal tastes and habits were truly repugnant.

An ambitious plot fails

King James soon found, however, that he was in a no-win situation. After their disappointment, a group of Catholics led by Guy Fawkes hatched the famous Gunpowder Plot of 1605. It was very ambitious, involving nothing less than blowing up the Houses of Parliament when King James and his ministers were in attendance.

The plot never got going. Guy Fawkes was discovered red-handed in the cellars of the Houses of Parliament, together with his stock of gunpowder. The plotters were hung, drawn and quartered as traitors. Ever since, Guy Fawkes Day has been celebrated in England on 5 November. Dummy models of Fawkes are displayed in the street. Children ask passersby to give them 'a penny for the Guy'. Fireworks displays take place all over England.

Guy Fawkes was caught red-handed with several barrels of gunpowder and was arrested on the spot. Though not the leader of the Gunpowder Plot, he has since become the focus of its commemoration in England on 5 November each year.

James believed in witchcraft. There had been a Witchcraft Act in Queen Elizabeth's time. But that was not enough for James. He changed the act to include cannibalism among the dark practices performed by witches.

'If any person or persons shall use, practice or exercise any invocation or conjuration of any evil or wicked spirit…or take any dead man or child out of his or her grave, or the skin, bone or any part of any dead person, to be employed or used in any manners of witchcraft…they shall suffer the pains of death.'

The king prefers gentlemen

Though he was married and had children, James was also homosexual. He used to prowl around his court looking for beautiful young males as lovers. When James took a fancy to one, the king would plant sloppy wet kisses on his cheeks. He would fondle him in full view of the court.

One who received this royal treatment was handsome George Villiers, who became Duke of Buckingham. Villiers was canny enough to know that being the king's lover was more than just a guarantee of a grand title. It could lead to wealth and power as well. James adored Buckingham. He pawed and petted him in public. He called him his 'sweet Steenie'. In letters to him, King James addressed Buckingham as 'sweetheart'. When Buckingham went abroad on a foreign mission, James wrote to him, saying: 'I wear Steenie's picture on a blue ribbon under my waistcoat, next to my heart.'

> **Sooner or later, the king would run out of cash. Then, Parliament could hit back. The king spent money like water. His coronation cost £20,000. His wife, Anne, went overboard with expensive clothes and jewels.**

But the king's advances were not always welcomed. The Earl of Holland, for example, turned aside and spat after James had 'sladdered' in his mouth. James's courtiers, looking on, were disgusted. A later historian, Thomas Babington Macaulay, called King James 'a nervous drivelling idiot'. He was not far wrong.

'Kings are chosen by God'

The English could just about put up with all this. After all, they had had some peculiar kings before and England had survived. What they could not stand, however, was a highly dangerous notion James had brought with him from Scotland. This was the Divine Right of Kings, which belief implied that James had been appointed as king by God. Only God could judge

King James I of England was also King James VI of Scotland. This illustration shows him dressed in state robes, holding the orb and sceptre that were part of the Crown Jewels and the regalia that signified his royal powers.

what he did. James considered himself above the law and told Parliament so in 1610:

'The state of monarchy', said James, 'is the supremest thing on earth. As to dispute what God may do is blasphemy...so it is seditious in subjects to dispute what a king may do....' He went on: 'Kings are not only God's lieutenants upon earth and sit upon God's throne, but even by God himself they are called gods.'

This was alarming rhetoric. English kings had never before been allowed to carry on in such a way. Parliament and its predecessors, the English barons, had fought a long battle for the right to advise the monarch. Now here was King James telling Parliament that they could 'go to hell': he chose his 'sweet Steenie', the Duke of Buckingham, as his one and only adviser.

Luxury lifestyle funded by the public purse

James also found a way around Parliament's chief power: their right to grant the king money. James obtained funds in other ways: he imposed taxes on imported goods, forced the aristocracy to accept loans, and sold offices to the highest bidder. All of this was illegal.

Parliament fumed. But they settled down to wait: sooner or later the king would run out of cash. When he did so, Parliament had the chance to hit back. The king spent money like water. His coronation had cost £20,000. His wife, Queen Anne, went overboard with expensive clothes and jewels. James gave cash away in handfuls to courtiers. Entertainments at his court were always lavish. The most popular, the masque, cost a fortune. Many such masques were staged at the court of King James.

King's surprising turnaround

Eventually, in 1621, James needed money so badly that he was forced to call a Parliament. The members got their shots in first. For a long time they had been angered by the partiality James showed to Roman Catholics. They wanted England to be Protestant through and through. Above all, they wanted an end to James's friendship with Catholic Spain. Their

Charles I looks very dandified in this portrait, wearing a long wig and broad-brimmed hat. The horse was posed with its head down, with its groom leaning to one side, to conceal the fact that the king was only 4 feet 7 inches tall.

demands, in the form of a 'Protestation', were entered into Parliament's journal. James was furious. He sent for the journal. He tore out the pages where the Protestation was printed. Parliament knew what they could do with their Protestation.

Then, quite suddenly, King James gave in. In 1624 he let Parliament have everything they had ever wanted. A say in foreign policy; an end to preference toward Catholics – even the right to make war.

'If I take a resolution, upon your advice, to enter into a war,' James told Parliament, 'then yourselves… shall have the disposing of the money. I will not meddle with it.'

Parliament, triumphant at last, voted the king the enormous sum of £30,000. James's turnaround had been amazing. But there were good reasons for it. He was only 57, but getting old. He had suffered a stroke. He was becoming senile and did not have long to live. Letting Parliament have what it wanted was the only way to get a quiet life. James died on 27 March 1625 at his country home, Theobalds in Hertfordshire.

Thirteen years earlier, James's heir, Prince Henry, had died of typhoid fever. This was not only a tragic loss for his parents, but for England as well.

Henry, only 18, had been a bright young man. He had up-to-date ideas about working with, instead of against, Parliament. He was a devout Protestant. When Henry came to the throne, so it was said, all the problems his father had caused would be cured. But it was not to be.

The runt of the litter

What England got instead of Henry was a new version of King James. King Charles I, James's second son, was a very small man, four feet seven inches tall. He was stubborn, shy, slow and stupid. All his life, he stammered. Worse, he took over the Duke of Buckingham as his own lover. Worse still, Charles was another 'Divine Right of Kings' adherent. Parliament cringed when Charles said: 'I must avow that I owe the account of my actions to God alone'. It might have been his father James talking.

There were all sorts of bad omens on 2 February 1626, the day Charles was crowned king. One of the wings on the dove topping Charles' sceptre broke off. A jewel popped out of the coronation ring. Most frightening of all, there was an earthquake. Superstitious people began speculating that there would be trouble ahead.

There certainly was trouble ahead. In the reign of James I, Parliament had argued fiercely with him. But they had always been loyal to him as king. Charles' Parliament was different. It was full of extreme Protestant Puritans. They were not willing to put up with King Charles – or any king. To them, all kings were tyrants.

Duke haters unite

This placed Charles in a very dangerous position. He made it worse by employing all his father's tricks. He imposed taxes on his people – some illegal. He clung to Buckingham, who practically controlled the king and so controlled England.

George Villiers, Duke of Buckingham, was widely hated. Slanderous ditties were written about him. Rude ballads were sung. On 28 June 1628, a mob gathered in London for a 'we-hate-the-Duke' meeting.

The duke was widely hated. Slanderous ditties were written about him. Rude ballads were sung. Seditious pamphlets were written. Then, on 28 June 1628, a mob gathered in London for a 'we-hate-the-Duke' meeting. Nearby was a playhouse where a performance had just ended. Someone spotted John Lambe, the duke's doctor, coming out one of the doors. The mob howled. Lambe ran. He darted from one tavern to another, desperately seeking shelter. But the mob caught up with him. They seized Lambe and beat him to death on the pavement.

Murdering the duke's doctor was the next best thing to killing the duke himself. But it wasn't good enough for one John Felton, who had a personal grudge against Buckingham.

The Duke of Buckingham was murdered by John Felton, who held a grudge against the duke. Felton became a hero: the death of Buckingham was welcome to many people who disliked his influence over King Charles.

he became a national hero. Londoners cheered and celebrated when they heard Buckingham was dead. Parliament was pleased, for they had wanted to get rid of Buckingham for years. Now he was gone, and King Charles was on his own.

By now his disputes with Parliament had reached new heights. They were on a collision course. Inside Parliament, on 2 March 1629, Charles' supporters and opponents actually brawled in the House of Commons chamber.

Charles soon put a stop to that. He dismissed Parliament and ruled without it for eleven years. He kept his cash flow going in the same way as had King James. A tax called 'Ship Money' became the most hated of his fundraising schemes. Ship Money was supposed to be a tax paid by coastal towns for building ships in times of national danger. There was no national danger when Charles demanded the tax. Furthermore, he demanded Ship Money from inland towns.

Ship Money was not sufficient, however. In 1640 Charles needed £300,000 for a war against the rebellious Scots. He summoned Parliament. Nothing had changed. All the old quarrels were still there: the king must stop imposing taxes, he must be tougher on Catholics, his ministers must be controlled by Parliament. King Charles refused to give in. Instead, he dissolved Parliament once again.

A heroic murderer

In 1627 Buckingham had refused to make Felton a captain in the Navy – and had been very insulting about it, too. Felton vowed revenge. On 23 August 1628, Felton waited for Buckingham outside the Greyhound Inn in Portsmouth. Buckingham had just finished breakfast when Felton rushed up and stabbed him in the chest. That one blow was enough. Buckingham fell to the ground dying.

John Felton was hanged for his crime, but

Ship Money and other taxes went on. Hatred of the king increased, and Parliament lost patience. On 23 November 1641, the Grand Remonstrance was passed by the House of Commons by a margin of 159 votes to 148.

The Remonstrance was the work of John Pym and four other members of Parliament. It contained a list of the many ways in which King Charles had abused his power. Nearly six weeks later, on 4 January 1642, King Charles went in person to the House of

In 1642, Charles I went to the Houses of Parliament hoping to arrest five members who had accused him of abusing his royal powers. He failed. A tradition followed of the monarch not being permitted to enter the House of Commons.

Commons. He took a strong guard of soldiers with him. His intention was to arrest the five authors of the Grand Remonstrance. They would then be charged with treason.

Charles told the Speaker of the House of Commons, William Lenthall:

'By your leave, Mister Speaker, I must borrow your chair a little.'

The Speaker's chair was on a raised dais. The king stepped up on it and scanned the faces in front of him. John Pym and his four friends were not there. They had been warned not to go to the Commons that day.

Charles asked Lenthall where they were. Lenthall replied: 'May it please Your Majesty, but as the House is pleased to direct me, whose servant I am here.' In

other words, Lenthall intended to give nothing away.

The king knew that he had lost. 'Well,' he said, 'since I see all the birds are flown, I do expect from you that you shall send them unto me as soon as they return hither.' Then he left. John Pym and others returned a week later, but no one was about to hand them over to King Charles.

Royalists versus Roundheads

Civil war looked certain now. King Charles, his queen, Henrietta Maria, and their children fled from London to Hampton Court Palace in Surrey, where it was safer. England's third and last civil war began on 22 August 1642. That day, King Charles 'raised the royal stand-ard' in Nottingham. Now it was his supporters, the Royalists, against Parliament, the Roundheads.

The war began well for King Charles and the Royalists. They won the first big battle, at Edgehill, in Warwickshire. But after that, it seemed neither side could finally defeat the other. Too many battles ended as draws. Sieges dragged on and on.

Families took sides in the civil war. Some members supported the king, others Parliament. Many had no choice. Royalists and Parliamentarians both introduced conscription: young men were forcibly hauled off to fight. In 1643, one of the Parliamentary leaders, Oliver Cromwell, recruited a troop of women. They were known as 'the Maiden Troops'. Their job was to 'stir up the youth' to fight for Parliament.

Many of the troops did not want to go to war. A group of them attacked one recruiting officer, Lieutenant Eures, in a tavern. They forced Eures to crawl out on a beam attached to the tavern sign. He was

A royalist stronghold under assault during the English Civil War, showing one woman deafened by the artillery barrage. Civil wars are often regarded as the most savage of all: this one brought terror to thousands of ordinary people.

BRAVE BRILLIANA

WIVES WERE LEFT TO defend their homes when their husbands went to war. One was Brilliana, Lady Harley. Brampton Bryan, her home in Herefordshire, in western England, was besieged for six weeks by Royalist forces. Royalists led by the Marquess of Hartford ordered her to surrender. She refused.

Before long Lady Harley, her servants and followers were in a fearful state. They ran short of food. Royalist soldiers entered the park surrounding her house. They stole cattle, sheep and oxen. They burned buildings and cottages. They killed one of her servants, Edward Morgan. Lady Harley's cook was also shot dead.

Royalists pounded Brampton Bryan with cannon fire, destroying most of the roof. The rain leaked in. Every room in the house was soaking wet.

But Lady Harley hit back. She had only 50 soldiers, but she ordered them to destroy the Royalists' defenses. She stole back much of the food the Royalists had taken. But the effort cost Lady Harley her life. She had an apoplectic fit on 29 October 1643, and died two days later. In the end, the Royalists gave up and withdrew.

beaten. Stones were thrown at him. Then he was flung onto a heap of rubbish. But he was not dead – not yet. He managed to stagger out, but his attackers spotted him and beat him savagely about the head until he died.

New Model Army stormtroopers

Oliver Cromwell was a country gentleman and farmer. He came from the same family as Thomas Cromwell, Henry VIII's doomed minister. He had fought in the civil war from the beginning. He soon recognized important facts about the Parliamentary army. It was untrained. It was undisciplined. Parliament was not going to win this war with an army like that.

In 1645, Cromwell set about creating a New Model Army. This was much more professional. They trained hard, lived hard, fought hard. All this made an enormous difference. On 14 June 1645, the New Model Army won the battle of Naseby in Northamptonshire. This was the beginning of the end for King Charles. He fled for safety to Hereford. But he knew that his cause was lost.

King throws himself on Scottish mercy

Charles cut his hair short, put on a false beard. Then, disguised as a servant, he went north, to Scotland. There he gave himself up. As King of Scotland as well as King of England, Charles hoped that the Scots would help him. But the Scots Presbyterians had no intention of doing so, unless Charles agreed to their

terms. They wanted him to impose their Presbyterian faith in England, but for Charles this was anathema: Presbyterians believed that kings should be accountable to the people, who held supreme power in the land. A monarch like Charles, who believed in the Divine Right of Kings, wasn't going to swallow that, and he refused. The Scots lost patience and handed him back to the English.

Charles cut his hair short. He put on a false beard. Then, disguised as a servant, he went north, to Scotland. There he gave himself up. As King of Scotland...Charles hoped the Scots would help him.

Parliament placed Charles under arrest at Hampton Court Palace. But he became afraid that his guards meant to kill him. On 11 November 1647, he escaped. He rode south as fast as he could go. After three days, Charles reached Carisbrooke Castle on the Isle of Wight, off the south coast of England. There he demanded protection from the governor of the castle, who let him in.

A year later, on 1 December 1648, army officers arrived at the castle. They forced King Charles to go with them. He ended up in Hurst Castle on the English south coast. His room was small and dark with only a slit for a window.

England's first royal trial by subjects

Meanwhile, Oliver Cromwell had given orders for the king to be tried in London's Westminster Hall. No king of England had ever been tried by his own subjects before. The trial opened on 20 January 1649.

The reenactment of Civil War battles is a popular activity among historically minded societies in England. Recreating the seventeenth century setting requires a great deal of careful research into costumes, hairstyles and weaponry.

Charles was accused that 'out of a wicked design to erect...an unlimited and tyrannical power...traitorously and maliciously levied war against the present Parliament and the people (they) represented.' The judges refused to call the king by his title. Instead, they called him plain 'Charles Stuart'.

ENGLAND'S FEMALE SNIPERS

KING CHARLES FORBADE WOMEN to fight in battle. But some of them did so, just the same. One was Jane Engleby, a farmer's daughter, who disguised herself as a man and fought alongside her husband at the battle of Marston Moor in 1644. Other women acted as snipers in Chester, Leicester and other towns. One woman, Lady Wyndham, took a potshot at one of the Roundhead leaders, Oliver Cromwell, during the siege of Bridgewater, in Somerset. She missed. If she had managed to kill him, the civil war might have turned out differently.

Defeat at the battle of Marston Moor on 2 July 1644 lost the royalists their support in northern England. Prince Rupert's men were defeated so severely that he had to hide in a bean field.

Charles I's death warrant, signed by 59 Parliamentary soldiers, including Oliver Cromwell. Many more were summoned to attend Charles's trial at Westminster Hall, but most of them baulked at the idea of passing a death sentence on their king.

Charles would not defend himself, since he did not recognize that the court had any right to try him.

'I would know by what power I am called hither....' Charles said. 'I would know by what authority, I mean lawful.... Remember, I am your king, your lawful king…a king cannot be tried by any superior jurisdiction on earth.'

The court was not impressed. All that remained now was to find Charles guilty and pass sentence. The sentence was death. Fifty-nine soldiers, including Oliver Cromwell, signed the death warrant. A large scaffold was built outside the Banqueting Hall in London's Whitehall.

30 January 1649 was a bitterly cold day. Charles asked for two shirts to keep him warm because, he said: 'The season is so sharp as probably may make me shake, which some observers may imagine proceeds from fear.'

Charles was taken to the scaffold. A vast crowd was there to watch. When he spoke to them, it was clear that for Charles, the Divine Right of Kings was still very much in force:

'I must tell you that the liberty and freedom [of the people] consists in having of Government, those laws by which their life and their goods may be most their own. It is not for having share in Government, that is nothing pertaining to them. A subject and a sovereign are clean different things.'

Charles laid his head on the block. The executioner's axe swung. He cut off the king's head with a single blow. As he did so, wrote an eyewitness, 'there was such a groan by the thousands then present, as I never heard before, and desire I may never hear again!'

Eight days later, Parliament abolished the title and office of king. On 19 May the monarchy was abolished, too. For the first and only time in its history, England had become a republic.

This painting by an anonymous Victorian artist depicts the future Lord Protector, Oliver Cromwell, gazing at the body of the executed Charles I. The king's head would have been reattached to his body before it was placed in the coffin.

A NOT-SO-MERRY MONARCHY

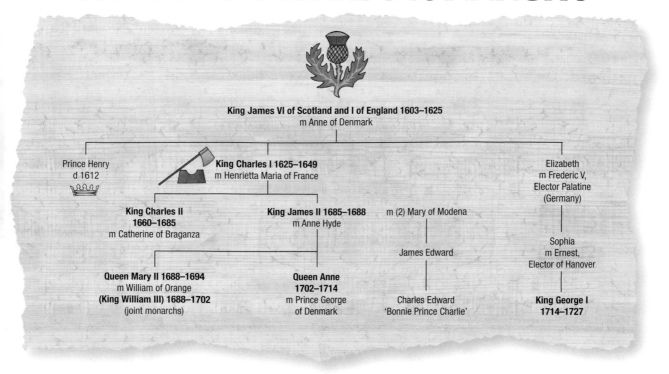

King James VI of Scotland and I of England 1603–1625
m Anne of Denmark

Prince Henry
d 1612

King Charles I 1625–1649
m Henrietta Maria of France

Elizabeth
m Frederic V,
Elector Palatine
(Germany)

King Charles II
1660–1685
m Catherine of Braganza

King James II 1685–1688
m Anne Hyde

m (2) Mary of Modena

Sophia
m Ernest,
Elector of Hanover

James Edward

Queen Mary II 1688–1694
m William of Orange
(King William III) 1688–1702
(joint monarchs)

Queen Anne
1702–1714
m Prince George
of Denmark

Charles Edward
'Bonnie Prince Charlie'

King George I
1714–1727

The English Republic was ruled by Parliament, which was dominated by Puritans. Strict believers, they sought to purify the country from sin and the excessiveness of remaining Roman Catholic practices.

◆

Adultery meant a death sentence. If a man killed his rival in a duel, he could be charged with murder. Puritans made special targets of swearing, gambling and drunkenness. They closed public houses on Sundays and fast days. Swearing was punished by fines. The amount depended on who had done the cursing. A duke was fined thirty shillings, a baron twenty shillings, a country squire ten and everyone else three shillings and four pence.

The crown, orb, sword and other regalia used at the coronation of Charles II had to be newly made for the event, because Parliament had sold off the existing regalia.

That was only for the first crime. All fines were doubled the second time around.

Fun is banned

Puritans were always on the lookout for wickedness and opportunities for same. This was why the playhouses – 'dens of vice and immorality' – were closed. Traditional pastimes such as bear baiting and cockfighting were stopped. So was 'lewd and heathen' maypole dancing.

Dyed clothing of any kind was out. It was against the law to be caught wearing lace, ribbons or decorative buttons. Puritans frowned on long hair, too.

England and its people had a very dismal time while Puritans ruled.

Public yearns for royal 'magic'

But the Puritans had made a big mistake when they abolished the monarchy. Monarchy and love of the monarchy were deeply ingrained in English tradition. There was a certain magic about the monarchy. People missed it so much that in 1657, Parliament made an unusual offer: they invited Oliver Cromwell, now Lord Protector, to become king. He laughed off the very idea. Cromwell knew the people did not want any old king: they wanted the real thing. And that meant Prince Charles, son of King Charles I, who was in exile.

Beyond this, Puritanism had a serious weakness. It depended on Cromwell and Cromwell alone. Once he died, in 1658, their regime fell apart.

England under 'Idle Dick' turns to anarchy

Cromwell's successor as Lord Protector was his son, Richard. Richard Cromwell was not the man his father had been. During the 20 months he was in charge, England sank into anarchy. One of the worst aspects was that many soldiers went unpaid. They began to wander around England, stealing food, money and anything else they needed.

Richard Cromwell was so useless that he was given the nickname 'Idle Dick'. He knew he was out of his depth. So he bolted. On 16 May 1659, Cromwell disappeared from London. He fled to Paris, then Italy. He even took a false name: John Clark. His wife never saw him again.

With Idle Dick gone, there was no one to rule England. It was now imperative that the king return. Charles had waited 11 years to get his throne back. He had made one attempt to seize it by force, in 1651, but it failed. After Charles' army was defeated at the battle of Worcester on 14 October, Charles had to go on the run. Oliver Cromwell published a poster offering £1,000 for his capture. Charles was forced to hide in an oak tree to escape his pursuers. Today, the many English pubs called 'Royal Oak' are reminders of this incident.

Hundreds of English public houses are named 'Royal Oak' after an incident that took place on 14 October 1651, when Charles II was forced to hide in an oak tree while escaping from his defeat at the battle of Worcester.

King returns in triumph

After his defeat in 1651, Charles disguised himself. He blackened his face and donned a shabby old suit of clothes. After skipping from town to town, with Cromwell's men in hot pursuit, he managed to sail back to France. But nine years later, Charles's great moment arrived at last: General Monck, a senior officer in the Army, invited him to return as king. On 29 May 1660, Charles's 30th birthday, he entered London in triumph. Londoners turned out by the thousands to welcome him. John Evelyn, the diarist, wrote:

'The triumph of above 20,000 horse and foot brandishing their swords and shouting with inexpressible joy: The ways were strewed with flowers, the bells ringing, the streets hung with tapestry, fountains ran with wine …trumpets, music and myriads of people flocking…so they were seven hours in passing the City (of London) even from two in the afternoon till nine at night.'

That night, there were fireworks and illuminations

A great moment for Charles II after 11 years of exile: he is being rowed towards Dover, where he landed back on English soil after being restored to his throne. Charles received a joyous greeting from his subjects.

over the River Thames. Spectators crowded into boats and barges. There were so many, Evelyn wrote, 'you could have walked across (the river)'.

King Charles had his own way of celebrating his return. Nine months later, on 15 February 1661, Barbara Villiers, one of his many mistresses, gave birth to a daughter. Known as Anne Palmer, she was one of the king's 15 illegitimate children.

'Pretty, witty Nell'

Taking mistresses was almost the only entertainment Charles had while in exile. He was not fussy about his choices. Any curvy, good-looking woman who caught his eye was invited to share the royal bed. The most humble, and the most delightful, was Nell Gwynn. She

Nell Gwynn was the most famous and least pretentious of Charles II's many mistresses. Charles first saw her at the theatre in London, where she was selling oranges to the audience. Later, Nell became one of England's first actresses.

came from the slums of London's East End. Her first job was hawking fish around the richer parts of London. She was spotted by one Madame Ross, a brothel keeper. So, at only 12 or 13, Nell became a prostitute.

But she was no ordinary prostitute. Nell Gwynn was a lively and amusing charmer. Later, Samuel Pepys, the diarist, called her 'pretty, witty Nell' and it suited her. She was ambitious, too. She did not intend to remain just another disposable girl in a brothel. London's stage gave her the chance to move on.

The playhouses reopened after King Charles' return. They showed new, sexy 'Restoration' comedies. These rude, crude, suggestive plays made Puritans rigid with disapproval. But King Charles loved them. He was often among the audience at one of the newest, The King's House, which opened in 1663. There he first saw Nell Gwynn. She sold oranges to members of the audience.

The charming Nell was eyed appreciatively by almost every man within range. She was an accomplished flirt and took several lovers. One was an actor, Charles Hart. He realized Nell would make a splendid actress. At this time, actresses were quite new to the English stage. Previously, female roles had been played by males.

Nell ruins rival's night of love

Another actress was Moll Davis, one of King Charles' mistresses. Moll hated Nell Gwynn and Nell hated her back. To get revenge on Moll, she played a wicked trick. One night early in 1668, Moll was about to sleep with King Charles. A few hours earlier, Nell invited Moll to eat some sweetmeats she had prepared. Moll did not know that the sweetmeats contained a hefty dose of the laxative jalap.

That night, the jalap went to work. Moll was seized by violent attacks of diarrhea. There was no lovemaking. What the king thought is not known. But he was probably amused by the joke – and the delightful young woman who had played it. Soon he had added Nell to his roster of mistresses.

Another 'prank' – though this one considerably more dramatic – that appealed to Charles' sense of fun was an attempt, in 1671, to steal the Crown Jewels

from the Tower of London. The would-be thief was Colonel Thomas Blood, son of an Irish blacksmith. Blood had led a vivid life. In 1670, he kidnapped the Duke of Ormonde, Lord Lieutenant of Ireland. Blood was sentenced to death and was about to be hanged at Tyburn in London when a last minute reprieve arrived. Blood fled. A reward of £1,000 was offered for his capture. But he was not caught and set out to steal the Crown Jewels.

Blood brothers

Colonel Blood disguised himself as a parson. He spent time getting friendly with Talbot Edwards, Master of the Jewel House at the Tower. Their friendship went so far that the two men agreed to a marriage between members of their families. This marriage was to have taken place at the Tower on 9 May 1671.

Colonel Blood seized the king's crown and used the mallet to flatten it so it would fit into the pocket of his cassock. One of his accomplices seized the orb and hid it inside his breeches.

That day, with two accomplices, Blood arrived at the Tower. Talbot Edwards suspected nothing until Blood produced a mallet from beneath his cassock and began to beat him over the head. Edwards fell unconscious to the floor.

Blood seized the king's crown and used the mallet to flatten it so it would fit into the pocket of his cassock. One of his accomplices seized the orb and hid it inside his breeches. Meanwhile, the other gang members tried to file the sceptre in half.

Just then, Edwards' son Wythe arrived unexpectedly. When he found his father lying on the floor bleeding, he raised an alarm. At this, Blood and his accomplices fled. But they were caught before they got away.

The Merry Monarch is amused

When King Charles was told what had happened, he was so amused he gave Blood a pardon. He also gave

VENGEANCE, EVEN AFTER DEATH

THERE WAS ALSO REVENGE against the dead. Puritans who had died before the King's return were dug up and their bodies thrown into a pit. Among them were Oliver Cromwell and John Bradshaw. Bradshaw had been the presiding judge at Charles I's trial. There was a special punishment for this pair.

On 30 January 1661, their corpses were dragged on hurdles to Tyburn, near London's Marble Arch. There they were hanged on a gallows until the sun went down. After that, their heads were cut off and stuck on poles on top of Westminster Hall. Cromwell's head remained there for 25 years until it was blown down by strong winds.

A portrait of the young Charles II, who fled to France in 1648, the year before his father, Charles I, was executed.

him a large pension of £500 a year and invited him to come to court. It was all part of the 'fun and games' that returned to England when Charles, the 'Merry Monarch', came back as king.

But the Merry Monarch's reign was not all fun. There was a vicious campaign of revenge against the men who had signed his father's death warrant. Ten of these king-killers were hung, drawn and quartered at Tyburn in London on 20 October 1660. One, a soldier, sat up while he was being drawn and hit his executioner.

Cunning scheme to oust Parliament

But King Charles had other scores to settle. His main purpose in life was 'never to go on his travels again'. He would do anything to keep hold of the throne he had waited for so long. The most important item was to get rid of Parliament.

Kings had always relied on Parliament for money. If Parliament did not like a king's policy, they would refuse to pay up. The solution was for Charles to obtain his own store of cash. In 1670, he signed the Treaty of Dover with King Louis XIV of France. Parliament was supposed to believe that with this treaty, Charles would help Louis with his wars in Europe. But there was a secret clause: Louis agreed to give Charles large sums of money. When Parliament became suspicious, Charles lied, declaring there were no secret clauses. But his hands trembled as he spoke.

All the same, Louis' money gave Charles what he wanted. He was able to dissolve Parliament in 1681. He ruled without it for the rest of his life. This killed two birds with one stone. Parliament could no longer blackmail the king by refusing him money. But they also could not stop his heir, his brother James, Duke of York, from succeeding to the throne.

James was a Roman Catholic. When he became

Titus Oates received far worse punishment than simply being pilloried, as shown in this illustration. Found guilty of perjury, he was imprisoned for life in 1685, but was released in 1688 after the dethronement of James II.

SADIST JEFFREYS'S BARBAROUS DECREES

THE EXECUTION OF THE MOVEMENT'S leader did not mean the end of revenge for Monmouth's rebellion. Even more gruesome punishments followed. In a series of trials, 300 people who had supported Monmouth were sentenced to death. One was Alice, Lady Lisle, aged 70: she was sentenced to burn for sheltering two of the rebels.

The trials became known as the 'Bloody Assizes'. George Jeffreys, one of James II's most brutal agents, presided over the trial in Bristol. He was already known as a bloodthirsty sadist. Jeffreys even profited from the deal. He made a fortune selling pardons to some of the rebels. But hundreds were flogged. Hundreds more were transported to the American colonies – a terrible punishment at the time. It was revenge on a grand scale.

The sentences given out by Judge Jeffreys at the 'Bloody Assizes' remain the benchmark for cruel and unusual punishment.

king, he sought to return England to the Catholic Church. This caused an uproar in Parliament. Several attempts were made to exclude James from the succession. None succeeded. James's most powerful backer was King Charles himself. James was the rightful heir, so he argued, thus James must be king.

Plots and intrigue

But anti-Charles conspirators were also at work. In 1678, two jokers, Titus Oates and Israel Tonge,

The Catholic James II caused tremendous upheaval and much violent protest with his attempts to return England to the jurisdiction of the Pope in Rome. He escaped the fate of his father, Charles I – execution on the block – but was forced into lifelong exile.

decided to stir things up. They hatched the 'Popish plot'. This plot was all hot air. It never existed. But people were so nervous that many believed it was true.

The 'plotters' were Catholic Jesuit priests who planned to kill King Charles. This would make sure Catholic James became king. Then the Popish Plot became known to a London magistrate. He looked into it and came to the conclusion that it was all lies. All the same, Titus Oates went on trial for perjury and was sentenced to life imprisonment.

Next, in 1683, a group of conspirators hatched another plan, the 'Rye House Plot'. This time they really meant to kill. Their targets were not only James, but King Charles as well. That, they thought, would eradicate the risk of having a Catholic king on the throne of England.

Rye House near Hoddesdon in Hertfordshire, which was at the centre of a republican plot hatched in 1683 to kill Charles II and his brother, James, Duke of York, on their way back from the horseracing at Newmarket.

One of the conspirators was James, Duke of Monmouth, King Charles' first illegitimate son. He was vain, stupid and ambitious. Monmouth wanted to be king himself and thought that this was the way to do it.

The plot focused on Rye House farm at Hoddeston, Hertfordshire. King Charles, a keen racegoer, was a regular visitor to the Newmarket races. A narrow lane near Rye House was on the route to Newmarket from London. When King Charles and his brother James used it to return from the races, the plotters intended to ambush and kill them.

But things did not work out as planned. A fire broke out at Newmarket while Charles and James were there. Racing was abandoned. This meant they left Newmarket and rode along the lane much earlier than expected. That, of course, saved their lives.

The conspirators were arrested. One, the Earl of Essex, committed suicide before his trial. But three others were found guilty of treason. There were suspicions that much of the evidence had been made up, and that some of the prosecution witnesses had lied. All the same, the conspirators were beheaded – except Monmouth. King Charles was too fond of him to punish him.

A new king, an old rebellion

Two years later, on 5 February 1685, Charles died. Just as he had always wanted, James became King James II. But soon thereafter, Monmouth tried again to seize the throne. He headed an armed rebellion against the new king. Monmouth's army was overwhelmingly defeated at the battle of Sedgemoor,

DEEDS
of
POWER

A SIMPLE MISTAKE LEADS TO CARNAGE

THE DISASTROUS EVENTS of January 1692 occurred purely due to a simple mistake about location, followed by hazardous weather. The chief of the MacDonald clan, Alisdair McIain, went to the wrong place, Fort William, to swear his oath of loyalty to William and Mary. Upon discovering his error he set off for the right place – Inverary – but snowstorms delayed him. He did not reach Inverary until January 6.

The Government would not listen to excuses or explanations. Instead, they took a savage revenge. On 13 February 1692, at Glencoe, soldiers of the Argyll regiment butchered the MacDonalds. They shot, stabbed and clubbed them to death. Their commander, Robert Campbell, lined up seven MacDonald prisoners and shot them in turn. Then he finished them off with his bayonet.

Alisdair McIain was shot in the back as he was getting out of bed. Dung was smeared over the bodies of the dead. Then they were thrown into the nearby river. Alisdair McIain's wife's fingers were bitten off so that soldiers could steal her rings.

In 1692, Glencoe in the Scottish highlands saw the most appalling massacre to take place on British soil, when the MacDonald clan was slaughtered by soldiers of the Argyll regiment.

Gulielmus Rex Maria Regina

in Somerset, on 6 July 1685. He managed to escape from the battlefield and went on the run.

Monmouth was found a week later, hiding in a ditch. He was accused of treason and executed on 15 July. But axeman Jack Ketch was a bungler. He chopped away at Monmouth's neck five times. Even then, he did not kill him. Monmouth's body was still twitching. Ketch threw down the axe in disgust. 'I cannot do it,' he said. 'My heart fails me.' In the end, a knife was used to hack off Monmouth's head.

Even though he had fought hard to make sure James succeeded him, King Charles knew exactly what would happen when he did. He predicted that James would ruin himself within three years. His calculation was perfect.

James lost no time returning England to the Catholic faith. Protestants seethed as he gave Catholics important government and other official posts. They gritted their teeth in rage as James opened negotiations with the Pope to return the English church to his jurisdiction.

The only comfort James' opponents had lay with his two daughters, Mary and Anne. Both were Protestants. Mary was married to the prominent Dutch Protestant, William of Orange. So even if they had to put up with the Catholic James for now, he would be succeeded in time by a Protestant reigning queen – maybe two.

An unwanted surprise

Then, in 1688, something happened that changed the whole picture. On 10 June, King James's second wife, Mary of Modena, gave birth to a son, James Edward, after 15 years of marriage. James Edward's birth after such a long time surprised everyone, even his parents. It also placed James II's enemies on alert.

James Edward was now heir to his father's throne. That meant an endless line of Catholic monarchs on the throne of England. It was too much. James had to go. A group of seven prominent Englishmen sent a secret message to William of Orange. They asked him to bring an army to England and throw James out.

This painting shows the joint monarchs William III and Mary II. William was invited by Parliament to save England from the Catholic 'menace' that threatened the country because of the 'popish' policies of King James II.

England must be saved

It was a desperate move. Undoubtedly these men were committing treason. But no one was going to accuse them of that when England had to be saved from the Catholic 'menace'.

William of Orange landed at Torbay, Devon, on 5 November 1688. As he advanced toward London, James's army retreated. During the retreat, they began to desert. James knew he was on a losing streak. He became terrified. He thought he was going to be beheaded, as had been his father, Charles I.

Now, nothing stood between Mary and the throne – except that her husband William did not want to be a mere consort.

James tried to escape. He attempted to cross the English Channel to France on 11 December 1688. Though disguised as a woman, he was recognized by fishermen who took him back to England.

William and Parliament did not want James back. They would have preferred it if he had escaped into exile. James was given every chance to try again. He managed to get to France on his second attempt, Christmas Day, 1688.

'The throne or nothing' for William

Now, nothing stood between James's daughter, Mary, and the throne – except that her husband William did not want to be a mere consort. He wanted to be king. It was King William or no William, he told Parliament. Otherwise, he threatened to return home and let the English stew.

Parliament had to agree, even though Mary was true heir to the throne. Parliament could not sidestep her, so the throne was offered jointly to William and Mary. They became King William III and Queen Mary II. It was the first and only time England had two monarchs at the same time.

Parliament's offer was not without strings, however. They had had more than enough of monarchs who ranted on about the Divine Right of Kings and did as they pleased.

In 1689, Parliament solved this problem by creating a 'constitutional' monarchy. Meaning that monarchs lost some of their rights, such as to make war or raise taxes. The only income they could have was that granted by Parliament. The polite way of describing constitutional monarchy was that the monarch reigned but did not rule. What it really meant was that Parliament 'fixed' the monarchy so it could no longer rock the boat.

The 'woman' descending the steps in this picture is no woman at all, but the fleeing King James II in disguise. Despite the deception, James was recognized the first time he tried to flee, but he was helped to get away a second time.

The first order of business for William and Mary was to get rid of ex-King James once and for all. In 1690, James brought an army to Ireland. But William easily defeated him at the Battle of the Boyne on 1 July. James fled back to France. He never tried to invade again.

In 1689, the Scots had tried to fight for him. They rebelled against the new king and queen. They were defeated, and the English were very suspicious of them. The Scottish clans were ordered to declare loyalty to William and Mary. The deadline was New Year's Day, 1692. But a terrible misunderstanding occurred and because of it, a shocking slaughter took place.

Scots never forgave King William for the Massacre

Queen Anne, second daughter of James II, was the last Stuart monarch. In 1694, after her elder sister Queen Mary II died, Anne waived her right of succession and allowed her brother-in-law, William III, to take the throne. She succeeded him after he died in 1702.

of Glencoe. But William's problems were getting worse. He had no children. And there was no hope of any children after Queen Mary died of smallpox in 1694. William was heartbroken. Outwardly, he was something of a cold fish. But he collapsed in tears when told Mary had smallpox. The shock was so great that William became paralyzed for a time.

William refused to marry again. This meant that Mary's sister, Anne, became his heir. Unlike Mary, Anne had given birth to many children – 17 in all. But something was terribly wrong with each of them. All died while still young. The last, William, Duke of Gloucester, survived longer than the others. But in 1700, when he was 11, William died, too. He suffered from water on the brain and was weak, slow and stupid. But as long as he lived, he was the last hope of the Protestant Stuart monarchy.

A Scottish toast to the heroic mole

Two years later, on 21 February 1702, William III was riding in Richmond Park, near London, when his horse stumbled on a molehill. At first, William's doctors thought the only damage was a broken collarbone. But the accident was much more serious than that. William's hand became swollen. He could not sign documents and instead had to use a stamp. His doctors tried everything – powdered crab's eyes, pearled julep and sal volatile. Nothing worked. William died on 8 March. For centuries afterwards Scots drank toasts to the mole – 'the little gentleman in the black velvet coat' – because it had caused the hated king's death.

Queen Anne – a ladies' woman

The plain, dull and obstinate Anne, who now succeeded to the throne, was the last of the Stuart monarchs. Although she was married and had given birth to many children, Anne was probably a lesbian. All her close companions were women. A crude pamphlet was written about Queen Anne's 'orientation':

> When as Queen Anne of great renown
> Great Britain's sceptre swayed
> Beside the church, she dearly loved
> A dirty chambermaid.

Anne, it seems, was the 'girl' in lesbian relationships. She was completely dominated by her most famous female companion, Sarah Churchill, Duchess of Marlborough, a very strong-minded woman and ancestor to Winston Churchill.

Sarah and her husband John had Queen Anne just where they wanted her. Anne and Sarah had been childhood friends. Sarah used their friendship to grab all sorts of titles and rewards. These titles came with plenty of money and land. Sarah also engineered a dukedom for her husband: he became Duke of Marlborough in 1689. Later, when Anne was queen, the duke won four splendid victories against the French. With this he shot to fame as England's greatest soldier. Blenheim Palace in Oxfordshire was built especially for him as a reward.

A game goes horribly wrong

Queen Anne disliked pomp and pageantry. She hated the formality of the royal court. So she relaxed by playing a game with Sarah Churchill. Anne called herself 'Mrs. Freeman'. Sarah called herself 'Mrs. Morley'. They pretended they were not queen and subject, rather two ordinary women who enjoyed a chat and gossip and a game of cards.

This was a mistake. Sarah took the game seriously. Anne was a bit of a mouse, plain and awkward. Sarah was a beauty and knew it. So it was not long before she was boldly ordering the queen around and throwing her weight about.

This could not go on indefinitely. In 1707 Anne and Sarah had a big row. Sarah stormed out of the court. The quarrel was so serious that Sarah and her husband left England, too. They did not come back until after Anne's death.

But someone else was waiting to take over from Sarah Churchill. Mrs. Abigail Masham was a relative of Sarah's. Indeed, it had been Sarah who arranged for Mrs. Masham to be appointed 'Woman of the Bedchamber' to Queen Anne. Sarah soon found it was the wrong move: Abigail Masham wormed her way into Queen Anne's affection, telling terrible tales about Sarah to the queen.

Sarah was furious. She wrote of 'the black ingratitude of Mrs. Masham, a woman that I took out of a garret and saved from starving.'

But Abigail remained Queen Anne's closest companion for seven years. In that time she lined her

Queen Anne was the last of the Stuart monarchs. When she failed to produce an heir, the country was thrown into intense debate. Her eventual successor, George I, was only 52nd in line to the throne, but at least he was a Protestant.

own pocket with profits from financial deals. She kept other would-be friends of the queen away by plotting against them. But when Anne died, Mrs. Masham's power vanished overnight.

Anne's health had never been good. It was made worse by her long series of miscarriages and stillbirths. The deaths of her children depressed her greatly. In 1708 her husband, Prince George of Denmark, died.

Queen Anne hated Sophia. She would not even allow her name to be mentioned at court. So she was delighted when Sophia died in June 1714.

Anne had adored him and was never the same again.

Anne's childlessness was not just a personal problem. It was a national one as well. In fact, it was an emergency. The Catholic Stuarts were still around, still aiming to seize the English throne. To prevent them from succeeding, a Protestant heir had to be found. The nearest was Sophia, Electress of Hanover in Germany. Her mother Elizabeth had been a daughter of King James I, the first Stuart monarch.

Queen Anne hated Sophia. She would not even allow her name to be mentioned at court. So she was delighted when Sophia died in June 1714, since she now would not be Queen of England. But within three months, Anne herself was dead.

German George gains Crown

The king who now succeeded to the throne as the first Hanoverian monarch of England was Sophia's son George, Elector of Hanover. George was Protestant, which is what Parliament wanted. It was enough to keep the English loyal to him when James Edward Stuart and his followers, the Jacobites, attempted but failed to seize the throne in 1715.

But George did not have much else about him to appeal to his subjects. They had endured bad kings, mad kings, despots, usurpers and weaklings. But, as the English were soon to discover, the Hanoverians were something else.

MISTRESSES AND MADNESS
A FEUDING FAMILY

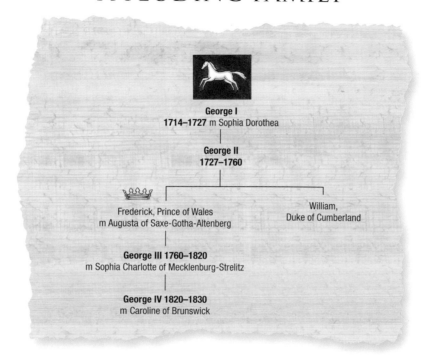

George I
1714–1727 m Sophia Dorothea

George II
1727–1760

Frederick, Prince of Wales
m Augusta of Saxe-Gotha-Altenberg

William,
Duke of Cumberland

George III 1760–1820
m Sophia Charlotte of Mecklenburg-Strelitz

George IV 1820–1830
m Caroline of Brunswick

All but one of the Hanoverian Kings were among the crudest, coarsest monarchs that England ever had. Their manners were dreadful and they showed little idea of how to behave.

In an age when the English expected monarchs to be gracious and dignified, the Hanoverians had no concept of what the words meant.

Even worse, King George I started a terrible family tradition. Each Hanoverian monarch clashed violently with his heir. These were not just family spats. They were vicious contests. Real harm was intended – and real harm was done.

George II was the last king of England to lead his troops into battle, at Dettingen in 1741. At the time he was 60, a lot older than this illustration makes him appear.

A boor with two gruesome girlfriends

The English were shocked to find out what George I was like. He was a dull man, with reddish features and bulging eyes. He was something of a savage – boorish and uncultured. He spoke very little English and had only three interests in life: women, horses and food.

George came to England with two mistresses. Both were incredibly ugly. One was Melusina von Schulenberg, the other Charlotte Sophia Kelmanns. King George was very fond of both. He lost no chance to show them off at court. This trio soon became a national joke in England.

This portrait of George I, the first Hanoverian monarch of Britain, was copied from a painting by a fellow German, Sir Godfrey Kneller. King George is shown in his robes of state, his crown on his head, and an ermine cloak.

The contrast between the two mistresses was hilarious. Schulenberg was nearly 60 years old and thin as a reed. She became known as 'the maypole'. Kelmanns was a huge mass of wobbling fat. She was called 'Elephant and Castle' after a district in south London. Both were dubbed 'ugly old trolls'. There was even extra-spicy gossip about Kellmanns: it was widely hinted that she was King George's half-sister.

George I was the first divorced King of England since Henry VIII. The tragedy surrounding his divorce fed gossips with endless tittle-tattle. George's marriage in 1682 had been a disaster from the start. George and his wife, Sophia Dorothea of Celle, had hated each other since they were children. But their marriage was a business arrangement: both families gained new lands because of it.

A marriage made in hell

Unfortunately, Sophia Dorothea was looking for happiness in her marriage. She found the opposite. George was dour, lumpish, and could not take a joke. Sophia, by contrast, was a bright spark. She was very pretty, lively and full of fun. George did not understand her, nor did he try. He was often away from Hanover, fighting wars. When at home, he preferred to play around with his mistresses.

Sophia was too young and impetuous to put up with such a situation. In 1686, while pregnant with her second child, she burst into George's study and demanded he get rid of his mistresses. George was furious. He

---

George took a terrible revenge on Sophia. In 1694, they were divorced. Sophia was forbidden to see her son and daughter.

---

seized Sophia and shook her violently, almost strangling her. Sophia became hysterical. Fortunately, her child, a daughter, was safely born in March 1687.

Prince Charming falls for queen

Around this time a Swedish count, Philip von Königsmarck, arrived at the court of Hanover. Königsmarck was everything George was not. He was 22 years old, very handsome and a real charmer. Men liked him. Women adored him. Königsmarck, a soldier, had come to Hanover for a job. Instead, he became Sophia Dorothea's lover. The two became attracted to each other at a ball given in Hanover in 1688. Königsmarck looked wonderful in a suit of pink and silver. Sophie wore a beautiful white dress and flowers in her hair.

It was all very romantic, even magical. Before long, Königsmarck was hopelessly in love with Sophia. He wrote her passionate love letters every day, sometimes twice a day.

Sophia kept trying to send him away. She realized taking a lover would be very dangerous. But eventually, he broke down her resistance. Sophia and Königsmarck became lovers sometime in 1691. The gossips soon got hold of the

story. From there, George's family learned about it. They placed Sophia under constant surveillance.

Tragedy for the lovers

On the night of 1 July 1694, the lovers met in Sophia's apartments at Leine Palace in Hanover. Königsmarck begged Sophia to run away with him. Apparently someone had seen him going into the apartment. But no one saw him coming out. In fact, no one ever saw Count Königsmarck again.

What had happened to him? People said that he was murdered on George's orders, and his body was chopped into pieces. The pieces were supposedly buried beneath floorboards at the royal country house, Herrenhausen.

George took a terrible revenge on Sophia. On 28 December 1694, they were divorced. Sophia was forbidden to see her son and daughter and was shut away for life in the Castle of Ahlden. She remained there for 32 years until her death in 1726.

Sophia Dorothea haunted George for the rest of his life. He was terrified she would escape from Ahlden. He destroyed all documents concerning their divorce. No one was allowed to speak of Sophia in his presence.

Herrenhausen Palace, in Hanover, Germany, was the summer residence of the Electors of Hanover. It was completed by Electress Sophia, mother of King George I. Destroyed in an air raid in 1943, it was rebuilt in 2013.

The son eclipses the father

George's son and heir, George Augustus, had been only 11 when he last saw his mother. But he never forgot her. And never forgave his father. When he came to England with his wife, Caroline, he kept two portraits of Sophia Dorothea hidden in their apartments. George Augustus became very popular in England. Unlike his father, he spoke English. Caroline was beautiful and gracious. It was no wonder people liked them.

Not so with King George. His subjects never liked him. They made fun of him and his mistresses. They wrote rude pamphlets about him. Journals published cartoons that made him look ridiculous. But George Augustus

A portrait of King George II. Throughout his long reign George hated England and did not travel very far in the country, preferring his beloved Hanover. Unpopular at first, he eventually gained the respect of his subjects.

and Caroline did not suffer this way. They were welcomed wherever they went.

The king grew jealous of them. When he hit back, he hit hard. Just before Christmas, 1717, he ordered George Augustus and Caroline to leave St. James's Palace in London. Worse, the king ordered them to leave their four young children behind. Unfortunately, the youngest child, a boy, died soon thereafter: he was only four months old. The autopsy showed he had a faulty heart. Even so, his parents blamed King George.

Rival court in the heart of London

George Augustus and Caroline set up a new home of their own in London. It became a popular meeting place for politicians and others who disliked King George and his ministers. People said that many plots to overthrow the king were hatched in Leicester House. If they were, nothing actually happened. But the rival 'royal court' increased the hatred between father and son.

The pair never truly reconciled. On occasion, they made a great show of affection in public, to convince everyone everything was all right. But it was not. This show was more difficult to sustain after Sophia Dorothea died in Ahlden on 2 November 1726.

After the news reached London, King George went to see a play with his mistresses. He showed every sign of enjoying himself. The 18th century was not an

The beautiful and lively Sophia Dorothea of Celle, the neglected wife of the future King George I, paid a terrible price for her infidelity – imprisonment for life in the Castle of Ahlden, where she died in 1726 after 32 years.

This illustration shows the execution of the defeated Jacobite rebels at Tower Hill after the Battle of Culloden. It had been a decisive victory for George II's second son William, the Duke of Cumberland.

age of tender feelings. It was a cruel, crude time. Even so, the audience was shocked. They did not expect their monarch to behave like such a cad.

Royal death foretold

King George and Sophia Dorothea had seemed linked in a curious way. George came to hear of a prophecy about them: when one died, so said the prophecy, the other's death would follow within a year. In June 1727, King George went back to his Electorate of Hanover for a visit. Some said that a letter written by Sophia Dorothea was thrown into his coach. It reminded him of the prophecy.

The letter was right. On the way to Hanover, the king suffered a stroke. His entourage managed to reach Osnabrück safely on 11 June. But that same night King George died.

The news took four days to reach England. Prime Minister Robert Walpole rode all the way from London

Sir Robert Walpole, painted by John Wootton against a rural background in the guise of a country gentleman. Walpole, usually regarded as Britain's first Prime Minister, was chief minister to George I and George II for a total of 20 years.

to Richmond, Surrey, to inform George Augustus – now King George II. The new king received the news without emotion.

New king damns his new kingdom

George II's first act was to order portraits of his mother, Sophia Dorothea, brought from their hiding place. The portraits were to be hung where all could see them. The new king seemed a welcome change from his father. He was much friendlier and much more gracious. But that was just a show. In fact King George hated England, the English and everything about them.

'I wish with all my heart that the devil take your (Prime) Minister,' he once exploded in a rage, 'and the devil take the Parliament, and the devil take the whole island, provided I can get out of it and go to Hanover!'

Hanover, of course, was his sanctuary. There, he could be free from 'that damned House of Commons'.

Hanover would allow him to rule as an absolute monarch, by Divine Right.

Queen and Walpole unite and rule

George's wife, Queen Caroline, was a great asset to her husband. She was beautiful, charming and clever. George adored Caroline. Even in public, he could hardly keep his hands off her. Caroline could easily have dominated him, but George would not have it. He wanted everyone to see he was boss. But everyone knew otherwise.

The truth was that Caroline, together with Prime Minister Robert Walpole, had the king on a string. The two used to discuss the latest political questions in private, and together would decide what the government's policy was to be. Then, Walpole would arrive at the palace to see King George. Queen Caroline would be in the room, stitching quietly at her embroidery.

While Caroline remained in the background, the two men talked. But the queen and Walpole prearranged a set of secret hand signals. During his conversation with the king, Walpole played with his hat. Or he took snuff. Or pulled out his handkerchief. Caroline sent a signal back by raising her fan or threading a needle. George never noticed a thing. Once he and Walpole had agreed about policy, he imagined it was all his own idea.

But there was something George and Caroline did agree about. Both detested their eldest son, Prince Frederick. They began to dislike him almost as soon as he arrived in England from Hanover in 1728.

The gentle prince with a brute of a brother

The trouble was, Frederick was not the heir to the throne his parents wanted. He was not the military type. He preferred writing poetry to fighting wars, and

was a talented musician. As far as King George was concerned, Frederick was a weakling. He far preferred his second son, William, Duke of Cumberland.

William was a soldier first and last. He was also very uncouth. He gained a terrible reputation for cruelty in the second Jacobite Rebellion in 1745. Then, the Stuart who tried to reclaim the English throne was Charles Edward, son of James Edward. Charles was known as 'Bonnie Prince Charlie'.

Wholesale slaughter at Culloden

The rebellion came to a shocking end at the Battle of Culloden in 1746. Highlanders who supported Charles were slaughtered by the hundreds, mainly by lowland Scots soldiers. Later there were executions and massacres. Scottish homes were looted and burned. Whole communities were destroyed.

Bonnie Prince Charlie had managed to escape back to Europe, aided by one Flora MacDonald. She disguised him as a woman, 'Betty Burke', an Irish spinning maid. Once it was all over, Scots dubbed William 'Butcher Cumberland' for his cruelty. Frederick presumably would not have acted like his brother. He was too kind-hearted. When Flora MacDonald was taken to London and locked up in the Tower of London, Frederick visited her and offered help. Because of Frederick, Flora was set free.

That, of course, did not please the king one bit. Here was his hated heir actually helping his Scottish enemies. Soon history began to repeat itself. King George and Frederick had vicious quarrels. Frederick was banned from his father's court and the royal palaces. A rival court gathered around Frederick and his wife, Princess Augusta. When told of it, King George flew into one of his violent rages.

'He is a monster and the greatest villain ever born,' he ranted. 'My first-born is the greatest ass and the greatest liar…and the greatest beast in the whole world, and I most heartily wish he was out of it!'

Unloved and unmourned

Tragically, Frederick soon fulfilled his father's wishes. Quite suddenly, in 1751, Frederick became seriously ill. While he was working in his garden, it began to rain and Frederick was soaked to the skin. Before long, he was suffering from pleurisy. Pleurisy turned to pneumonia. Then, on the night of 20 March 1751, he suddenly clutched his chest and cried out: 'I feel death!' Minutes later, Frederick was dead. He was 44.

An anonymous poet had the last word about Frederick – and the Hanoverian family.

'Here lies Fred,
'Who was alive and is dead.
'Had it been his father,
'I had much rather;
'Had it been his brother,
'Still better than another.
'Had it been his sister,
'No one would have missed her.
'Had it been the whole generation,
'Still better for the nation.'

King George was playing cards when told his son was dead; he continued his game. He was glad Frederick was gone, and the son was not given a proper funeral for an heir to the throne. Suspicion was that King George had ordered it that way. No member of the Royal Family

attended. Nor did any English lord or bishop. There was only a brief ceremony, without music.

Frederick's successor as heir was his eldest son, 13-year-old Prince George – the future King George III. George was forced to live with his grandfather at Hampton Court Palace. He was a stubborn boy. The king often complained that his grandson 'lacked the desire to please'. In other words, he would not do as he was told. George frequently had his ears boxed for disobedience.

Cleaning up the act

Although young, Prince George had learned much from watching his father and grandfather. Though both were devoted to their wives, they were also great womanizers. Young George vowed that when he became king, he would clean up the royal act. There would be no mistresses, immorality at court, gambling or extravagance. George III set the pace himself. He was still unmarried when he became king at age 22 in 1760. But he immediately gave up his teenage love, Lady Sarah Lennox. Although Sarah was aristocratic – her brother was Duke of

> **A rival court gathered around Frederick and his wife, Augusta. When told of it, King George flew into a violent rage.**

Richmond – her rank was not high enough to become queen. Giving up Sarah caused George a great deal of pain. But he was also mindful of the dignity of the British Crown. So the woman he married in 1761 was much more highly ranked: Princess Charlotte of

George, Prince of Wales, the future Prince Regent and George IV, was the embarrassing heir every royal parent dreaded: an irresponsible renegade, undignified, profligate, selfish and immoral.

Mecklenburg-Strelitz. King George was totally faithful to her for the 57 years their marriage lasted.

A motley crew

George and Charlotte had 15 children – seven sons and eight daughters. But if George thought he was going to bring back good old-fashioned family values with his many offspring, he was sadly mistaken. The king kept his daughters at home, ostensibly to save them from the so-called wicked world. But his sons were a disgrace.

One of them, William, Duke of Clarence, seduced two of the queen's Maids of Honour when he was only thirteen. Later, he had ten illegitimate children by his mistress, the married actress Dorothea Jordan. Another son, Ernest, Duke of Cumberland, had a child by his own sister, Princess Sophie. The youngest son, Edward, Duke of Kent, lived for 30 years with his French mistress, Madame Laurent. Two other sons were eccentric and badly behaved, frequently making nuisances of themselves in the House of Lords. On one occasion they had to be removed, swearing and making rude gestures.

The worst of a bad bunch

Undoubtedly the worst of the sons was the eldest, George, Prince of Wales. No vice seemed beyond him. He was vain, arrogant and inconsiderate. He bedded a long series of unsuitable mistresses, including other men's wives. He was already an experienced hand at gambling, drinking and creating scandal by age 17.

As if this were not enough, the Prince of Wales was wildly extravagant. 'Spend, spend, spend!' might have been his motto. In 1787, he was in the red to the tune of £220,000. This was not merely a personal problem, it was a matter of royal prestige. It did not look good to have tradesmen and other creditors pounding on the door of the heir to the throne, demanding payment. Or, just as bad, refusing him credit.

REGAL PROFILES

CURED – ALMOST TO DEATH

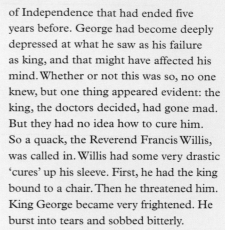

THE FIRST SYMPTOM of King George's strange illness was a painful jaw. It was so painful it prevented him from sleeping. Next, he had a stomach upset, shooting pains in his back and breathing difficulties. Things got worse. His eyesight failed. He became deaf. He started talking nonsense incessantly. He talked to trees. He talked to his dead ancestors. Before long Queen Charlotte became terrified of being alone with her husband. His veins stood out on his face. His eyes had a dangerous glint. He foamed at the mouth.

The king's doctors were baffled. Possibly, he had been affected by the loss of the American colonies in the War of Independence that had ended five years before. George had become deeply depressed at what he saw as his failure as king, and that might have affected his mind. Whether or not this was so, no one knew, but one thing appeared evident: the king, the doctors decided, had gone mad. But they had no idea how to cure him. So a quack, the Reverend Francis Willis, was called in. Willis had some very drastic 'cures' up his sleeve. First, he had the king bound to a chair. Then he threatened him. King George became very frightened. He burst into tears and sobbed bitterly.

Willis's strategy continued. Every time King George had a problem – difficulty in swallowing, loss of appetite, or sweating – he was strapped into a straitjacket. Then he was tied down to his bed and left there for hours.

Willis raised blisters on the king's legs to 'drive out the evil humours'. The blisters caused King George agonizing pain. He tore them off only to be strapped into a straitjacket once again. The blisters were reapplied by force. Before long, King George came to believe Willis was trying to murder him. He began to pray for a cure. If he could not be cured, he prayed instead for death.

But somehow, King George started to recover. Early in 1789, his crazy talk began to stop. His personality returned. He was able to shave himself again. He was given back his knife and fork at mealtimes. Soon the king was back to normal.

Nigel Hawthorne brought the troubles of the British monarchy to life in Alan Bennett's 1991 play *The Madness of George III* and its subsequent film adaptation.

King George did not have sufficient funds to pay his son's debts. So Parliament had to bail out the prince and pay his bills. But the prince was not cured – far from it. He kept on spending, fancying himself as something of a dandy and expending vast sums on clothes. The prince was also fond of building projects, jewels, expensive parties and expensive women.

The son breaks all the rules

Then, in 1784, Prince George committed the greatest of all his follies. He fell madly in love with Mrs. Maria Fitzherbert, a twice-widowed commoner. He asked her to become his mistress. But she was a devout Roman Catholic and a respectable woman. She refused. It was marriage, or nothing. So George and Maria were married in 1785 – in secret. The parson who performed the ceremony was released from debtors' prison for the specific purpose.

It was thanks to his sons and their mistresses that George III had an army of illegitimate grandchildren. But what he did not have was a single legitimate grandchild to continue the Hanoverian dynasty.

With this marriage, George had broken two very important laws in England. One was the Act of Settlement of 1701, which stated that no one in line of succession to the throne could marry a Roman Catholic. The other was the Royal Marriage Act of 1772, which banned royals from marrying before age 25 without the monarch's permission. George was 23 when he married Maria. This did not stop him from living openly with his wife. From time to time, he found a new mistress and wandered off. But he always returned to Maria. He called her 'the wife of my heart and soul'.

Maria was undoubtedly good for the Prince. She civilized him. She made him cut down on his drinking. She put a stop to some of his more boorish habits – such as picking his teeth in public.

Then, in 1788, King George became very sick. No

Caroline of Brunswick, wife of King George IV, was even more outrageous than her husband. The couple lived together for barely a year until after the birth of their daughter, Princess Charlotte, in 1796. Afterwards, Caroline embarked on a career of blatant adultery and scandal.

one knew what was wrong. He had to endure many months of bizarre and painful 'quackery' before he recovered fully.

Parliament strikes deal with prince

By 1794, the Prince of Wales was in big trouble again. He had built up another huge mountain of debts. He became bankrupt, owing £630,000. Once again he had to ask Parliament to pay. Parliament agreed, but with strings attached.

Thanks to his sons and their mistresses, King George III had an army of illegitimate grandchildren. What he did not have was a single legitimate grandchild to continue the Hanoverian dynasty. Parliament offered the Prince of Wales a deal: his debts would be paid, but he had to marry legally and produce legitimate heirs to the throne.

The Prince was trapped. He had to agree – and Mrs. Fitzherbert therefore had to go. Instead, he would marry the wife his father now chose for him. Princess Caroline of Brunswick was the king's niece and the prince's first cousin. But she was the worst possible choice the king could have made. Her family background said it all. She came from an unhappy home. Her parents were constantly at war with each other. Two of her brothers were mentally retarded.

Trouble in store

Caroline had grown up thoroughly spoiled. Her conversation was peppered with swear words. She was vain, rebellious and immoral. It was as if King George was allowing his son to marry a wild beast.

Prince George knew nothing of any of this. He and Caroline had never met before she arrived in England for their wedding. But when he saw her for the first time, he went into shock. 'Harris,' he gasped to his attendant, Lord Malmesbury, 'I am not well, pray get me a glass of brandy!'

But the shock the prince received at Greenwich was nothing compared to what followed. He did not know it yet, but the stage was set for the most outrageous royal scandal England had ever known.

13
BATTLE ROYAL

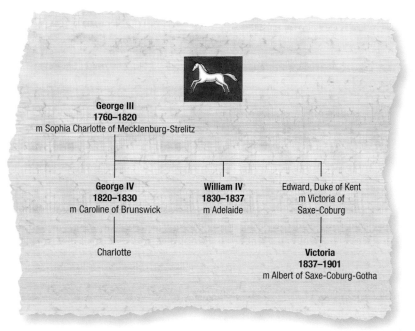

George III
1760–1820
m Sophia Charlotte of Mecklenburg-Strelitz

George IV
1820–1830
m Caroline of Brunswick

William IV
1830–1837
m Adelaide

Edward, Duke of Kent
m Victoria of
Saxe-Coburg

Charlotte

Victoria
1837–1901
m Albert of Saxe-Coburg-Gotha

A glass of brandy may have dulled the shock for a time,
but an awful reality was still there when the effect wore off. Prince George's
future bride stood before him at their first meeting
looking an absolute fright.

✦

Caroline was dressed in a robe and cloak with a beaver hat on her head. The robe was in a shade of sickly green with satin trimmings, festooned with fussy loops and tassels. This was the best her attendants could do to hide her pudgy figure.

A frump decked out in finery

Caroline's face was covered with garish makeup. Somewhere underneath were her fine, fresh complexion and rosy cheeks. She looked like a clown.

The Royal Pavilion, Prince George's exotic home in Brighton, East Sussex, was greatly influenced by oriental styles of architecture, with an Indian exterior and a Chinese interior.

And that was not all. Close up, Caroline reeked. She smelled unwashed. Prince George reeled. He was very strict about hygiene and regular bathing.

Somehow, Prince George managed to compose himself and behave graciously. But it took a stupendous effort. The prince had to contain himself again when he took Caroline to a pre-wedding dinner. She prattled on and on about the latest gossip, including talk about the prince's latest mistress, Lady Jersey. Her language was crude, coarse and smutty.

After a while, George could stand the situation no longer and got thoroughly drunk. He was still hung over when the marriage ceremony took place on 8 April 1795. George spent most of his wedding night in a drunken stupor, asleep on the floor next to the fireplace. But somehow – though he probably never remembered how – he fulfilled his royal duty. Caroline, the new Princess of Wales, became pregnant on her wedding night.

Royal pair make an effort

In truth, Caroline was not all that impressed with George, either. At one time, he had been a slim young man, and handsome too. Not any more. At age 33, years of self-indulgence and overeating had taken a toll. Caroline was disappointed to see how fat and puffy he had become.

In spite of having a distinct aversion to one other, George and Caroline made some effort to live together. They spent the summer and autumn of 1795

Cartoonists often caricatured Prince George. His huge bulk was due to constant overeating. He fancied himself as a dandy and wore exotic clothes. This contemporary caricature shows him with an equally gross 'friend'.

Maria Fitzherbert was the great love of King George IV's life. He broke the law in 1785 when he married her without his father's permission. George left her from time to time to dally with mistresses, but he always returned.

at Brighton Pavilion, on England's southern coast. This lavish, oriental-style building – still one of the major sights of Brighton – had once been George's most expensive extravaganza. But while the couple were there, George's drinking pals descended on them, along with their women. The quiet honeymoon in Brighton turned into a riotous drinking party.

This did not help George and Caroline learn to tolerate each other, and soon they stopped trying. Caroline was spoiled, rebellious and vain. It had once been said that unless she were kept on a tight leash, she would go wild. George did not bother trying to rein her in.

Once their daughter, Princess Charlotte, was born on 7 January 1796, Prince George made moves to distance himself from his marriage. Charlotte was

but a few days old when her father drafted a will disinheriting Caroline.

After his fling with Lady Jersey, George was struck with a yearning for Maria Fitzherbert once again. In a nearly hysterical mood, he wrote vowing eternal love for 'my wife in the eyes of God and who is and ever shall be mine.' Another letter, this time to Caroline, was totally different. It began 'Madam', and went on to state his desire for a total and permanent separation.

George and Caroline never lived together again. But they were never divorced, nor was this the end of their relationship. The couple would be bound together in mutual hatred for the next 25 years.

The Queen's amorous adventures

Caroline was not the sort of woman to retire to a quiet, discreet life in the country, where everyone might forget about her. She was too vulgar, too outlandish, for that. She did move to the country, but that was about it. Her new home was in Blackheath, on the southern edge of London.

Before long, Caroline was shocking the locals with her antics. She received a stream of 'gentleman callers'. Tales of multiple adultery began to circulate and spread. Caroline got her clutches on one William

---

With Parliament against him, the prince had to give in. But he hit back by throwing Caroline out of her Kensington Palace apartments. He also forbade Charlotte to see her – no matter what Parliament said.

Austin, young son of a dockyard worker, and claimed he was her and Prince George's son. Fortunately, government investigators proved the story false. They went on to dig up evidence about Caroline's sex parties. But they were unable to prove anything, despite the gossip.

The indecisive lover

Meanwhile, Prince George's longing for Maria Fitzherbert had worn off again. He took a new mistress, Lady Horatia Seymour. After that, it was back to Maria again. She held George off for four years, possibly to teach him a lesson. But in 1801, she agreed to live with him again. Maria managed to hang on to George for ten years – a record for him. But he wandered off again, this time with yet another mistress, Lady Hertford.

King loses his mind – for good

In 1811 King George III's illness returned and he became permanently mad. He had violent fits. He refused to eat. He imagined that his son Augustus, who had died in 1783, aged four, was still alive. He lost all sense of time, place or reality and lived in a dream world. The one thing he remembered, it seems, was how to play the harpsichord.

This time, it was hopeless. The king was declared incurably insane in 1812. He was shut away in his palace and spent his days wandering around his rooms, mumbling to himself and clutching the Crown Jewels.

Caroline senses trouble ahead

George was appointed Prince Regent at last. He took the oath on 6 February 1811. But he still had to deal with the troublesome Caroline. The king's madness had been a disaster for her, for in spite of everything, King George had protected her. Now, that protection was gone, and she was in the hands of a husband who detested her. He soon made the most of it.

He used Princess Charlotte as a psychological weapon with which to beat his wife, refusing to let her see their daughter. Caroline was up to the challenge. She had allies in Parliament and used them to force a Parliamentary debate. The vote went to Caroline.

With Parliament against him, the prince had to give in. But he hit back by throwing Caroline out of her apartments at Kensington Palace. He also forbade Charlotte to see her – no matter what Parliament said.

Queen wins public's affection

Caroline's response was to make several well-publicized public appearances. She posed as the victim of a cruel husband, but cheerfully so. The ploy worked. Crowds cheered her. At the same time, they booed the Prince Regent.

The warfare between George and Caroline moved on to the next round. George decided that Princess Charlotte should marry Prince William of Orange.

This cartoon shows 'the Royal Extinguisher' – King George IV – who finally triumphs over his dreadful wife Caroline by placing a cone made of paper over her and a crowd of Jacobites – supporters of the ousted House of Stuart.

William was an unpleasant young man. Even so, Charlotte was expected to obey her father. But, as was her mother, she was stubborn and loud-mouthed. It was not long before she had picked a quarrel with William.

Charlotte fled to Caroline's house in Connaught Place, London. Caroline was not there. She was at Blackheath. The Prince Regent's brothers came after her. They badgered her to obey her father. By this time her war with the Prince Regent had exhausted Caroline. This latest fight was too much. She joined in and told Charlotte to stop making trouble and marry William.

Charlotte had her own cunning way of dealing with William. She blackmailed him by demanding that, as second in line for the English throne, she must remain in England after their marriage. Next she told William that Caroline must come and visit whenever she wanted. That was it. The very thought of sharing living space with Europe's most scandalous mother-in-law was the last straw for William. He refused her requests. Charlotte broke off the engagement.

Princess Charlotte eventually married another prince, Leopold of Saxe-Coburg-Gotha, in 1816. However, she died after giving birth to a stillborn son. Caroline was in Italy when she heard the news and immediately went into deep mourning for her daughter. In England, the Prince Regent collapsed in a dead faint on hearing the tragic news. He recovered, but was so distressed he was unable to attend the funeral.

THE PARTY QUEEN WHO LOVED TO SHOCK

BY 1814, AFTER NEARLY 20 YEARS OF FIGHTING her husband, Caroline longed to get away. The time was right. England's long wars against Napoleon Bonaparte and the French were coming to an end after 22 years. It was now safe to travel in Europe. Despite her experiences in England, Caroline still had plenty of bounce left in her. She wanted to be free to enjoy herself.

But for Caroline, that meant she would spin even more out of control than before. News soon reached England of a long series of spicy scandals. Bonaparte's family were now in disgrace. Caroline went out of her way to seek them out. They became so friendly that Caroline even took Joachim Murat, Napoleon's brother-in-law, for her latest lover.

Caroline moved on to Italy. There, she squeezed her fat bulk into skimpy dresses with necklines down to her waist. The skirts rose well above her plump knees. Caroline appeared at parties and gala balls wearing a huge black wig. She painted her cheeks blood red and stuck sequins on them.

Caroline became an attraction wherever she went. She went about wearing long pink feathers, riding in a coach shaped like a shell. Somewhere along the way, Caroline acquired an extraordinary companion. Bartolomeo Bergami had flashing eyes, curly black hair and an outsized moustache. He was an Italian adventurer of mysterious origins.

Bergami became Caroline's secretary and, of course, her lover. The pair journeyed around the Mediterranean, ending up in the Middle East. There Caroline made a pilgrimage to Jerusalem mounted on a donkey. Considering her vast bulk and the donkey's small size, it was a sight to behold.

Caroline and Bergami settled down to live together in Pesaro, Italy.

Like her husband, Princess Caroline was a frequent target of cartoonists and pamphleteers. Here she is cavorting around with her lover Bartolomeo Bergami and, right, on the arm of Alderman Wood. Caroline died in 1821, the year these caricatures were published.

Urgent quest for an heir

This, though, was not merely tragic family loss. It created a crisis. Charlotte had been the only heir to the throne in her generation. The other heirs to mad King George III were Charlotte's elderly uncles and aunts, none of whom had any legitimate children.

So Parliament sent a petition to four of Charlotte's uncles to marry and produce legitimate heirs. It meant leaving their mistresses, which caused them pain. All the same, they did their duty for the sake of the Hanoverian line. They took wives and had children. Unfortunately, many of the infants died.

For a time, even the Prince Regent considered divorcing Caroline and marrying again. But Caroline refused to let him. She did not think her sexual adventures in Europe were sinful, and prepared to fight any divorce action the prince might bring.

> **Time for the new king to act was limited. He had to get rid of Caroline before his coronation. In fact, the coronation was postponed while the king made yet another attempt to unhitch himself.**

The prince set up a commission to find grounds for divorce. Caroline responded by promising to create a storm of protest in England. It was a shrewd move. Details of the prince's own private life were bound to come out. All the same, Caroline tried another tack. She offered to set aside her rank as Queen of England when George became king. In return, she wanted George to give her a large sum of money. He refused, ending thoughts of divorce. The couple remained married, shackled together in mutual loathing.

Death of a pitiful old man

Caroline was still on course to become Queen of England. As long as King George III was still alive, that remained a remote possibility. But on 29 January 1820, King George died. He had become a tragic figure, far

This drawing of King George III depicts him at the age of 72, in his Golden Jubilee year of 1810. But tragedy was fast approaching at this time: King George went mad once again, and this time there was no chance that he would recover.

gone into madness. He was deaf and blind. His white, gaunt face was sometimes observed, staring out the palace window, seeing nothing. His beard had grown long and straggly. He knew nothing about the death of Princess Charlotte, or the marriages of his sons. He was even unaware his queen, Charlotte, had died in 1818.

George fails to ditch Caroline

The Prince Regent succeeded his father as King George IV. As far as her rights were concerned, Caroline was now queen. But as far as her husband was concerned, he was not going to let her anywhere near the throne.

Time for the new king to act was limited. He had to get rid of Caroline before his coronation. In fact, the coronation was postponed while the king made another attempt to unhitch himself from his outrageous queen. He asked Parliament to pass a Bill of Pains and Penalties. This set out Caroline's numerous sins. The attempt failed. The only evidence offered was circumstantial – albeit Caroline's sexual antics had been the subject of frequent gossip. The Bill of Pains and Penalties had to be dropped. Londoners, who loved Caroline, went wild with joy and celebrated for three days and nights.

The toast of London once more

Caroline chose this moment to make a triumphant return to England. Everywhere she went she was fêted and saluted. George IV, by contrast, was subjected to vile insults. Obscene graffiti were scrawled on the walls of Carlton House, his private London residence. And not only there. 'The queen forever! The king in the river!' were slogans scrawled on the walls of the Russian Embassy in London. George IV got the message. He left London for his country cottage at Windsor, Berkshire. There, he waited for 'Caroline fever' to die down.

Nine weeks passed before George thought it safe to return to London. To make sure, he took a troop of Life Guards with him. He was relieved that the crisis seemed to have passed. When he went to a play at London's Drury Lane, he was applauded. The same happened when he went to see another play at Covent Garden.

DEEDS of POWER

NO ENTRANCE TICKET FOR THE QUEEN

ON CORONATION DAY, the interior of Westminster Abbey was decorated with brocade, lace, silks and satins, velvet and feathers – an opulent display for a great royal occasion. Outside, the crowd of sightseers was large and excited. Sellers of coronation souvenirs did a vast trade. Pickpockets moving unnoticed among the sightseers also had a very good day.

Suddenly, a row broke out at an entrance to the abbey. Caroline was there, but the doorkeeper had orders from the king. He was to stop the queen from getting in. His reason?, The queen did not have a ticket. Caroline tried another door. It was locked. She could not get in that way, either. It was the same at each of the abbey's many doors. Stone-faced doorkeepers barred her. They were not the least impressed when she told them who she was.

Caroline was not going to stand for this without making a big fuss. But the crowds soon tired of her. Caroline was making a nuisance of herself and spoiling the fun. They hissed and booed her. No one helped Caroline as she desperately went from door to door, trying to get in.

The row became so great that guards were called in. They stood in a line in front of every doorway. Finally, the last door was shut in Caroline's face. By this time Caroline was red-faced with shame and fury. In the end she was forced to return to her carriage and drive home to Brandenburg House. Two days later, she wrote a furious letter to the king.

'The queen must trust that after the public insult Her Majesty has received this morning, the king will grant her just right to be crowned next Monday....' There was no reply.

Determined to be acknowledged as queen, Caroline attempted to gate-crash the coronation of her husband, King George IV, in 1821. He managed to stop her from getting in and she had to return home, frustrated.

King bans queen from his coronation

After this, the king felt confident enough to fix another date for his coronation – 19 July 1821. Queens of England had their own special coronation, after the king's. But George was confident enough now to tell Caroline she could not take part. Her name had already been removed from the prayers to be said at the coronation ceremony. She had been pestering him to have her name put back, to tell her what robes she should wear, to name the attendants who would carry her train.

But George IV was determined that his coronation would be a one-man show. Caroline was not deterred. She was determined to crash the ceremony, planned for London's Westminster Abbey. Failing that, she would create mayhem. Caroline was counting on her popularity with London crowds. The king knew she would make a terrible scene, so he took precautions to prevent her even from entering the abbey.

The end of a feisty queen

Twelve days after his coronation, George IV went aboard the royal yacht for a state visit to Ireland. The yacht was at anchor off the Isle of Anglesey, north Wales, on 6 August 1821, when news arrived that Caroline was dying. She had been taken ill at Drury Lane. Medical treatments at this time were extremely brutal, often causing the patient's death. But such treatments were all Caroline's doctors knew. So they bled her and gave her hefty doses of calomel and castor oil.

William IV succeeded his brother George IV on the throne in 1830. He had never expected to become king and was so delighted that he drove around London in his carriage greeting his subjects and shaking them by the hand.

Queen has the last word

The doctors believed she would somehow recover. Instead, she died on 7 August. For once, George IV acted decently. He remained on Anglesey during the week of Caroline's funeral. Five days of official mourning had been declared. The king waited until they had passed before making his entry into Dublin.

But it was Caroline who had the last word. At her own request, her coffin was inscribed with the words: 'Caroline of Brunswick, the Injured Queen of England'. Even the King of England was unable to do anything about that.

George IV was King of England for ten years, until his death at Hampton Court on 26 June 1830. His heir was his brother William, Duke of Clarence, who became King William IV.

An unruffled royal oddball

Like other sons of King George III, William was a bit of an oddity. He even looked peculiar. Aged 64, William had a round face, very red cheeks and a distinctly unroyal quiff. When the coins of his reign were minted, designers deliberately left out the quiff.

William was awakened at six in the morning and told he was king. He showed no emotion. Instead, he shook the messenger's hand and went back to bed. His only comment was that he had 'always wanted to sleep with a queen'. His wife Adelaide had, of course, just ascended from Duchess of Clarence to Queen Consort of England.

Later the same day, he stuck a small piece of black crepe in his hat and went out riding at Windsor. But William IV was not as nonchalant about succeeding to the throne as he pretended to be. As a younger son of a king, he had never really expected to be king himself. When it actually happened, he was thrilled.

No heir but Victoria

A few days later, he went riding around London in his coach. He stopped here and there to buttonhole passers-by, shake them by the hand and tell them how delighted he was to be their king. It was embarrassing, but somehow heartwarming.

Unfortunately, William IV came to the throne without legitimate heirs of his own. As Duke of Clarence, William had married Adelaide in the royal rush for a wife after the death of Princess Charlotte. They had two daughters, but both died in infancy, and there were no children after that.

William's heir was his niece, Princess Victoria. She was the daughter of his younger brother, Edward, Duke of Kent – another participant in the royal rush to marry. Victoria's mother, Victoire of Saxe-Coburg, kept her daughter strictly under her control. Victoire's main

Victoria, niece of George IV and her predecessor William IV, came to the throne at age 18 in 1837 determined to repair the good reputation of the royal family after the outrageous activities of the Hanoverian kings. The result was an era of strict morality.

aim was to keep the girl well away from the influence of disreputable Hanoverian relatives.

Predictably, William IV became at odds with Victoria's mother. His greatest wish was to live long enough for Victoria to reach the age of majority, 18: if he could do that, he could prevent her mother from becoming Regent. The king just made it. William IV died on 20 June 1837. Victoria had turned 18 the month before, on May 24.

A pair of right royal prudes for England

Not surprisingly, Princess Victoria grew up to be narrow-minded and self-opinionated. She was also a terrible prude, and tended to be obsessive. In 1840, she married her first cousin, Prince Albert of Saxe-Coburg-Gotha, who was even more of a prude than she was. He once said that the thought of adultery made him feel physically sick.

> **Victoria's heir, the future Edward VII, was pure Hanoverian. Strict morality meant nothing to him. Both as Prince of Wales and as king he became the greatest royal womanizer since Charles II.**

Albert set the pace for his wife's reign and for their private life. Hanoverian sleaze was out. Strict Puritan-style morality was in. Family respectability was to become the motto of Victorian England. More than that, the nine children of Victoria and Albert were to be role models for a new society: their example, so their parents resolved, would stand as a lesson on how to be royal, yet lead a pure life.

But there was one great big flaw in this plan. Victoria's heir, the future King Edward VII, was pure Hanoverian. Strict morality meant nothing to him. Both as Prince of Wales and as king, he became the greatest royal womanizer since King Charles II. He gambled, he drank, he smoked – all to excess. His life was one long round of scandal that horrified his parents and left their high-minded plans in ruins.

14

SCANDAL BEHIND CLOSED DOORS

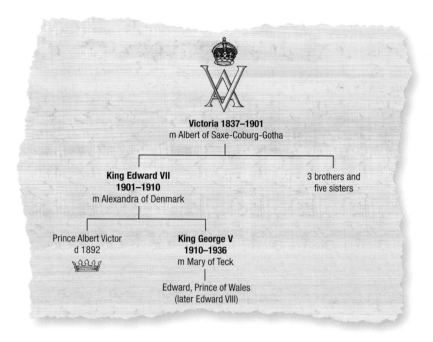

Victoria 1837–1901
m Albert of Saxe-Coburg-Gotha

King Edward VII 1901–1910
m Alexandra of Denmark

3 brothers and five sisters

Prince Albert Victor d 1892

King George V 1910–1936
m Mary of Teck

Edward, Prince of Wales (later Edward VIII)

Edward, Prince of Wales, known in the royal family as Bertie, began his life of scandal at a young age. In 1861, when he was 19, he was sent for military training to an army camp at the Curragh, in Ireland. It was there that he lost his virginity.

Bertie had spent his childhood in confinement at home, with his family. He was held captive by a very strict system of education. But more study and more application were required of him than he could reasonably manage. Bertie was not stupid, he was simply unacademic. Book learning, which he came to hate, meant nothing to him. He reacted by throwing tantrums, attacking his tutors and working himself into wild rages.

Three royal generations: Queen Alexandra and King Edward VII (standing), the future George V and Queen Mary, and their son Edward (later King Edward VIII and, after his abdication in 1936, Duke of Windsor).

'Bertie's Fall'

But in 1861, this repressed young man had his first taste of what the outside world was really like. First of all, he met other young men, all training to be army officers. He found they had habits he had never heard of. One was making use of the services of the camp prostitute, a pretty young actress named Nellie Clifden.

One night, officers at the Curragh moved Nellie into the prince's bed. The inevitable happened. Nellie made a man of him. But when the news reached Bertie's parents, they were horrified. The incident became known as 'Bertie's Fall', and Bertie was never allowed to forget it.

Prince Edward shocked his parents and Victorian society with his sexual antics and his association with high-life scandal. Less prudish types, however, had a sneaking admiration for Bertie, who broke the rules and got away with it.

Bertie gets the blame

Even worse, there was a tragic sequel. Not long after 'Bertie's Fall', his father, Prince Albert, fell seriously ill. His doctors had no idea what was wrong. He had probably caught typhus from faulty drains at Windsor Castle.

Albert died on 14 December 1862, aged only 42. Queen Victoria went half-mad with grief, for she had idolized him. She went into mourning and remained so for the next 40 years, until she died. Bertie and his 'Fall' were blamed for causing Albert's death. Victoria never forgave him.

But before Albert died, a cure for 'Bertie's Fall' had already been arranged: marriage to a sensible wife who would keep tabs on him and stop his straying.

A hand-picked beauty

The royal houses of Europe were searched for a suitable bride for Bertie. Finally, the choice became the 18-year-old Princess Alexandra of Denmark. She had the one asset Bertie's parents most wanted: she was extremely beautiful. Victoria firmly believed Alexandra's physical beauty alone would make Bertie mend his ways. Victoria – and Alexandra – soon discovered differently.

REGAL PROFILES

FUN-LOVING PRINCE WITH GIRLFRIENDS GALORE

Bertie was naturally attracted to fun-loving, pleasure-seeking high society types. He could dance until dawn. He would gamble and bet on horses and play flirtatious games all night. Bertie loved every minute of it. Before long, Bertie and Alexandra were leading separate lives.

Alexandra stayed at home with their children. She supported many charities. Meanwhile, Bertie lived it up. He was off to the races. He went to Paris, where he took a French princess for a mistress. He cavorted openly with opera stars and actresses. When he came back to England, he brought with him semi-pornographic pictures of popular French singers. Gossip soon did the rounds about his illegitimate children. Bets were placed on who his next mistress would be and how long she would last.

Although Bertie was pure Hanoverian, he was not irresponsible, like his ancestors: he had a strong sense of royal dignity and the need to maintain it.

Bertie and Alexandra were married on 10 March 1863 at St. George's Chapel, Windsor. Queen Victoria cast gloom over the ceremony by attending clad entirely in black and observing from a high balcony.

What Victoria had not realized was that in having Bertie married, she was freeing him from her apron strings. Now, he would have his own household. In fact he had two homes, Marlborough House in London and Sandringham in Norfolk. He also soon had his own family: his first son, Prince Albert Victor, known as Eddie, was born in 1864. Above all, Bertie could now make his own social life. And a very riotous – not to say scandalous – social life it would be, too.

> John Brown was often alone with the queen. He came to her bedroom after breakfast and sat with her while she looked through papers in confidential government 'boxes' – a task she had to perform every day.

Queen Victoria, meanwhile, was involved in a scandal of her own. Victoria was a very emotional woman given, on occasion, to melodramatic conduct. She had not simply loved her husband, Prince Albert, she had adored and worshipped him. It was the same – according to gossip of the day – with her personal servant, or gillie, Scotsman John Brown. Brown was never anything but a best-liked servant. But after Albert's death Victoria became so attached to him that it gave rise to gossip.

Courageous and well-respected companion

John Brown was based at Balmoral, the royal home in Scotland. He was no ordinary gillie. His intelligence was above average and he was a very good judge of human nature. Besides that, he had a way of talking Victoria liked. She hated all the bowing and scraping when royals were around. Brown, by contrast, spoke his mind. And he knew how to do it without being rude. For Victoria, he was a breath of fresh air.

Brown was unusually thoughtful and considerate. He knew Victoria loved white heather. So he kept an eye out for it in the countryside around Balmoral. Victoria was thrilled to receive bouquets of her beloved flower from her much-loved servant.

Despite her high position as Queen of England, Victoria was a dependent type of woman. She liked and needed to be cared for. Brown fulfilled her requirements. He became her constant companion, accompanying her wherever and whenever she wanted.

Brown also saved her life. On 29 February 1872, Victoria was about to go through the garden entrance to Buckingham Palace when a man named Arthur O'Connor pointed a pistol at her. John Brown leapt on him and knocked the weapon out of his hand. Brown pinned the man down until police arrived.

Later the queen awarded Brown a gold medal for his courage.

John Brown was often alone with the queen. He came to her bedroom after breakfast and sat with her while she looked through papers in confidential government 'boxes' – a task she had to perform every day. She saw more of Brown than of her own children.

Victoria's children became jealous. They spoke of Brown as 'Mama's lover'. They may even have believed the gossip that Victoria and John Brown were secretly married. For a while, it became an 'in' joke to refer to the queen as 'Mrs. Brown.'

'Mrs. Brown' widowed again

After more than 20 years of devotion to the queen, John Brown died in 1883. Victoria was almost as distraught as when Prince Albert died. Her reaction was, of course, excessive. She put up a statue to Brown at Balmoral. She planned to write a poem in his praise. She ordered that Brown's room should be kept exactly as it had been when he died. A fresh rose was to be placed on his pillow every day. The orders were carried out: a new rose appeared on the pillow every day for 18 years, until Queen Victoria died in 1901.

Bertie, of course, thoroughly disapproved of all this 'romantic nonsense' over John Brown. Victoria, in turn, thoroughly disapproved of Bertie. If anyone was disgracing the royal family name, so she thought, it was he.

Judi Dench as Queen Victoria and Billy Connolly as John Brown in _Mrs Brown_, a film made in 1997 about the relationship between Victoria and her 'gillie', or Highland servant. Some said that Victoria and Brown were married.

Bertie's near-miss

She had a point. Bertie, as always, lived dangerously. Mostly his activities were kept under wraps. But it was inevitable that sooner or later, there would be a scandal that could not be hidden. The time arrived in 1870.

In February of that year, Lady Harriet Mordaunt confessed to her husband, Sir Charles, that she had committed adultery with several men. One of them had been Bertie.

Bertie protested his innocence. He knew the Mordaunts well. It was true he had written several letters to Harriet. But they were friendly, so he said, no more than that. Unfortunately, Sir Charles Mordaunt was not like other members of the English aristocracy. Most did not mind if the prince bedded their wives. They regarded it as a sort of compliment. But Sir Charles did not see why Bertie should get away with it. He threatened to name the prince as a co-respondent in his divorce case. This caused horror all around. It was one thing to gossip about royal goings-on, quite another to have it all spelled out in public.

But Bertie was saved when Sir Charles' divorce case

Bertie and Alexandra, Prince and Princess of Wales, photographed in 1882. Alexandra was famous for her beauty, which lasted all her long life, but her physical attractions were not enough to keep her husband faithful or virtuous.

failed. Not because his wife was not guilty, but because she had been declared insane. Her 'lovers', royal and otherwise, were found to be in her imagination. It was a tragic outcome, but it got Bertie off the hook. After the divorce case, he had to put up with booing, hissing and catcalls whenever he appeared in public. But at least he had not been named as an adulterer by the court.

This did not mean he was out of trouble. Bertie was never out of trouble. Six years later, he had another lucky escape. In 1876, the Earl of Aylesford sued his wife for divorce. Bertie was not named as co-respondent this time. The man named by the earl was Lord Blandford, heir to the Duke of Marlborough. But Bertie had written letters to the Countess of Aylesford. Read a certain way, some suggested a very close, maybe sexual, relationship.

Unfortunately for Bertie, Lord Blandford had a fiery younger brother, Lord Randolph Churchill. When Lord Randolph worked himself into a temper, sparks flew. Randolph threatened to publish Bertie's letters. But then the Duke of Marlborough stepped in and put a stop to the divorce proceedings. It had been a narrow escape.

Another close call for Bertie

By now, there was talk that Bertie was not fit to succeed his mother on the throne. That faded after a while. But in 1890, Bertie added fuel to the fire once again. In September that year, the prince was staying at Tranby Croft, country home of his rich friend Arthur Wilson and his wife.

On 8 September, after dinner, it was decided to play a round or two of baccarat, the card game. Baccarat was illegal in England at the time. Even so, bets were placed, and the game commenced.

One of the players was Sir William Gordon Cumming, a distinguished army officer with many medals to his name. Cumming had been a friend of Bertie's for 20 years. They shared interests in womanizing and gambling.

During the evening, other players thought they

had seen Cumming cheating. At that time, cheating at cards was one of the worst social crimes possible to commit. It was made even worse because the prince was there. Bertie was told what had happened.

First thoughts were to protect him from a 'horrible scandal'. Two courtiers had accompanied Bertie to Tranby Croft. One, Major Owen Williams, thought of a way out. Gordon Cumming had to sign a document saying he would never play cards again. It made him sound guilty. But that could not be helped.

Gordon Cumming signed the document, but under fierce protest. He claimed he was innocent. But he was assured nothing more would be said on the matter. He had to be content with that.

But the story got out. Late in 1890, Gordon Cumming received an anonymous letter from Paris. This revealed that far from being hidden, gossips were

The Baccarat or Tranby Croft Scandal, in which Bertie was involved in 1890, shocked society both because his friend Cumming was accused of cheating and because baccarat was illegal. It hardly reflected well on the prince's probity.

having a field day talking about the 'baccarat scandal'. No one ever found who had talked. But Gordon Cumming was furious. He decided to clear his name through the courts. He would demand that his hosts at Tranby Croft, the Wilsons, withdraw the accusation of cheating. Otherwise, he would sue them for slander.

The case was to be heard in English civil court. This meant Bertie could be subpoenaed as a witness. For a member of the royal family to appear in a witness box was unheard of. It was a scandal in itself. Desperate attempts were made to persuade Gordon Cumming to withdraw the case. But he refused.

The case opened at the Chief Justice's Court in London on 1 June 1891. Press and public were packed tightly in galleries above the courtroom. Bertie entered the witness box on the second day of the trial. Other witnesses, including Gordon Cumming himself, had been mercilessly cross-examined by prosecution lawyers. But they went gently when it came to Bertie. They did not try to pin him down, but attempted to gather his evidence as quickly as they could.

But there was one man on the jury, Goddard

Clarke, who was not prepared to pussyfoot around. He stopped Bertie just as he was leaving the witness box. In a sharp cockney voice, he asked the prince questions the lawyers had avoided.

> **There was one last cure Eddie's parents had not tried yet. They would find him a nice, sensible wife to act as his minder.**

Had the Prince actually seen Gordon Cumming cheating at cards?

'No,' the Prince replied.

'What was your Royal Highness' opinion… about the charges of cheating made against Gordon Cumming?' Goddard Clarke wanted to know.

All Bertie could say was: 'I felt no other course was open to me but to believe what I was told'. It was a lame answer and it made him look foolish. But it turned the case against Gordon Cumming. The jury decided if the heir to the throne of England believed his friend was guilty, then he must be. Gordon Cumming lost the case. The consequences were dire.

Bertie tainted by grubby trial

Cumming's social life was at an end. He was thrown out of clubs. He was banished from the British Army. No one in high society would speak to him, or of him. He might as well have been dead. And all because he had dared to involve a future king of England in a grubby court case.

But Bertie did not get away scot-free. He received much criticism from the press – for gambling, for keeping bad company, for betraying his friend, for setting a bad example.

'If he is known to pursue in his private visits a certain round of questionable pleasures', thundered The Times of London, ' the serious public…regret and resent it.'

This was mild compared to a cartoon in German newspapers ridiculing Bertie's emblem – the tall, white, Prince of Wales feathers. The Prince of Wales' motto was also depicted, but the inscription had been changed from 'I Serve' to 'I Deal'.

The French press made the most of the scandal. They printed gossip that hinted Bertie was about to leave his mother's court and abdicate, giving the crown to his eldest son, Prince Eddie. But what even the prying French press did not know was that Eddie on the throne of England would have been a downright disaster, for he was the royal family's darkest, most embarrassing secret.

Utterly hopeless Eddie

Born in 1864, Prince Eddie grew up idle, weak and backward. His tutors found it impossible to teach him anything. He was unable to concentrate for any length of time. And he did not give a damn. If anyone tried to discipline Eddie or give him instructions, he replied with an idiotic grin or a shrug of the shoulders.

Experts and specialists were called in. But they could not tell what was wrong. Eddie's parents, Bertie and Alexandra, were in despair. They tried a few cures of their own. Eddie was sent to Cambridge University in the hope that somehow it would spark an interest in something. But this idea failed. One of Eddie's tutors described him as 'abnormally dormant'. Another remarked: 'He hardly knows the meaning of the words "to read".

Next, Eddie was placed in the army. But his instructors soon realized he could not manage even the simplest parade ground drills. After that, Eddie became a cadet in the Royal Naval College, Dartmouth, in 1877. The results were no better.

Final attempt to stabilize son

There was one last cure Eddie's parents had not tried yet. They would find him a nice, sensible, down-to-earth wife who would act as his minder. This was the same trick Queen Victoria had used on Bertie himself. It had not worked then. But Bertie and Alexandra were so desperate by this time, they could not think of anything else to do.

The wedding that was never to be

The girl they chose was Princess May of Teck, a cousin of Eddie's and a descendant of George III. May was

The Prince of Wales is pictured here in 1901, just before he succeeded to the throne. He loved the pomp and ceremony of royalty and relished wearing medals and orders, carrying his sword and wearing his plumed hat.

25; young, but not too young. She was very disciplined and dutiful. She would make a first-class watchdog. Eddie and May became engaged on 3 December 1891. Their wedding was fixed for the following February. But it never took place. Eddie went down with influenza the day before his 28th birthday, on 7 January 1892. The following day, he only just managed to stagger downstairs to look at his birthday presents.

From then on, his health became worse and worse. Later, Princess May remembered the scene at Eddie's bedside. It was like some ghastly tableau. The grieving

> **When the king and Mrs. Keppel were invited to a weekend house party in the country, their hosts quietly gave them adjoining rooms. Everybody knew what was going on. But no one breathed a word.**

mother, Alexandra, the tormented patient, Eddie, the helpless doctor and the family watching it all over a specially erected screen. Eddie died at 9:45 A.M. on 14 January while his mother held his hand. Later, at Eddie's funeral, Princess May's wedding bouquet decorated his coffin.

It was all very sad. Eddie's short life had been wasted. His parents became ill with grief over the tragedy. But it had surely crossed several minds that tragedy now was better than disaster later. Many people, including Queen Victoria, believed that if Eddie had ever become king, the English monarchy would have come to an end.

Bertie becomes king

With Eddie's death, his younger brother Prince George became their father's heir. In 1893, George married Princess May. Eight years later, Queen Victoria, last of the Hanoverian monarchs, died. Bertie, by now

The aged Queen Victoria in this photograph did not appear on her postage stamps. Throughout her 63-year reign, she appeared as the pretty 21-year-old she had been in 1840, when Britain's first stamp, the Penny Black (right), was issued.

almost 60, became King Edward VII, first king of the House of Saxe-Coburg-Gotha. The name of the ruling dynasty was changed in memory of Prince Albert, who hailed from the Duchy of Saxe-Coburg-Gotha in Germany.

But nothing else changed for the new king. His high-flying social life went on. He still journeyed to Biarritz every spring. He still visited the health resort of Marienbad later in the year. Then there were the shooting season in England, regular visits to the races, rounds of golf, card-playing sessions and a new royal craze – motoring.

Throughout the year Edward VII would play host at enormous banquets. The menu typically consisted of turtle soup, salmon steak, chicken, mutton, snipe stuffed with goose liver, fruits, ices, caviar and oysters. There was plenty of claret, champagne and brandy to drink. At the end of the banquet large cigars and cigarettes were passed out. King Edward himself was a very heavy smoker: he could get through twelve cigars and twenty cigarettes a day. That was in addition to heavy drinking and overeating.

The king still had his mistresses, notably the charming Mrs. Alice Keppel. As with all his affairs, Edward's liaison with Mrs. Keppel was carefully protected by their friends. When the couple were invited to a weekend house party in the country, their hosts quietly gave them adjoining rooms. Everybody knew what was going on. But no one breathed a word.

Alexandra's generous gesture

Queen Alexandra, of course, knew all about Mrs. Keppel. She also knew that King Edward truly loved her. In 1910, the king's long years of overeating and high living at last caught up with him. He suffered a series of heart attacks. Alexandra remained with him until he died on 6 May at 11:45 P.M.

Before his death, however, Queen Alexandra called in many of his good friends to say a last goodbye. Among them was Mrs. Keppel. Alexandra knew how to be generous.

Edward VII loved the theatre. Here he is in the front row of the audience, sitting between his mistress Mrs. Keppel and the Duchess of Devonshire at a theatrical event at Chatsworth, the Devonshires' country mansion.

King George V and Queen Mary in full coronation robes. George V, who succeeded his elder brother Eddie as their father's heir in 1892, came to the throne after the death of Edward VII on 6 May 1910.

Diplomatic name change for new king

Edward was succeeded by Prince George, who became King George V. Princess May became known as Queen Mary. King George began as the second monarch of the House of Saxe-Coburg-Gotha, but the name would be changed again, in 1917.

The world war with Germany and its allies was being fought at the time. Horrific tales of slaughter were coming back from the battlefields in France. In England, this caused such hatred of Germany that it became embarrassing for members of the royal family to have German names and titles. So George V changed the family's name again – to Windsor, after the royal castle in Berkshire.

King George was the opposite of his father. He was very shy and did not like the high life. He was utterly devoted to Queen Mary, so much so that if he didn't see her for a while he felt physically ill. He took no mistresses.

Although he had loved his father, Edward VII, George had strongly disapproved of his way of life. Like the young King George III before him, he was determined to wipe out the disreputable image of the king as playboy and make the royal family respectable once again.

But like George III, his plans went haywire. The culprit was exactly the same; the heir to the throne. George V's eldest son and heir, Prince Edward, was arguably worse than all the other troublesome heirs put together. He very nearly destroyed the monarchy.

A LOOSE CANNON

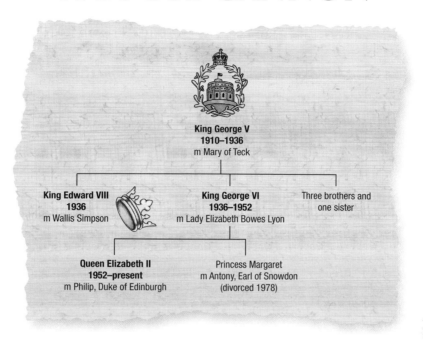

King George V
1910–1936
m Mary of Teck

King Edward VIII
1936
m Wallis Simpson

King George VI
1936–1952
m Lady Elizabeth Bowes Lyon

Three brothers and
one sister

Queen Elizabeth II
1952–present
m Philip, Duke of Edinburgh

Princess Margaret
m Antony, Earl of Snowdon
(divorced 1978)

Quarrels between monarchs of England and their eldest sons had been going on for almost two centuries when King George V came to the throne in 1910. George and his son and heir, Prince Edward, would carry on in the same way.

ut their quarrel was much more serious than any before. So grave, so fundamental was this particular dispute that the royal family themselves believed they were finished.

The unwilling royal

Essentially, the problem with Prince Edward – known as David within the royal family – was that he did

Edward VIII came to the throne determined to make divorcee Wallis Simpson his queen. He met stern, unyielding opposition that ultimately forced him to abdicate.

not wish to be a prince. He wanted nothing to do with the pomp and pageantry that went with being royal. Royal duties bored him. He hated formality. He hated privilege. What he wanted was to be ordinary, something no royal could ever hope to be.

All this set David on a collision course with his parents, King George V and Queen Mary. Their devotion to duty was total. If it meant making personal sacrifices – lack of privacy, limited choice of friends – that was too bad. Rules had to be obeyed.

David, of course, wanted to toss out royal rules. The first public sign of how he felt came in 1911. That year, aged 16, he was invested Prince of Wales at a grand

Glum-looking Prince Edward, known as David, is seen here with his parents, King George V and Queen Mary at his investiture as Prince of Wales at Caernarvon Castle in 1911. He later referred to the robes as a 'preposterous rig'.

ceremony at Caernarvon Castle in Wales. Photographs of the event show him looking sulky and glum. Later on, David did everything he could to test the limits placed upon him by royal birth. During World War I, he insisted on going to France and the front line of the fighting. Everyone was horrified. Suppose David were taken prisoner by the enemy? Suppose he were killed? It would not do. The heir to the throne had to be protected.

Battling prince is 'one of the boys'

David would have none of it. He went to France. He went right to the front line. And he was there, in the trenches, while British soldiers were under fire.

'The prince is always in the thick of it,' one soldier wrote home to England. 'Only last night he passed me when the German shells were coming over.'

Despite the dangers and risks, David loved every minute of it. At last, he could be with ordinary men, sharing their problems, talking with them as if he were their equal. The king definitely did not approve. He believed royals should remain aloof and dignified. He told David: 'The war has made it possible for you to mix with all manner of people. But don't think this means you can act like other people. You must always remember… who you are.'

The king was already too late. In 1918 David had taken refuge in an air-raid shelter in London while German Zeppelins were dropping bombs. There, he met a young married woman, Freda Dudley Ward. David fell madly in love with her. Within a short while, they were all but living together.

Playboy prince revels in high life

For a prince to have a mistress was, of course, nothing new. But Freda Dudley Ward was David's entree to the sort of social life where he at last felt at home . It was not the stiff, starchy circle of 'good' families approved by his parents. It was the so-called *'demi-monde'*, the 'twilight' world of wild all-night parties, fashionable nightclubs, loose morals and shady people. They included social climbers, gold diggers and profiteer millionaires. These were not the sort, according to the

king, that his son should have had anything to do with.

David's parents tried to 'cure' him by sending him on overseas tours, but the cure never worked. On his return to England David simply took up again where he had left off. He was back at the parties and night-clubs almost as soon as he got off the ship.

After a while, David took on another mistress, a beautiful American, Thelma, Lady Furness, a sister of Gloria Vanderbilt. Thelma, too, had a large circle of fun-loving friends. In 1931, she introduced David to two of them, Wallis Simpson and her second husband, Ernest.

David, seen here in army uniform, relished the chance to mix with ordinary young soldiers in the trenches of World War I. He longed above all to be ordinary himself, but his royal birth made that impossible.

Prince falls for Mrs. Simpson

At first, the Simpsons were just two more of David's acquaintances. But in 1934, Thelma had to return to the United States. She left 'the Little Man', as she called David, in the care of Wallis Simpson. It seemed a safe bet. Wallis was plain, scrawny and a little sour-faced. Thelma reckoned she was no competition.

Little did she know. While Thelma was away, David fell in love with Wallis. She was more womanly, more protective and a much stronger character than his other women. At a time when England was hard hit by the Depression, she shared David's concern for the plight of ordinary people.

'Wallis,' David told her, 'you're the only woman who's ever been interested in my job!' She was just what David wanted.

But Wallis Simpson was just what David's parents did not want. It was not because she was American, it was because she was a divorced woman and, as David's passion for her grew, was likely to be divorced again. At this time, divorce was considered immoral in England. Members of the royal family were not supposed to know or even speak to anyone who had gone through a divorce.

Now here was the heir to throne involved in a romance with a divorced woman while she was still married to her second husband. The shock was tremendous. But Wallis was no passing fancy. Edward wanted to marry her and make her his queen.

Father despairs over the future king

King George and Queen Mary were helpless. They forbade David to bring Wallis to the royal palace. David thought his father was a stuffy old prig. The king thought his son was a cad. Queen Mary thought Wallis an 'adventuress'. This seemed to be a general opinion about Wallis, who was branded a fortune hunter and a loose woman out to get as much as she could grab from her royal connection. The British

secret services, who kept Edward and Wallis under close surveillance, certainly thought so. Early in 2003, their reports were made public for the first time, and revealed that Wallis was very careful to feed Edward's

> ## Now that he was king, Edward VIII did not have to worry that the royal family, royal officials – and his mother – did not like Wallis. Far from it. He could show Wallis off to everyone.

infatuation for her. She kept secret from both the prince and her husband, Ernest Simpson, that she was having an illicit affair with a car salesman named Guy Trundle, and fended off all other women who might get near her royal lover. Meanwhile, the public in England knew nothing of the growing royal crisis. There was no television. Cinema newsreels were carefully censored, so too were radio broadcasts. Few people took holidays abroad, where the foreign press was full of the story. By general agreement, newspapers in England kept quiet about the whole affair. But sooner or later, the truth was bound to come out.

On 20 January 1936, King George V died. David, the queen and other members of the royal family were at his bedside. Queen Mary curtsied to her son, in recognition of him as the new king, Edward VIII. But she could not help remembering what her husband had once said: 'The boy will ruin himself within the year'. How right he was.

King parties on regardless

Now he could show Wallis off to everyone, and the way he did it was outrageous. In May 1936, when he hired a yacht, the *Nahlin*, for a cruise in the eastern Mediterranean, he and Wallis were accompanied by several of their 'unsuitable' friends. What happened next

This illustration of Wallis Simpson flatters her. The British public found it almost impossible to understand how the sour-faced, middle-aged woman pictured in their newspapers could rock the throne of England and the royal family.

According to royal officials, this was not how the King of England should appear in photographs: a bare-chested King Edward VIII is pictured with Wallis Simpson during the cruise of the yacht *Nahlin* in the Mediterranean.

The king could not have cared less. What he wanted to do, he did – and damn what anyone else thought.

'To oppose him over doing anything,' Queen Mary wrote, 'is only to make him more determined to do it. At present, he is utterly infatuated (with Mrs. Simpson), but my great hope is that violent infatuations usually wear off.'

Plans to wed Wallis

It did not wear off. In July 1936, while the king and Wallis were still cruising on board the *Nahlin*, her divorce proceeding was already underway. The case was due to be heard in court on 27 October. Simple arithmetic was all that was needed to guess what was in King Edward's mind. The divorce would be final in six months, on 27 April 1937. The king's coronation was fixed for 12 May. There was just enough time for Edward and Wallis to get married and be crowned king and queen soon thereafter.

Royal affair sparks national crisis

The royal scandal became a serious national crisis. Prime Minister Stanley Baldwin was called in. He tried to persuade the king to give up Mrs. Simpson. He failed. The king's own relatives tried. They failed. So did the Archbishop of Canterbury. And the governments of the Dominion countries of the British Commonwealth – Australia, New Zealand, Canada and South Africa – all failed.

By early December, King Edward VIII had become a man none of his friends wanted to know anymore. They realized the biggest royal scandal of the century was about to break and did not want to be involved. Suddenly the king's friends started turning down invitations to Fort Belvedere, his personal home. They made excuses not to attend parties, or go on royal picnics. They had never liked Wallis Simpson, they said. As for the king, they thought he must be crazy.

filled the foreign newspapers with smut and scandal for many weeks. The *Nahlin's* passengers, including the king, arrived at various ports of call drunk and barely dressed. They gave noisy parties on board the yacht. King Edward and Wallis Simpson did not care who saw them kissing and cuddling. All of it was considered a grossly undignified way for the King of England to behave.

This is the abdication document signed by Edward VIII on 10 December 1936. Edward signed himself 'RI': Rex Imperator (King Emperor), but it would be for the last time. His three brothers, Albert, Henry and George, signed the document as witnesses.

INSTRUMENT OF ABDICATION

I, Edward the Eighth, of Great
Britain, Ireland, and the British Dominions
beyond the Seas, King, Emperor of India, do
hereby declare My irrevocable determination
to renounce the Throne for Myself and for
My descendants, and My desire that effect
should be given to this Instrument of
Abdication immediately.

In token whereof I have hereunto set
My hand this tenth day of December, nineteen
hundred and thirty six, in the presence of
the witnesses whose signatures are subscribed.

SIGNED AT
FORT BELVEDERE
IN THE PRESENCE
OF

THE KING STEPS DOWN FOR LOVE

DESPITE HIS RELUCTANCE TO BE KING, there was no escape for Bertie. His brother signed the Document of Abdication on 10 December. Having done so, he became Prince Edward once more. The next day the former king made an historic broadcast from Windsor Castle:

'A few hours ago I discharged my last duty as king and emperor, and now that I have been succeeded by my brother, the Duke of York, my first words must be to declare my allegiance to him. This I do with all my heart.

'You all know the reasons which have impelled me to renounce the throne. But you must believe me when I tell you that I have found it impossible to carry the heavy burden of responsibility and to discharge my duties as king as I would wish to do without the help and support of the woman I love.

'...This decision has been made less difficult to me by the sure knowledge that my brother, with his long training in the public affairs of this country and with his fine qualities, will be able to take my place.... And he has one matchless blessing, enjoyed by so many of you, and not bestowed on me – a happy home with his wife and children.

'...And now, we all have a new king. I wish him and you, his people, happiness and prosperity with all my heart. God bless you all! God save the king!'

THE DAILY MIRROR, Friday, December 11, 1936

Daily Mirror

No. 10306   Registered at the G.P.O. as a newspaper   ONE PENNY   LATE·LON·ED

EDWARD VIII'S RADIO FAREWELL TO-NIGHT

THE NEW KING ARRIVES IN HIS CAPITAL

London Cheers George VI

Edward VIII will broadcast to the Empire and the world to-night as Mr. Edward Windsor, a " private individual owing allegiance to the new King."

This will follow the signing of his abdication papers and the succession to the Throne of his brother, the Duke of York, who will be 41 on Monday.

The time has been fixed tentatively for 10 p.m. During the evening Edward VIII is expected to leave the country.

THE capital welcomed its new King — who will reign as George VI—for the first time just before midnight when he arrived back at his home at 145, Piccadilly, after dining with his brother at Fort Belvedere.

A crowd of 20,000 which had waited for hours burst into wild and prolonged cheering.

The King's arrival was so sudden that his car was caught up in the home-going theatre traffic.

Two taxis barred his entrance into his home, and though hundreds of police struggled wildly, they could not keep the surging crowd back.

People ran shouting round the royal car waving their hands, hats and handkerchiefs in the King's face.

Tired and Pale

He sat well back in his car, looking tired and pale. Obviously he was moved by the tremendous demonstration and he smiled wanly and bowed once or twice.

After being held up for quite five minutes in the crowd the car edged its way into the courtyard.

When the King stepped from the car there was more tremendous cheering. By this time the crowd was quite out of hand and swept right up to the railings of the house.

Further police were rushed to the scene and they helped to restore order.

After the King had gone indoors the great multitude stood outside and sang the National Anthem and "For He's a Jolly Good (Continued on back page)

Britain's new King, the Duke of York, arriving home at 145, Piccadilly, last night, after dining at Fort Belvedere with his brother. Huge crowds gave the new Monarch a great welcome to his capital. (See back page).
Picture pages are 8, 12 14, 16, 17, 19 and 28.

A historic edition of the London *Daily Mirror*. The trepidation on the face of the new king, George VI, was genuine.

Wallis begs to be set free

All this happened within a few days. The English poet Osbert Sitwell dubbed it 'Rat Week'. But as the rats deserted the ship, the ship was sinking. When the silence of the English newspapers was broken on December 3, the king was on his own. The next day, Wallis fled for safety to France after stones were thrown at the windows of her home in London. From there, she begged the king to let her go rather than give up his throne for her sake.

He would not even think of it. 'No matter where you go,' he told Wallis, 'I will follow you!'

What Edward VIII wanted was the throne of England and Wallis, but if he had to choose between them, then the throne would have to go. The throne went on 10 December 1936 when Edward VIII became the first king of England to abdicate of his own free will.

His decision caused anguish in the royal family. The heir to the throne, Edward's younger brother Bertie, became terrified at the thought that now he would be king. He burst into tears and sobbed on his mother's shoulder. His wife, Elizabeth – the late Queen Mother – said, 'It was like sitting on the edge of a volcano.'

Another unwilling king

Bertie had never been trained to be king. He was nervous. His health was poor. He suffered from a stammer. Appearing in public was agony for him. He had a nice, quiet life with his lovely wife and two daughters, Elizabeth and Margaret. Now all that was to end. No wonder Bertie was so upset.

Royal snub for Wallis

The former king crossed the English Channel into lifelong exile on the night of his abdication. On 3 June 1937, he married Wallis Simpson at a château in northern France. No member of the royal family was there. The couple were given new titles – Duke and Duchess of Windsor. But there was one thing they did not get. Bertie, who took the name King George VI, refused to make Wallis a 'Royal Highness'. He reasoned that, with two failed marriages behind her, the chances of the third one lasting weren't all that good.

Edward and Wallis never forgave King George or his family. Although Edward had no authority to do so, he himself gave Wallis the title which King George had kept from her. He insisted that everyone address his wife as 'Her Royal Highness, the Duchess of Windsor'.

Government wants the Windsors out of the way

Back in England the duke was offered the governorship of the Bahama Islands. The position carried little prestige. The Bahamas were the most insignificant colony in the whole British Empire. Usually, its governor was a minor civil servant or a retired army officer. But the islands had one great advantage: they were well away from the war zone. It was a good place to park the Windsors for as long as the war lasted.

Trouble follows wherever they go

Once in the Bahamas, the Duke of Windsor still could not stay out of trouble. The worst thing that happened while he was governor was the murder of Sir Harry

After the war ended, the Windsors returned to Europe. Still shut out by the royal family, they became stars of the rich social scene, moving from one fashionable resort to the next.

Oakes, a mining millionaire. Oakes was a shady character. He lived in the Bahamas to avoid paying taxes and had secret arms dealers for friends.

In 1943, Sir Harry was savagely murdered. The duke personally took charge of the investigation. He had no experience in such matters. As a result, he bungled the case so badly that an innocent man – Oakes' son-in-law – was framed for the crime. Fortunately, he was found not guilty at his trial. The real killer was never discovered. But there were hints about Mafia involvement in the affair.

Champagne lifestyle for globe-trotting pair

Ever since his abdication, the duke had wanted to serve his country in a 'top job'. But yet again, he had become embroiled in scandal. The sordid business of Oakes and his kind had rubbed off a little on him. Beside this, he had proven himself incompetent. The mess he made of the Oakes affair made sure that the duke was never offered an official post again.

After the end of the war in 1945, the Windsors returned to Europe. Still shut out by the royal family, there was only one place for them to go. They became stars of the rich, well-heeled social scene. They moved from one fashionable resort to the next – Biarritz, Venice. They dined at Maxim's, the Paris restaurant, twice a week. Photographs of them enjoying themselves in nightclubs and luxury hotels appeared in newspapers. They lived the high life to the fullest.

Sad Wallis can never say goodbye

But it all came to an end in 1972, when the duke died in Paris. After that, if anyone still thought of Wallis as a greedy gold digger, out for all she could get, they were proven wrong. For a time, she refused to admit that the duke was dead and had to be forcibly removed from his bedside.

'He was my entire life,' she said at her husband's funeral at Windsor.

'He gave up so much for me. I can't begin to think what I shall do without him.'

She could not do without him. Wallis was never able to put her life back together again. She would sit alone for hours in the duke's room, which was kept exactly as it was when he died. 'Goodnight, David!' she would say before going to bed.

Wallis went into a steady decline. She ended up paralyzed and crippled. She spent her last years lying in bed surrounded by pictures of herself and her husband. She lived in the past, dreaming of the years they had spent together. Wallis died in 1986, aged 89. She was buried next to Edward at Windsor. Queen Elizabeth II and her family attended the ceremony.

The duke had always wanted Wallis to be accepted into the royal family. In death, she had managed it

The Windsors' nightlife was avidly followed by the press. The duchess was of particular interest to newspaper readers. She was usually wearing magnificent jewels from the collection showered on her by the duke.

As Duke and Duchess of Windsor, David and Wallis concentrated on an energetic social life, appearing in all the 'right' fashionable places in the 'right' fashionable company. Here they are following the play at a golf tournament.

at last. But there was still no official 'HRH' title. The plate on her coffin read simply 'Wallis, Duchess of Windsor 1896–1986'.

A dutiful king

George VI had died 20 years before his elder brother, in 1952. The good name of the English royal family had taken a frightful battering in the abdication crisis of 1936. The royals themselves believed they were finished. But in his reign of 15 years, King George and

FACT or FICTION

DID THE DUKE SUPPORT THE NAZIS?

EVEN IN EXILE, the Windsors had a knack for creating sensational headlines wherever they went. In 1938 they were invited to visit Nazi Germany, where they met Führer Adolf Hitler and his henchmen. There was outrage in England when newsreels showed the duke giving the Nazi salute. Stories arose that the duke and duchess were Nazi sympathizers, but secret surveillance reports released in 2003 contained no evidence that this was true.

The Nazis, however, didn't require proof. The former king of England gave them a chance to spread innuendoes about his supposed Nazi sympathies. There was also gossip about a Nazi plot to kidnap the Windsors. Then, so the story went, once they had invaded and conquered England, the former king would be placed on the throne again – as a Nazi puppet.

The Germans never invaded England. But the duke and duchess showed no interest in their plans anyway. They just wanted to get away from the war zone. They managed to escape to neutral Spain. From there, they returned to England. But they were not to stay.

Pictures such as this showing the Windsors meeting Hitler gave rise to gossip that the duke and duchess were Nazi sympathizers.

his admirable Queen Elizabeth had done a first-class repair job. The royal family became respectable once again. This time there was no troublesome heir to ruin the effort. The love and affection King George felt for his heir, Princess Elizabeth, was so great that his eyes filled with tears whenever he spoke of her. The long series of royal quarrels was over.

Dark cloud in a clear blue sky

This did not mean that Elizabeth II was going to escape trouble and scandal. Trouble made its appearance very early on, on the day of Elizabeth's coronation, 2 June 1953. That same day, outside Westminster Abbey, her younger sister Margaret was caught on camera picking a piece of fluff off the uniform of Group Captain Peter Townsend of the

The seemingly perfect royal family. George VI and Queen Elizabeth (later the Queen Mother) with their daughters, Princess Elizabeth and Princess Margaret. This picture of domestic bliss was in total contrast to the high jinks of the duke and duchess.

Royal Air Force. It seemed the sort of thing a woman did when she regarded a man as 'hers'.

Townsend was a royal servant, a former wartime fighter pilot and an equerry to the new queen. Beady-eyed journalists watched the scene and took note. A new royal romance was in the air. But so was a new scandal. Peter Townsend was a divorced man and an untitled commoner. By the royal rules of the time he had no business romancing the sister of a queen.

A MODERN MONARCHY?

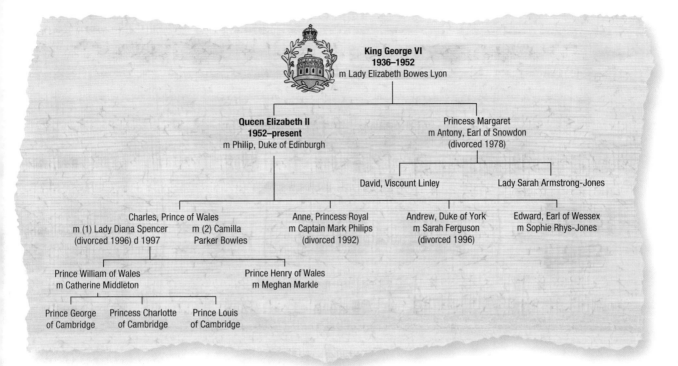

King George VI
1936–1952
m Lady Elizabeth Bowes Lyon

Queen Elizabeth II
1952–present
m Philip, Duke of Edinburgh

Princess Margaret
m Antony, Earl of Snowdon
(divorced 1978)

David, Viscount Linley

Lady Sarah Armstrong-Jones

Charles, Prince of Wales
m (1) Lady Diana Spencer   m (2) Camilla
(divorced 1996) d 1997   Parker Bowles

Anne, Princess Royal
m Captain Mark Philips
(divorced 1992)

Andrew, Duke of York
m Sarah Ferguson
(divorced 1996)

Edward, Earl of Wessex
m Sophie Rhys-Jones

Prince William of Wales
m Catherine Middleton

Prince Henry of Wales
m Meghan Markle

Prince George
of Cambridge

Princess Charlotte
of Cambridge

Prince Louis
of Cambridge

Princess Margaret was the live wire of the royal family. If she had not been born a princess, she could have had a brilliant career on the stage – as a mimic, singer or pianist.

✦

She had charm, she had zest. She had personality. And, as Peter Townsend himself said, she was 'intensely' beautiful. What Margaret did not have was luck. Margaret first met Peter Townsend in 1945, when she was 15. He had just become equerry to her father, King George VI. Townsend was handsome and charming. He was a war hero. Margaret fell deeply in love with Peter Townsend and set her heart on marrying him.

24 February 1981 was the day that years of royal wedding speculation ended. Charles, Prince of Wales announced his engagement to the pretty 19-year-old Lady Diana Spencer.

Forced to choose between duty and love

Margaret was delighted when she found that Townsend loved her in return. But there were tremendous obstacles. Townsend was divorced. The social barriers divorced people faced were bad enough. But the English church did not even recognize divorce. It was an impossible idea that the queen's sister should marry a man whose first wife was still living, and become stepmother to his children.

The queen, supreme head of the Church of England, could not possibly give permission for such a marriage. The only way it could go ahead was for Margaret to give up her royal title, cut herself off

Peter Townsend (left) and Princess Margaret were often photographed together during royal engagements. But their romance was doomed from the start. It was not yet acceptable for royals to marry commoners.

love would cool. That did not happen. When Townsend returned to England in 1955, the romance was still very much 'on'.

English newspapers went into a frenzy of speculation. Would the couple marry or not? 'Come on, Margaret, make up your mind!', ran one newspaper headline.

But Margaret was not in a position to make up her mind. She was bombarded with reasons not to marry Townsend. The church was against it. The royal family did not like it. The people were divided. Some thought that as a war hero, Townsend would make an admirable husband for a royal princess. Others believed that Margaret should put her royal duty first.

Royal duty won in the end. The announcement came on 31 October 1955. Margaret had decided not to marry Peter Townsend.

'Mindful of the Church's teaching that Christian marriage is indissoluble, and of my duty [to the queen], I have decided to put these considerations before all others.'

from her family, and leave England to live abroad for the rest of her life.

Queen Elizabeth did not want that to happen to her beloved sister. So she tried another way. Peter Townsend was given a job in Belgium. It was only just across the English Channel, but far enough away to separate him from Margaret. The queen hoped their

Margaret parties to forget sorrows

It was the worst moment of Margaret's life. She never got over it. She plunged into a frantic round of parties. She became the star of the fun-loving jet set. She went to nightclubs. She shocked everyone by drinking and smoking in public. She made friends with people royals were not supposed to mix with – actors, actresses and pop stars.

Then, in 1959, Townsend wrote to Margaret that he was going to marry a Belgian girl, Marie-Luce. No one was surprised that Marie-Luce looked almost exactly like Princess Margaret. Margaret, meanwhile, had received a proposal of marriage from the English society photographer, Antony Armstrong-Jones.

'I received the letter from Peter in the morning,' she said later, 'and that evening, I decided to marry Tony. I didn't really want to marry at all. Why did I? Because he asked me!'

A marriage doomed to failure

In time, the reason proved not to be good enough. Margaret and Tony, as they came to be known, were married at Westminster Abbey on 6 May 1960. It was

Margaret never got over the Townsend affair, though her marriage to photographer Antony Armstrong-Jones in 1960 concealed that fact. Ironically, Margaret became the first of the Windsors to divorce when that marriage ended in 1978.

a splendid royal occasion. The couple later had two children, but the marriage was doomed. Armstrong-Jones, who became Lord Snowdon, came to hate his link with the royal family. It got in the way of his career. The couple had terrible rows. Each took lovers. At last, in 1976, they decided to give up. Margaret and Tony separated and in 1978 they were divorced.

Margaret never married again. She drank and smoked even more than before. She took much younger men as lovers. She held high-life parties at her villa on the island of Mustique.

A sad life and an untimely end

At home in England, Margaret received occasional visits from Peter Townsend. But he died in 1995. At last, it all caught up with her. Her health began to fail. She suffered a series of strokes. Outside her family and

friends, no one knew how badly she was affected until 4 August 2001, the day her mother, the Queen Mother, celebrated her 101st birthday. There was the Queen Mother, looking fit and sprightly, waving to crowds cheering her outside her London home, Clarence House. And there was Princess Margaret, sitting in a wheelchair, half-paralyzed and partially blind. Princess Margaret died six months later, on 9 February 2002, at the age of 71.

By that time, the royal family had been rocked by another scandal even greater than the Townsend affair, and almost as serious as the abdication of King Edward VIII. It was a story of betrayal, bad faith and hole-in-the-wall affairs. Once again, people wondered if the English monarchy would survive. Once again, they watched with a mixture of horror and fascination as the fearful story unfolded.

A fairy tale for the nation

This, though, was the last thing on anyone's mind on 29 July 1981, when Prince Charles, heir to the throne, married Lady Diana Spencer at St. Paul's Cathedral in London. The press pronounced it the 'fairytale'

After the end of the Townsend affair, Princess Margaret indulged in the high life. Her excessive smoking and drinking produced serious health scares and she was accused, quite unjustifiably, of neglecting her royal duties.

The kiss on the balcony at Buckingham Palace, the romantic climax to the 'fairytale wedding' of the Prince and Princess of Wales. The marriage, however, was no fairytale: for the Windsors, it marked an era of unprecedented scandal.

marriage of the century. The fresh-faced 20-year-old Diana became an overnight star. Everywhere she went, she was greeted by huge crowds. She was the most famous, most photographed woman in the world. The public loved her. The press loved her. Everyone loved her. Except for her husband, Prince Charles.

Groom still loves 'ex'

No one knew it at the time, but Charles was in love with someone else: Camilla Parker-Bowles, who had once been his girlfriend. Charles could have married Camilla as far back as 1973. But he had thought

she was not quite 'pure' enough for a future queen of England. She had had lovers. She was too much of a 'go-getter' to settle down to the dull round of royal duties. So Charles let her go and Camilla married someone else. Even then, Camilla was not completely out of Charles's life. They remained friends and occasional lovers. Camilla boosted Charles's confidence, made him feel good and accepted him as he was. Before long, Charles realised that by marrying Diana, he had married trouble.

Insecure Diana craved love

Lady Diana Spencer, youngest daughter of Earl Spencer, was the child of a broken marriage. When she was only six, her mother, Frances, suddenly disappeared from home and never came back. The divorce that followed was so brutal that Frances would never speak about it. In a fight for custody of their four children, Earl Spencer won by blackening his wife's character. The effect on Diana and her younger brother, Charles, was devastating.

Diana grew up insecure and longing for love. She wanted a husband who would be hers and hers alone, who would love her and protect her, and always be there for her. But Charles could not give Diana the attention she craved. Being Prince of Wales was not a nine-to-five job. Charles had royal duties to perform and was often away from home.

There was plenty of media speculation that all was not well in the household of the Prince and Princess of Wales. It was easy to laugh off the talk as gossip, but in fact, the media were right. By 1986 Charles and Diana's marriage was crumbling fast.

Little in common

Moreover, Charles and Diana were very different people. Charles loved opera. Diana preferred pop music. Charles liked reading books about philosophy or history. Diana read romantic novels. None of this would have mattered had there been enough goodwill between them. But goodwill was difficult when Charles' friends thought Diana was 'an airhead'. Her friends thought Charles was stuffy and dull.

It did not take long for relations between Charles and Diana to become strained. Diana came to believe that if only she could get Charles away from Camilla, everything would be all right. But the more Diana nagged him to give up Camilla, the more Charles clung to Camilla.

Charles runs from rows

Diana staged dramatic tantrums. While she was expecting their first child, Prince William, Diana threw herself downstairs to prevent Charles from going out riding.

Unfortunately, Charles was not the sort of strong-minded man to cope with a wife who behaved like this. Charles's solution was to run to Camilla, which only made matters worse. Royal duty demanded that, in public, Charles and Diana must put a brave face on the situation. Even so, there was plenty of media speculation that all was not well in the household of the Prince and Princess of Wales. It was easy to laugh off the talk as gossip, but in fact, the media were right. By 1986 Charles and Diana's marriage was crumbling fast. Charles later confessed that by that time he was no longer sleeping with his wife. In 1987 Diana seemed to give up hope that Charles would ever give her the attention she wanted. She began to look for it elsewhere, with other men.

No joint celebrations

In 1991 came the tenth anniversary of Charles and Diana's wedding. A date to celebrate? No, it was not. No one felt like celebrating. On their wedding anniversary, they were apart, Charles in London, Diana in Wales. The tenth anniversary party Queen Elizabeth wanted to give for them never took place.

The mouse finally roars

Meanwhile a time bomb was ticking that would burst the bubble of the so-called 'fairytale' marriage forever. Sometime in the winter of 1991–2, Diana gave the royal reporter Andrew Morton long, detailed interviews about what was really going on in her marriage. She told him everything. No holds were barred. Morton's book *Diana: Her True Story* was published in London on 7 June 1992. It was a bombshell. Morton painted a picture of Charles as cold and arrogant. He was supposedly jealous of Diana's success and popularity.

Even worse was to come. The book revealed that Diana had attempted to commit suicide five times. She suffered from the eating disorder bulimia. She had mutilated herself on several occasions.

Diana colluded with author

When Morton's book was published, there were denials all around that Diana had had anything to do with it. But who else could have known about the marriage in such detail? Morton's fellow journalists and others with inside information guessed the truth, but the public was unaware for another five years, until shortly after Diana's death.

Public reaction to *Diana: Her True Story* was extraordinary. Many readers were convinced it told the truth. If Diana had taken lovers – which she had – Charles's behaviour had driven her to it. Nothing seemed to be too bad to say about Prince Charles, who was now cast as Public Enemy Number One.

The queen's terrible year

But even this was not the end of the scandals of 1992, which Queen Elizabeth later described as her *annus horribilis* – horrible year. On 19 March, the queen's second son, Prince Andrew, Duke of York, separated from his wife, Sarah Ferguson. They had married in 1986, but the marriage soon degenerated into a terrible tale of neglect, irresponsibility and adultery. Then, on 13 April, the queen's only daughter, Princess Anne, began a divorce action against her husband, Captain Mark Phillips. With that, the marriages of three of the queen's four children were on the rocks.

But the main spotlight was on Charles and Diana. *Diana: Her True Story* had been the end of the line. There could be no forgiveness. Prince Charles felt grossly betrayed. The queen was angry at all the dirty linen Diana had washed in public.

Media feeding frenzy

Charles's friends responded to Morton's book in a magazine article written by the journalist Penny Junor. This told the prince's side of the story. It

pictured Diana as paranoid and jealous. She had kept Prince William and Prince Harry away from their father. She swore at Charles and pulled every dirty trick known in the annals of shrewish wives.

By this time, the media were daily reporting accusation and counter-accusation, claim and counter-claim. No one knew any longer who was telling the truth and who was lying. Scandalous revelations came

'Camilla,' Diana said, 'was always there.' Camilla Parker-Bowles had been an important presence in Charles's life since 1973, and their relationship continued even after his marriage to Diana.

thick and fast. Smutty conversations on secret tapes, involving both Charles and Diana, were transcribed and published. The headlines were lurid. 'My Life of Torture', 'Love Tapes Upset Diana', and worse.

The end of a fantasy

After all this it was impossible for the 'fairytale' marriage to go on. The end came near the close of 1992. On 9 December, Charles and Diana's separation was announced in the House of Commons by Prime Minister John Major. The divorce followed nearly four years later, on 28 August 1996.

Now that Diana was no longer royal, she lost her title of 'Her Royal Highness' and no one had to curtsey to her any more. But she was still a headline-

Diana: Her True Story by Andrew Morton first appeared in 1992. After Diana's death in Paris in 1997, the book was re-published and the fact, formerly denied, that she had fully cooperated with Morton became public knowledge.

maker and was going to make more sensational news after July 1997, when she received an invitation from the Egyptian billionaire Mohamed Al Fayed, owner of Harrod's, the luxury London store. Al Fayed offered Diana and her two boys his villa at St. Tropez, complete with his yacht, *Jonikal*, and a companion, his handsome and personable son Dodi.

No sooner had Dodi and Diana got together in St. Tropez than the press was weaving a romance about them. Sensing a major story, boatloads of newsmen and photographers descended on St. Tropez. Dodi and Diana fled, first to the Mediterranean island of Corsica, then to Sardinia and finally, on 30 August, to Paris. But word of their arrival had gone ahead of them and the paparazzi, who made a living taking and selling photographs of celebrities, were waiting for them.

Dodi and Diana were the greatest celebrities the paparazzi had encountered in a long time. A group of them followed the couple to their Paris hotel, and then laid siege to it. The couple managed to escape by a back entrance, but the paparazzi were soon on their tail.

Death of an Icon

It was nearly midnight. Dodi ordered his driver, Henri Paul, to step on it and a high-speed chase began through the streets of Paris. As Henri Paul reached an underpass close to the Place d'Alma, his Mercedes was doing close to 135 miles per hour. The Mercedes shot into the underpass. Soon Henri Paul, who, according to reports, was drunk, lost control of the car. It skidded across the tunnel, crashed into a pillar, bounced off and hit the opposite wall. The car ended up a tangle of twisted metal and broken glass.

Dodi was killed at once. So was Henri Paul. Diana lived through the crash, but her injuries were too severe for her to survive. She was pronounced dead at the hospital at 4:00 A.M. the next morning. She was 36.

A nation in mourning

When the news reached Britain, people went into shock. They stood in the streets, tears pouring down their cheeks. Thousands descended

on London, and laid so many flowers for remembrance outside the royal palaces that the sidewalks disappeared under a thick carpet of blooms. Many of the mourners stood in line for hours to sign books of condolence. There was open criticism of the 'cold-hearted' Queen and her family who were spending their regular holiday at Balmoral in Scotland and were still there, instead of heading immediately for the capital.

Eventually, the royals gave in. They returned to London and the Queen gave a short tribute to Diana on television. For her pains, members of the public pronounced her speech 'not emotional enough'.

Queen Elizabeth suffered appalling embarrassment over the revelations contained in Andrew Morton's book. In it, she was pictured as aloof and unhelpful toward her daughter-in-law, the Princess of Wales, although in fact the opposite was true.

THE CAMPAIGNING PRINCESS

EARLY IN 1997 DIANA HAD ASKED the media to become her allies in a new cause on behalf of the Red Cross. The recent civil war in Angola, West Africa, had left behind acres of land thickly strewn with anti-personnel mines. Although the fighting was over, the mines were still there and thousands of local people were dying, losing legs, hands, eyes whenever they stepped on one.

With the press looking on and taking photographs and making newsreels, Diana went into the minefield area. She was protected by a visor and bulletproof vest. As the cameras rolled, she walked past notices placed every few yards which read: 'Danger! Mines!' Above each notice was the warning sign of a skull and crossbones.

The pictures were shown all over the world, on television, in cinemas and in newspapers. The Red Cross could not have had better publicity. Eight months later, in August 1997, Diana went to Bosnia, in southeast Europe. Here, too, a civil war had recently ended. Here, too, the land was filled with mines. And here, too, the press took pictures of Diana continuing her campaign.

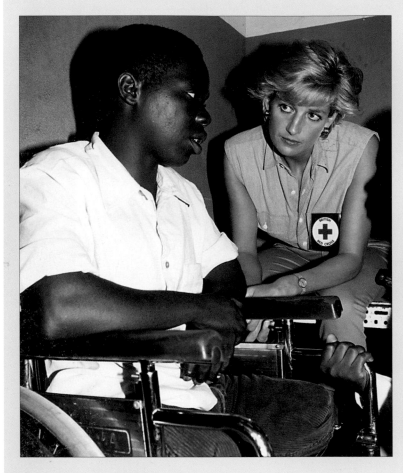

In the last year of her life, Diana worked to promote public awareness of the injuries inflicted by anti-personnel mines and campaigned against their continued use.

'GOODBYE, ENGLAND'S ROSE!'

Diana's funeral took place on 6 September. London virtually closed down for the day. Huge crowds lined the streets as her coffin was driven to Westminster Abbey for a short service. They were still there when the cortège made its way out of London heading for Northamptonshire and Diana's childhood home. Althorp House. There, in a private family ceremony, she was buried on an island in the middle of a lake.

'Goodbye, England's rose,' the opening words that Elton John sang for his friend at the funeral, became the next day's headlines as newspapers were filled with reports of one of the most emotional tear-filled days the United Kingdom had ever seen.

Charles still cast as villain

But this was by no means the end of the Diana story. The intrusive, gossip-hungry media soon saw to that. Charles and his long-time love Camilla Parker-Bowles were still around and therefore still susceptible to reports that Diana's army of fans had never, and would never, forgive the Prince for the way he had treated his wife.

Even six years after Diana's death, millions were still willing to feed on any 'news' that painted the Prince as a villain. In January 2004, for example, a newspaper report appeared about a letter purportedly written by Diana. In this, she stated that Charles was planning a car accident in which she would suffer 'a serious head injury'. Unsurprisingly, the letter was later revealed to be a crude forgery, but not before it had convinced millions that Charles was a potential murderer.

The public were regularly polled for their opinions, and these showed that a majority rejected Charles as their future king. They preferred his son William as heir to the throne instead.

More than seven years after Diana's death, when Charles at last married Camilla Parker-Bowles on 9 April 2005, the numbers who wanted William for king had dropped, but still stood at 42 per cent, 8 per cent higher than in 2001.

Diana's continuing influence was evident from the moment Charles and Camilla became engaged in February 2005. It was announced that instead of being called 'Princess of Wales' after the marriage, Camilla would take her future title, HRH the Duchess of Cornwall, from Charles's estate, the Duchy of Cornwall. She would not be Queen when he became King, but 'Princess Consort'.

 These efforts to avoid comparisons with Diana did not prevent the late Princess's fans from sending hundreds of pieces of hate mail to Camilla before the wedding. It was feared that on the day there might be demonstrations against the newlyweds outside the Registry Office in Windsor, Berkshire, where the ceremony was performed. Consequently, Charles and Camilla bypassed the crowd of spectators waiting to greet them, and drove off as soon as the ceremony was over.

The marriage of Charles and Camilla in 2005 was a very quiet affair compared to his state wedding to Diana in 1981. The ceremony took place a day later than originally planned, because Charles had to travel to Rome to represent the Queen at the funeral of Pope John Paul II.

Butler's revelations

Charles and Camilla were by no means the only avenue through which the media kept the Diana story going. In 2002, for example, there was the sensational trial of Diana's butler, Paul Burrell, who was accused of stealing items belonging to Diana, Charles and their two sons. The trial was stopped and Burrell acquitted after the Queen recalled a conversation in which the butler told her he was keeping safe the items he was later charged with appropriating. Rumours soon flourished that the Burrell trial had come too close to revealing evidence that might have embarrassed Her Majesty.

Harold Brown, another royal butler whose trial on similar charges was also halted, refused to 'sell his story' to the Press. Paul Burrell had no such qualms. He became a headline celebrity with fresh revelations of royal misbehaviour. According to Burrell, Diana's erstwhile father-in-law, Prince Philip, wrote her insulting letters, calling her a 'harlot' and a 'trollop'. Philip, backed up by Rosa Monckton, Diana's close friend, hotly denied these allegations.

Was love-rat major Harry's father?

The year 2002 also produced one of the most titillating
of Diana stories. James Hewitt, one of her ten alleged
lovers, was known to the tabloid press as a 'Love-Rat'
for going public about their affair. A former major
in a cavalry regiment of the British Army, Hewitt
was forced to resign over the revelations. In 1998,
Hewitt announced that he would never sell the 64
love letters Diana had written him, but four years

**Prince Harry, furious at the intrusion into his private life,
attacked a photographer who was trying to take his picture
outside a London nightclub in October 2004. During the
scuffle that followed, Harry was hit in the face by a camera.**

later he was asking a massive £10 million for them.
The price included some salacious titbits, including
the nicknames Diana gave to their private parts and
details of the sex toy she sent him while he was serving

in Kuwait during the first Gulf War in 1991. Although Hewitt received offers, they fell far short of his asking price: the highest bid reached only £4 million.

Also in 2002, a rumour circulated that Hewitt, not Prince Charles, was the father of Diana's second

---

in January 2005 Harry was pictured at a fancy-dress party wearing a Nazi uniform – complete with an arm-band swastika.

---

son, Prince Harry. There was certainly a resemblance between Hewitt and Harry, who was born on 15 September 1984. They had the same neat facial features and both of them had red hair. In September 2002, Hewitt publicly denied the rumours. Then news came to light that in 1985, the Royal Family had ordered a DNA test to prove paternity. Diana, it was said, was incensed, but the test proved that, after all, Prince Charles, not Hewitt, was Harry's father.

Harry the hell-raiser

By this time Prince Harry was 18, old enough for some hell-raising of his own. Harry gave the press plenty of material. He indulged in drinking while below the legal age. He smoked 'pot'. He scuffled with a photographer outside a nightclub. But none of these compared with the furore that ensued in January 2005 when Harry was pictured at a fancy-dress party wearing a World War II German Army uniform – complete with an arm-band bearing the Nazi swastika.

Harry was savaged in the press for his insensitivity regarding the Holocaust and for insulting the memory of his great-grandparents, King George VI and Queen Elizabeth (the Queen Mother), who had been symbols of British defiance of the Nazis during World War II. Harry apologized, but the criticisms continued. A furious Prince Charles ordered him to visit Auschwitz-Birkenau, the largest of the Nazi concentration camps.

In July 2006, stories emerged about Harry's infidelity towards his long-term girl friend, Chelsy

Davy. This time, the tabloid newspaper *The Sun* reported that Chelsy was 'putting a brave face' on the news that the Prince had enjoyed a wild night out at a party at the Art Bar in London where he romanced an older woman, Catherine Davies, a 34-year-old mother of two. To make matters worse, this was apparently the fourth time that her boyfriend had 'seduced' another woman, leaving Chelsy 'furious'.

It was June 2010 before another British newspaper, the *News of the World*, reported that Harry and Chelsy had finally broken up. Subsequently, Harry went on as he had begun – more boisterous behaviour in nightclubs and bars. In July of 2011, *Hollywood News*, which normally specializes in movie star gossip, reported that he was dating a lingerie model, Florence Brudenell-Bruce. Then, in 2012, he was photographed in Las Vegas playing strip billiards with six young women.

Not all partying

But while in his youth Prince Harry was much more of a party animal than his elder brother, Prince William, what the two princes did have in common was an active preoccupation with charity work. This reflected the interest which made their late mother such an icon during and after her marriage to their father. The two princes carried on the British Royal Family's philanthropic traditions as presidents or patrons of several organizations and, in September 2009, set up their own foundation to co-ordinate their work in this area.

A further royal tradition that the two princes shared was military service. Despite his wishes, as second in line to the throne, William's long term military career was considered out of the question, so after officer training at Sandhurst he went on to become an RAF search and rescue helicopter pilot, allowing him an active role in the armed forces without risking combat operations.

Harry, on the other hand, followed officer training at Sandhurst with active service in Afghanistan. He first served there for 77 days, only being pulled out when an Australian magazine made him a target by publishing news of his presence there. Four years later, he returned to Afghanistan for a 20-week deployment with the Army Air Corps, reaching the rank of captain and serving as an Apache helicopter co-pilot/gunner.

By the time he left the Army in 2015, Harry was already working on one of his new causes. The previous year he had launched the Invictus Games, an international Paralympic-style sporting event for injured servicemen and women. Following the first games in London in 2014, subsequent games were held in the USA, Canada and Australia.

While the Royal Family could at times be faulted for being stiff and out-of-touch with the country, a more mature Harry was proving to have a winning cheek and, like his mother, a more natural touch at connecting with people beyond royal circles.

The future King

Harry might have been forgiven for some of his more wayward moments, but Prince William, two years older than Harry, was destined for a highly onerous responsibility: in the course of time he would become King of England, as William V.

William was mindful of the sufferings his mother, Princess Diana, had endured from a rabid popular press during and after her marriage. He promised Catherine's parents that he would never allow such a thing to happen to their daughter.

Fortunately, in contrast to his brother, William had the advantage of a long relationship with a steady girlfriend, Catherine Middleton, who, unlike Diana whose parents went through a painful divorce, came from a happy family background. William and Kate, as they were popularly known, first met in 2002, when they were students at St. Andrew's University in Scotland. William had first seen Catherine when she appeared in a fetching see-through dress at a university fashion show, and was riveted by her superb figure.

In 2008, during their courtship, William got himself into trouble with the RAF authorities by landing his £10 million helicopter in a field close to

> **William had the advantage of a long relationship with a steady girlfriend, Catherine Middleton, who, unlike Diana, came from a happy family background.**

the Middleton family home in Berkshire. The same year, he used a Chinook helicopter to fly himself and Harry to a stag party on the Isle of Wight.

Despite these pranks and a brief period in 2007 when William and Kate apparently parted, their relationship survived and they married on 29 April 2011 at London's Westminster Abbey. A popular person with the public, Kate, now known as the Duchess of Cambridge, gave birth to a son, George, in 2013, a daughter, Charlotte, in 2015, and another son, Louis, in 2018.

Nearly pipped by Pippa

The Duchess, though, briefly risked being upstaged at her own wedding by her younger sister Pippa, whose eye-catching figure and bridesmaid's dress made her suddenly world famous. She seemed to love the attention and soon picked up deals writing books and magazines articles, as well as work as a television presenter. But she was to feel the downside of fame, too. Her party planning book received negative reviews and sold poorly. Also, her television career didn't take off and her private life was closely scrutinized.

By 2016, Pippa had wound down her media career. Reports suggested that she had been reined in by Prince William, who was sensitive to the poor publicity her work in the commercial sphere might bring to the Royal Family. Instead, she shifted her focus to charities, working as an ambassador for The British Heart Foundation, among other causes.

'Air Miles' Andy

Controversy continued to surround Charles's brother, Prince Andrew, whose role as the United Kingdom's Special Trade Representative involved him travelling the world promoting British business. This led to accusations that he was too close to countries with poor human rights records, such as Azerbaijan and Kazakhstan, and that he personally profited from the deals that followed. He was also dubbed 'Air Miles' Andy by the tabloid press for his frequent trips, some of which included golfing jaunts at public expense.

Married in 2011, Prince William and his wife Catherine have three children: George, born in 2013, Charlotte, born in 2015, and Louis, born in 2018. George is third in line to the British throne after his grandfather, Prince Charles, and his father.

Then there was the matter of Andrew's Berkshire home. After the break-up of his marriage, both he and his former wife, Sarah Ferguson, had, by 2006, left their marital home, Sunninghill Park, a house built for them near the Queen's residence at Windsor Castle. The following year the house was sold for £15 million – £3 million above the asking price – to an offshore trust in the British Virgin Islands. It was later revealed that the buyer was Timur Kulibayev, the billionaire son-in-law of the Kazakh president, Nursultan Nazarbayev. Why Kulibayev had paid so much for the property wasn't clear, but it fuelled speculation about the close links between Andrew and Kazakhstan's ruling elite. Then, Kulibayev allowed the empty house

ROCKY ROAD TO THE CHAPEL

ON THE WEDDING DAY, it was not Thomas Markle Senior who gave Meghan Markle away, but her soon-to-be father-in-law Prince Charles. Thomas Markle, who had divorced Meghan's mother when their daughter was six, pulled out of the wedding at the last minute because he had suffered two heart attacks. Although that was true, just days earlier the former Hollywood lighting director had profited from a paparazzi photo shoot. That must have displeased Buckingham Palace.

It was later revealed that three months after the wedding Meghan wrote to her father, who now lives in Mexico, asking him to 'stop victimising me through the media so we can repair our relationship'. Once devoted to Thomas, Meghan then seemingly cut him out of her life, failing to respond to his efforts to contact her.

Mr Markle didn't help matters by giving further interviews to the press, telling them that Meghan 'has always been a very controlling person'. In vain, he also appealed to the Queen to intervene and end the ever deeper rift.

Upon her marriage in May 2018, Meghan Markle became 'Her Royal Highness The Duchess of Sussex'.

to fall into ruin, becoming, for some, a symbol that there was something wasteful and rotten about the relationship. With permission granted to replace it with a larger property, the dilapidated house was finally demolished in 2015.

Andrew's reputation suffered again through his friendship with American billionaire hedge fund manager and philanthropist Jeffrey Epstein. In 2008, Epstein was sentenced to 18 months imprisonment after agreeing a plea bargain over child prostitution charges. Although Epstein lost many of his friends in the scandal, Prince Andrew wasn't among them. Following the sex offender's release, he was photographed in 2011 strolling through Central Park with the prince. The furore that this caused led to Andrew finally quitting his role as UK trade envoy.

The Markle Sparkle

Prince Harry met Meghan Markle on a blind date set up by friends in 2016. At the time, Meghan was best known as an actress in the American TV series *Suits*. Although beautiful and, as something of a campaigner and charity worker, already used to a role in public life, much about Meghan was highly unconventional for a royal match. Firstly, she is three years older than Harry. Secondly, she was a divorcee, having been in a relationship with TV producer Trevor Engelson from 2004 to 2013, and married to him for the final 18 months they were together.

Thirdly, she, like Kate Middleton, isn't an aristocrat, and, unlike Kate, is American. For some people this had worrying echoes of the earlier American divorcee to marry into the royal family,

Wallis Simpson, and the constitutional crisis that that caused with Edward VIII's abdication in 1936. Fourthly, Meghan is mixed race, her mother Doria Ragland being descended from African-American slaves. Nevertheless, in November 2017, Meghan and Harry announced their engagement and were married on 19 May 2018. Upon their marriage, the couple became the Duke and Duchess of Sussex.

Within months, however, some had dubbed Meghan 'Duchess Difficult'. It was suggested that she was struggling with the confines of around-the-clock personal security and that she had an imperious manner that had caused the premature departure of a number of her royal staff.

It's alleged, too, that there were tensions within the Royal Family. Although both the extrovert Meghan and the rather shy Kate were popular with the public, rumours emerged that the two didn't get along. According to one story, Meghan's abrupt manner regarding the bridesmaid's dress to be worn by William and Kate's daughter Charlotte reduced a heavily pregnant Kate to tears. Both couples lived at

Kensington Palace, but before the end of the year it was announced that Harry and Meghan would move to a cottage in the grounds of Windsor Castle after the birth of their first child in the spring of 2019. William and Harry had previously been inseparable. Had Meghan caused a rift between the princes?

The other Eden
In 2015, the Queen surpassed the reign of her great-great-grandmother, Queen Victoria, to become the longest-reigning British monarch and the longest-reigning queen regnant in world history.

Whether happy or sad, deplorable or felicitous, these royal episodes and the personalities involved in them provide the latest happenings to add to the long tale of dark deeds, dirty doings and foolish fancies that have marked a thousand years of English royal history.

The British royal family in the 21st century has broken with the confines of earlier conventions regarding class, race and marriage. On his wedding day, Prince Harry stands with his mixed-race American divorcee wife Meghan and her African-American mother.

INDEX

Page numbers in *italics* refer to illustrations; page numbers in **bold** refer to the main reference

PICTURE CREDITS